STUDIES IN

AFRICAN AMERICAN HISTORY AND CULTURE

edited by

GRAHAM HODGES
COLGATE UNIVERSITY

A GARLAND SERIES

THE MUSIC IN AFRICAN AMERICAN FICTION

ROBERT H. CATALIOTTI

GARLAND PUBLISHING, Inc.
New York & London / 1995

Library of Congress Cataloging-in-Publication Data

Cataliotti, Robert H., 1955–
    The music in African American fiction / Robert H. Cataliotti.
        p.   cm. — (Studies in African American history and
culture)
    Includes bibliographical references (p. 231) and index.
    ISBN 0-8153-2330-1 (alk. paper)
    1. American fiction—Afro-American authors—History and
criticism. 2. Afro-Americans—Songs and music—History and
criticism. 3. Music and literature—United States. 4. Songs,
American, in literature. 5. Afro-Americans in literature. I. Title.
II. Series.
PS374.N4C38 1995
813.009'357—dc20
                                                            95-35215

Printed on acid-free, 250-year-life paper
Manufactured in the United States of America

For
Abbey Lincoln Aminata Moseka
George "Big Nick" Nicholas
&
Albert "Budd" Johnson.
Thanks for the music
and
for taking the time to
tell me the story behind the songs.

Contents

Introduction

"It don't mean a thing if it ain't got that swing."
- Duke Ellington

In many ways the study of African American literature is like learning the words to a song. You know the song's melody, "the way it goes," but when you learn the words the meaning comes clearly into focus. Music has always occupied a central position in black American life. It has been the music that has preserved many elements of both African and African American culture throughout the black experience in America. In a country that has attempted to eradicate not only their culture, but also their essential humanity, African Americans have held on to and developed their music as a way of remembering, a way of enduring, a way of celebrating, a way of protesting and subverting, and, ultimately, a way of triumphing. African American literature tells this same story with the technical mastery, powerful spirit and sense of heritage found in the music. As with almost every aspect of black culture in America, the African American literary tradition, from its inception, has felt the influence of the culture's music.

There is dual intention in this study's examination of *The Music in African American Fiction*. It traces the manner in which black music and musicians have been represented in the fiction produced by African American writers. In addition, it analyzes how the "represented" music and musicians have been representative of the sensibilities of African Americans and provided paradigms for the artistic productions of black writers in the formulation of an African American literary tradition.

African American culture has its roots in an oral tradition, and music has been the most expressive, vibrant and inventive form to emerge from that tradition. The continuum that encompasses spirituals, blues, jazz, gospel, and rhythm and blues emerges from the earliest experiences of black people in America, and these forms are distinctive products of the folk processes of the oral tradition. What makes this unique cultural production genuinely amazing is both the fact that the social, political and economic conditions under which the creators labored were incredibly horrendous and that these forms reached spectacular heights of artistic sophistication in a relatively short time frame. Of course, African American culture did not develop in a vacuum; an ongoing interchange between African and European derived sensibilities has marked the history of this country. However, it is apparent that the music-making impulse in the African heritage has dominated the European, and the music that comprises this continuum is regarded as the outstanding form of artistic expression that has been produced in America. For this reason music that is characteristically African American is considered characteristically American throughout the world. Because the forms that make up this continuum have been recognized—both within and outside of black culture—as the most distinguished manifestations of the African American music-making impulse, they have been pervasively represented by black writers and thus are the focus of this study.

Ironically, mainstream white American culture has simultaneously co-opted these forms while attempting to diminish the achievements of black musicians—if not completely deny their source in African American culture. But black Americans have always known the truth about the music. Even though different forms appeal to different people, African Americans are aware of the music's function as a touchstone for racial identity and recognize the expressiveness, the inventiveness and the resiliency that enables the music to renew itself. This study attempts to identify and analyze what it is that makes up this special relationship between African Americans and their music by examining how black writers have represented music and musicians in their depictions of black life in America.

African American literature, like the music, is the product of the melding of different cultural sensibilities unique to the American experience. It evolved as the oral tradition of the African heritage was adapted to a literary tradition—a tradition with its roots in the European heritage. Music, being the most eloquent and articulate vehicle for black artistic expression, has provided a model for many African American writers. The attraction to the music surely lies in its sense of communal heritage, its original and masterful techniques, its seductive rhythmic sophistication and its spontaneous improvisational brilliance. Yet, beyond all these elements, the one characteristic of African American music that is its true mark of distinction is its capacity for emotive expression, its ability to communicate feeling—joy, sorrow, anger, protest, frustration, desire, and triumph. The ineffable, almost magical power to express feeling is at the heart of the attraction to this music. Call it soul. Call it swing or funk or the groove. Call it mumbo jumbo or diddy-wah-diddy or boogie-woogie or hi-de-hi-de-hi-de-ho or jock-o-mo-fee-nah-hey or be-bop-klook-mop-bam-boom. It's the spirit in the dark. Its source lies in the heart of the African sensibility and its distinctiveness results from the tempering of the American experience. The goal of many black writers has been to capture this spirit in the dark through written expression. The pursuit of this feeling in the development of an African American literary tradition which maintains a link to the oral folk heritage is evidenced in all the imaginative literary genres—poetry, drama and fiction. The creativity required to produce imaginative forms of writing invests them with the capacity to express the magic and mystery that are the essence of the music's soul. While poetry and drama are forms that are amenable to the influence of orality, particularly musical elements and techniques, the attempt to create fiction that bridges the literary and oral traditions is perhaps the greatest challenge to African American writers and is the most telling index of their success in forging a distinctly black literary tradition.

This study is an historical analysis of the tradition of representing music in African American fiction. The impact of evolving musical styles and innovative musicians on black culture is also examined as it is manifested in the literature. The analysis begins with the slave narratives and the emergence of the first black fiction of the antebellum years and moves through the Reconstruction. This is followed by analyses of definitive fictional representations of African American music from the turn-of-the-century through the Harlem Renaissance, the Depression and World War II eras through the 1960s and the Black Arts Movement. The representation of black music shapes a lineage that extends from the initial chronicles written in response to subhuman bondage to the declarations of an autonomous "black aesthetic" and dramatically influences the evolution of an African American literary tradition.

Baltimore, MD.
Aigust 1995

R.H.C.

Acknowledgments

I am indebted to a number of colleagues and friends for the realization of *The Music in African American Fiction* as the interdisciplinary project that I envisioned. Billy Joe Harris was invaluable in helping me crystallize the conception and scope of the study. Stacey Olster and Paul Newlin provided essential feedback throughout the composition process. And I have to give special thanks to Stacey Olster for her meticulous editing. Finally, Jerry Nelson's contribution to this study must be singled out. His hard work and constant advice to be myself and do my own thing gave me the confidence and drive to get the job done.

The deepest gratitude is expressed to the following family and friends for their encouragement and support: Arpege LaShawn Hunter, Don "Bar BQ Bob" DeBacker, Terry Kelsey, Robb Galasso, Marian Lynch, Carmen and Marie Cataliotti. I would also like to honor the memory of Josephine Cataliotti for her care and generosity during the writing of this book.

Last but certainly not least—for this study would not exist without them—I want to thank all the musicians who have enhanced my life. A partial roll call includes: Thelonious Monk, Billie Holiday, Lester Young, Bud Powell, Dexter Gordon, Miles Davis, Sonny Stitt, Louis Armstrong, Duke Ellington, Count Basie, Milt Hinton, Charlie Rouse, John Coltrane, Sarah Vaughan, Charlie Parker, Jay McShann, Muddy Waters, Professor Longhair, B. B. King, Robert Johnson, the Mardis Gras Indians tribes, Neville Brothers, Aretha Franklin, James Brown, Irma Thomas, Fats Domino, James Booker, Gladys Knight, Betty Carter, Randy Weston, Eddie Jefferson, Frank Foster, Sonny Rollins, Art Blakey, the Marsalis family, LaVerne Butler, Lois Dejean, Dizzy Gillespie, Tadd Dameron, Max Roach, Ben Webster, Elmore James, Earl King, Jimi Hendrix, Clifton Chenier, Snooks Eaglin, Dirty Dozen Brass Band, Blind Willie McTell, Mississippi John Hurt, Leroy Jones, Shannon Powell, Sonny Terry, Brownie McGhee, Lightnin' Hopkins, Sonny Boy Williamson, Howlin' Wolf, Mississippi Fred McDowell, Little Walter Jacobs, Solomon Burke, Marvin Gaye, The Marvelettes, The Shirelles, Tina Turner, The Staple Singers, Mahalia Jackson, James Cleveland, John Lee Hooker, Danny Barker, Marcus Roberts, Bobby Watson, Donald Harrison, Big Jesse Yawn, Bruno Carr, Major Holley, Carmen McRae, Buddy Tate, Harry "Sweets" Edison, Buck Clayton, Al Grey, Eddie "Lockjaw" Davis, Barry Harris, Roland Hanna, Benny Powell, C. Sharpe, Dinah Washington, Otis Redding, Chaka Khan, Bessie Smith, McCoy Tyner, Sun Ra and, of course, Abbey Lincoln, Big Nick Nicholas and Budd Johnson. . . .

xiii

The Music in
African American Fiction

I
"They Sang a Song of Triumph"

"To those songs I trace my first glimmering
of the dehumanizing character of slavery."
- Frederick Douglass

"And when they reached the other side,
  Let my people go;
They sang a song of triumph o'er,
  Let my people go."
- "Go Down, Moses"

"Alas! had it not been for my beloved violin, I
scarcely can conceive how I could have endured the
long years of bondage. . . . Often, at midnight, when
sleep had fled affrighted from the cabin, and my soul
was disturbed and troubled with the contemplation of
my fate, it would sing me a song of peace."
- Solomon Northup

"O, gracious Lord! when shall it be,
That we poor souls shall be free;
Lord, break them slavery powers—
Will you go along with me?
Lord, break them slavery powers,
Go sound the jubilee!"
- "Song of the Coffle Gang"

"Your country? How came it yours? Before the
Pilgrims landed we were here. Here we have brought
our three gifts and mingled them with yours: a gift of
story and song—soft, stirring melody in an ill-
harmonized and unmelodious land; the gift of sweat
and brawn to beat back the wilderness, conquer the
soil, and lay the foundations of this vast economic
empire two hundred years earlier than your weak
hands could have done it; the third, a gift of the
Spirit."
- W.E.B. DuBois

1.
"GO SOUND THE JUBILEE":
SLAVE NARRATIVES WILLIAM WELLS BROWN
& MARTIN DELANY

The integral role that music has played in African American culture is reflected in the fledgling efforts of non-fiction and fiction produced by black Americans during the nineteenth century. The music evolved from an oral tradition in a white-controlled society that stonewalled and often completely outlawed literacy as a mode of communication and expression for the black populace. While traditional African musical forms were usually proscribed, the slaves developed work songs and spirituals which were acceptable to the masters.[1] Ironically, the dominant white power structure in America was oblivious to the complexity and significance of this newly evolving music in the lives of black Americans, and often perceived it as a sign of contentment and actually encouraged its production. But as African Americans achieved literacy and began to use the written word to explore their position in American society they were quick to acknowledge the importance and power of music in their culture.

In what must be considered one of the cornerstones of African American literary expression, *Narrative of the Life of Frederick Douglass, An American Slave.* (1845), the extraordinary impact of the music on the consciousness of a black individual is clearly pointed out. The "wild songs" which Douglass heard black men and women create and perform while in slavery are credited with triggering a genuine revolution of the mind: "To those songs I trace my first glimmering conception of the dehumanizing character of slavery. I can never get rid of that conception. Those songs still follow me, to deepen my hatred of slavery, and quicken my sympathies for my brethren in bonds" (263). The music not only inspired Douglass to transcend the physical bonds of slavery but also provided him with a new, elevated perception of himself as a man. Before all other influences, these songs reached him and pushed him to initiate the process of taking control of his own life.

In the three paragraphs which he devotes to describing and interpreting the songs of the slaves Douglass provides a remarkably compact overview of many important issues concerning the characteristics and role of music in African American culture and its interaction with the dominant culture—issues that in many ways have remained valid and of concern to black writers today. He points out a basic duality in these songs which reveals "at once the highest joy and the deepest sadness." The spontaneous, improvisational nature of African American music-making is also illustrated: "They compose and sing as they went along, consulting neither tune nor time." Douglass hints at the existence of a nonliteral meaning in the songs, an aural subtext: "The thought that came up, came out—if not in the word, in the sound; —and as frequently in the one as in the other." And this subtext is exclusionary; the emotions, feelings and meanings are communicated in a kind of communal insider code: "They would sing, as a chorus, to words which to many would seem unmeaning jargon, but which, nevertheless, were full of meaning to themselves" (262-63).

Yet, Douglass states that when he was a slave he did not understand "the deep meaning of those rude and apparently incoherent songs. I was within the circle; so that I neither saw nor heard as those without might see and hear" (263). It seems that what he came to understand in retrospect about this music is that the songs provided the slaves with a direct outlet of expression and captured the essence of his people's response to slavery. He had been so thoroughly indoctrinated into the acceptance of that experience, so circumscribed by this oppressive system that he had missed the "deeper meaning." What he finally came to understand and what the oppressors failed to comprehend was that the music was ultimately subversive: "Every tone was a testimony against slavery, and a prayer and complaint of souls boiling against slavery, and a prayer to God for a deliverance from chains." When Douglass revised his *Narrative* in 1855 with *My Bondage and My Freedom* he added a section on the exclusionary nature of the songs' meanings. He states that when the slaves sang of "Canaan," it was with "something more than a hope of reaching heaven. We meant to reach the *north*—and the north was our Canaan." Of another spiritual he explains: "In the lips of some, it meant the expectation of a speedy summons to a world of spirits; but, in the lips of *our* company, it simply meant a speedy pilgrimage toward a free state, and deliverance from all the evils and dangers of slavery" (Douglass's italics) (278-79).

The Southern slavemaster was not alone in misinterpreting the music, for Douglass states that Northern white listeners also missed the point: "I have often been utterly astonished since I came to the north, to find persons who could speak of the singing, among slaves, as evidence of their contentment and happiness. It is impossible to conceive of a greater mistake" (263). But this tendency of the white audience to miss the "deeper meaning," the complexity of the music and to regard it, one-dimensionally, as simple entertainment enhanced the music's ability to wear the mask of "unmeaning jargon" and be that much more effective as an instrument of subversion for African Americans. Foremost among Douglass's objectives in writing his narrative was to attack, undermine and bring about the abolition of the system of slavery in the United States. The music created by the slaves not only provides Douglass with the initial impulse to break free physically and spiritually from this bondage but is also held up as a potent, persuasive tool in winning others over to the anti-slavery cause: "I have sometimes thought that the mere hearing of those songs would do more to impress some minds with the horrible character of slavery, than the reading of whole volumes of philosophy on the subject could do" (263).

Other African American slave narrative authors included music in their depictions of slave life. Solomon Northup's *Twelve Years A Slave* (1853) provides a particularly insightful look at how music functioned in nineteenth-century black life in America. Northup, a free black born in New York and an accomplished fiddler, was kidnapped and sold into slavery because of his music-making abilities. When Northup was put up for sale by various masters his musicianship was emphasized as a marketable commodity.[2] He eventually was brought to the Red River area of Louisiana and gained renown with his performances for both masters and slaves throughout the neighboring plantations. Northup gives detailed, firsthand descriptions of music he encountered, including a Chickasaw Indian dance and a slave dance featuring "patting," a polyrhythmic, call and response performance. He speaks of the importance of music to the black community and engages in a bit of braggadocio that anticipates the proud swagger of modern jazz musicians who emerged triumphantly from the "cutting contests" engaged in at all night jam sessions: "The African race is a music-loving one, proverbially; and many there were among my fellow bondsmen whose organs of tune were strikingly developed, and who could thumb the banjo with dexterity; but at the expense of appearing egotistical, I must, nevertheless, declare, that I was considered the Ole Bull of Bayou Boeuf" (344).[3]

But what is perhaps most striking about Northup's musical observations is the significance that music played in his own struggle for survival. Northup says that "had it not been for my beloved violin, I scarcely can conceive how I could have endured the long years of bondage." His musical abilities provided him with a source of income that allowed him to ease the physical deprivations of slavery with "conveniences for my cabin" and often removed him from backbreaking labor so that he could be hired out to perform. Yet, even more importantly, that violin provided him with a means to soothe his soul. Music-making becomes an outlet for personal expression that allows him to transcend the oppressive situation in which he finds himself:

> It was my companion—the friend of my bosom—triumphing loudly when I was joyful, and uttering its soft, melodious consolations when I was sad. Often, at midnight, when sleep had fled afrightened from the cabin, and my soul was disturbed and troubled with the contemplation of my fate, it would sing me a song of peace. On holy Sabbath days, when an hour or two of leisure was allowed, it would accompany me to some quiet place on the bayou bank, and lifting up its voice, discourse kindly and pleasantly indeed. (344)

Northup echoes Douglass's identification of a happy/sad duality in the music, and his description of the violin having a "voice" and the ability to "discourse" hints at the presence of a non-literal subtext in musical sounds.

Ironically, the music could also be used by slave masters as a tool of oppression and torture. In *Narrative of the Life and Adventures of Henry Bibb, An American Slave, Written by Himself* (1849), Bibb reports that: "When they [slaveholders] wish to have a little sport . . . they go among the slaves and give them whiskey, to see them dance, 'pat juber,' sing and play on the banjo" (68). Likewise, Northup describes Master Epps frequently returning drunk to his plantation and summoning Northup and his fellow slaves to the great house for "merry-making." Epps, whip in hand, would force his exhausted slaves to dance and Northup to fiddle all night, as his "portly form mingled with those of his dusky slaves, moving rapidly through all the mazes of the dance" (323).

Yet no matter how white Americans might misinterpret the meaning of the songs or try to appropriate them, for black Americans the music provided a vehicle for protest and transcendence. Harriet Jacobs's *Incidents in the Life of a Slave Girl* (1861), published under the pseudonym of Linda Brent, contains a scene where the slaves go to a religious service to "sing their own songs and hymns" after being left waiting by the Reverend Mr. Pike:

> It was so long before the reverend gentleman descended
> from his comfortable parlor that the slaves left, and went
> to enjoy a Methodist shout. They never seem so happy as
> when shouting and singing at religious meetings. Many
> of them are sincere, and nearer to the gate of heaven than
> sanctimonious Mr. Pike, and other longfaced Christians,
> who see wounded Samaritans, and pass by on the other
> side. (398)

A common strategy that slave narrative writers employed in subverting
the existence of the slave system in America was to expose the
hypocrisy of Christian acceptance of this system. Jacobs accomplishes
this with her description of the "sanctimonious" reverend who only
deigns to meet the slaves in a kitchen and then leaves them waiting,
along with her reference to supposed "Samaritans" who ignore the
plight of their fellow humans. She says the slaves *"seem"* happy and
describes them singing "as though they were as free as the birds that
warbled round us" (399). Yet, like Douglass, she points out that the
contentment and happiness often perceived in the songs of the slaves
were deceptive: "Precious are such moments to the poor slaves. If you
were to hear them at such times, you might think they were happy. But
can that hour of singing and shouting sustain them through the dreary
week, toiling without wages, under constant dread of the lash?" (400).
While the songs might provide temporary relief, the ultimate answer to
her question is obviously "no," exposing the unjust and cruel nature of
the system and pointing to emancipation as the only genuine relief.

The slave narrative author who perhaps best recognized the
importance of music to African American culture both as a survival
mechanism and as a subversive medium was William Wells Brown. In
his *Narrative of William Wells Brown, A Fugitive Slave* (1847), he
includes a scene depicting the separation of family members, which
was considered a potent rhetorical device in attacking the slave system.
Working as an assistant to a slave trader on a coffle gang, a group of
slaves chained together in a caravan for transport, Brown relates how
the slaver decided to give a woman's child away because he was
annoyed by the infant's crying. The frantic woman pleaded with the
slaver but to no avail. At this point in his narrative Brown inserts the
lyrics to a song:

The following song I have often heard slaves sing, when about to be carried to the far south. It is said to have been composed by a slave.

> See these poor souls from Africa
> Transported to America;
> We are stolen, and sold to Georgia,
> Will you go along with me?
> We are stolen, and sold to Georgia,
> Come sound the jubilee!
>
> See wives and husbands sold apart,
> Their children's screams will break my heart; —
> There's a better day a coming,
> Will you go along with me?
> There's a better day a coming,
> Go sound the jubilee!
>
> O, gracious Lord! when shall it be,
> That we poor souls shall be free;
> Lord, break them slavery powers—
> Will you go along with me?
> Lord, break them slavery powers,
> Go sound the jubilee!
>
> Dear Lord, dear lord, when slavery'll cease,
> Then we poor souls will have our peace; —
> There's a better day a coming,
> Will you go along with me?
> There's a better day a coming,
> Go sound the jubilee! (197)

Certainly within the context of Brown's narrative the song reflects the sorrow and anguish brought about by slavery's brutish separation of family members. Yet these lyrics probably composed, as Brown indicated, by an enslaved black man or woman are particularly telling in their expression of the slaves' perception of their position in America. They exhibit an awareness of the historical and economic ramifications of the enslavement of Africans. There is an implicit refusal to accept the status quo and a hope for transcendence. But that hope is not cloaked in the imagery of some spiritual "better day"; it is very much linked with the concrete ability to "break the slavery powers." The sound of the jubilee is not to be a herald of some heavenly reward but a celebration of emancipation.

Authenticity was of paramount importance for the slave narrative writer, and this was often achieved through documentation or testimony from white abolitionists.[4] The insertion of a genuine slave song into Brown's narrative also provides a degree of authenticity. In fact, one year after Brown published his narrative he compiled and published *The Anti-Slavery Harp: A Collection of Songs for Anti-Slavery Meetings.* His assembly of such a collection testifies to Brown's belief in the proselytizing power of music in attacking the slave system. Among the forty-eight songs in his compilation, many of which are published anonymously, appears "Song of the Coffle Gang" credited to "A Slave." The lyrics are almost exactly the same as those of the song which appears in Brown's narrative. The editorial note with which he introduces the lyrics reinforces the appropriateness of the song's positioning in the narrative: "This song is said to be sung by Slaves, as they are chained in gangs, when parting from families for the far off South—children taken from parents, husbands from wives, and brothers from sisters" (30).

While Brown's insertion of an actual slave song contributes to the documentary aspect of his narrative, his inclusion of the full set of lyrics seems to call upon the reader to imagine the effect of hearing this song performed by black singers. Of course, he simply states that he has "often heard the slaves sing" this song in similar situations, rather than portraying the woman losing her child singing the song. But he is appealing to the reader's imagination and setting up a multi-textual discourse against slavery, a rhetorical strategy which extends beyond straightforward presentation of documented fact. He is asking his readers to step outside the text of the written narrative and imagine the aural text of a black musical performance. Blacks who were writing their own stories during the ante-bellum years moved toward the use of imagination, despite white editors insisting on verifiable facts, because they saw the potential of drawing white readers into vicariously experiencing the inhumanity of slavery.[5] Certainly Brown recognized the emotional power of his people's music, and by evoking the sound of a black mother singing the incisive lyrics of "Song of the Coffle Gang" in the reader's imagination, it seems he was hoping to bring home the cruelty and injustice of the slave system in a far more poignant manner than could be achieved through a simple recounting of the incident.

The representation of music in the narratives of these different African American writers implies that these writers were aware of each other's texts and shared common concerns as well as rhetorical strategies. An important characteristic common to these narratives is their dual expression of the individuals' story and the collective story of their race in bondage.[6] It is interesting to note that this individual/communal duality that exists in the fledgling efforts of the African American literary tradition corresponds to a similar duality in the music which the slaves had created and were continuing to develop. The call/response pattern of the spirituals and work songs, a retention from African musical forms, relies on the lead singer or soloist giving his or her version of a musical "story" while the whole group participates in the shared presentation of this "story." This dualistic pattern that is so characteristic of the African and African American oral traditions informs the earliest efforts of the developing literary tradition.

One concern that seems to be shared by the above mentioned slave narrative authors in their representation of music in slave life is the interaction that occurs between black and white culture through the performance of this music. Northup and Bibb comment on the white man's use of the music for his own entertainment and as an instrument of oppression. Jacobs and Douglass recognize the transcendental potential in the songs but are also concerned with the misinterpretation by white culture. What singles out Brown from the other writers is that he does not merely report his observations of this interaction and interpret the results. In his narrative Brown *creates* the interaction. He invokes the music to produce a desired effect on his readers. He wants to reinforce his case against slavery by getting the reader to imagine the sound of a black singer delivering a specific set of lyrics in a particular situation. Brown realizes that the music can be used to persuade white readers (listeners) and he incorporates the full text of one of these songs and its imagined performance as a subversive strategy in his rhetorical attack on the American slave system.

The use of imagination by Brown in his non-fiction narrative anticipates his own and other black writers' shift to the creation of fiction as a vehicle for depicting their experiences and voicing anti-slavery arguments. The shift from non-fiction to fiction was a logical progression in the development of the African American literary tradition.[7] The representation of music as an integral part of African American culture was carried over to the fiction created by black writers.

With *Clotel; Or, The President's Daughter: A Narrative of Slave Life in the United States* (1853), Brown transformed and augmented his personal experiences in slavery into the first novel written by an African American.[8] As previously stated, Brown's insertion of the "Song of the Coffle Gang" in his *Narrative* served both as an imaginative bridge between narrator and reader and an authenticating document, creating a multi-textual discourse. This narrative strategy, employing imagination and multi-textuality became even more complex as Brown wove fact and fiction together in *Clotel*.[9]

Another carry over to the novel was Brown's interest in music, which informed *Clotel* in two important ways. First, the event that provides the catalyst for the plot of the novel—the slave auction sale of Thomas Jefferson's mulatto daughters—was a long-standing rumor which Brown became at least partially familiar with through a song that he had published in *The Anti-Slavery Harp*.[10] Brown introduces the text of "Jefferson's Daughter" in his collection with the attribution "From Tait's Edinburgh Magazine" and also includes a quotation from the "Morning Chronicle": "'It is asserted, on the authority of an American Newspaper, that the daughter of Thomas Jefferson, late President of the United States, was sold at New Orleans for $1,000.'" The lyrics to "Jefferson's Daughter" encapsulate one of the overriding themes of *Clotel*: the hypocrisy and duplicity of America's architects of liberty and equality.[11]

Can the blood that, at Lexington, poured o'er the plain,
    When the sons warred with tyrants their rights to uphold,
Can the tide of Niagara wipe out the stain?
    No! Jefferson's child has been bartered for gold!

Do you boast of your freedom? Peace, babblers—be still ;
    Prate not of the goddess who scarce deigns to hear;
Have ye powers to unbind? Are ye wanting in will?
    Must the groans of your bondman still torture the ear?

The daughter of Jefferson sold for a slave!
    The child of a freeman for dollars and francs!
The roar of applause, when your orators rave,
    Is lost in the sound of her chain, as it clanks.

Peace, then, ye blasphemers of Liberty's name!
    Though red was the blood by your forefathers spilt,
Still redder your cheeks should be mantles with shame,
    Till the spirit of freedom shall cancel the guilt.

But the brand of the slave is the tint of his skin,
  Though his heart may beat loyal and true underneath;
While the soul of the tyrant is rotten within,
  And his white the mere cloak to the blackness of death.
Are ye deaf to the plaints that each moment arise?
Is it thus ye forget the mild precepts of Penn, —
Unheeding the clamor that 'maddens the skies,'
  As ye trample the rights of your dark fellow-men?

When the incense that glows before Liberty's shrine,
  Is unmixed with the blood of the galled and oppressed,
O, then, and then only, the boast may be thine,
  That the stripes and stars wave o'er a land of the blest.
(23-24)

Brown's depiction of the sale of Jefferson's fictional mistress, Currer, and the two daughters who were the "products" of the relationship, Clotel and Althesa, sets up the three-pronged thrust of the novel. The separation of family members sends the mother to Natchez, the younger daughter to New Orleans and leaves Clotel near Richmond, allowing Brown to examine the horrors of slavery throughout the American South.[12] Brown draws upon an anti-slavery song to set the plot of *Clotel* in motion and establish the geographic scope of the novel.

The second way that music informs *Clotel* comes through Brown's depiction of slave life in Natchez. Although Currer virtually disappears from the novel, the Natchez plot provides Brown's most effective anti-slavery fictional material.[13] While the African American characters in the New Orleans and Richmond parts of the plot are light skinned mulattoes, in Natchez Brown creates a dark-skinned, vernacular figure, the servant Sam.[14] What may be the first fictional representation of African American music by a black writer is achieved through this character.

In the early stages of the Natchez plot Sam is depicted as the "master of ceremonies" among Mr. Peck's slaves but also as a man who disdains dark colored skin, uses fresh butter to straighten his hair, takes great pride in wearing his master's cast off clothes and insists on having white blood in his ancestry. He is considered a prodigy by his fellow slaves because of his ability to read and has "a great wish to follow in the footsteps of his master, and be a poet; and was, therefore, often heard singing doggrels [sic] of his own composition" (112). However,

this rather fawning, assimilationist portrait of a black man is turned
upside down by the narrator with the description of Sam leading his
fellow slaves in song in reaction to the death of their master.

After Peck's death his daughter Georgiana, who has radical
abolitionist beliefs, and Carlton, a friend of Peck's from the North who
has fallen in love with the daughter, are walking across the plantation
when they hear the slaves somewhere off in the woods singing. On
hearing the singing Carlton remarks, "'How prettily the Negroes sing.'"
Georgiana replies that she is sure Sam is there because "'he's always on
hand when there's any singing or dancing.'" She also warns Carlton,
"'We must not let them see us, or they will stop singing.'" When Carlton
wants to know where they get their songs from she explains, "'Oh, they
make them up as they sing them; they are all impromptu songs'"(133).
Carlton then suggests that they stop and listen to one. Sam is leading
and the others are responding in the chorus.

Sam.
'Come, all my brethren, let us take a rest,
    While the moon shines so brightly and clear;
Old master is dead, and left us at last,
    And has gone at the Bar to appear.
Old master has died, and lying in the grave,
    And our blood will awhile cease to flow;
He will no more trample on the neck of the slave;
    For he's gone where the slaveholders go.

Chorus.
'Hang up the shovel and the hoe—
Take down the fiddle and the bow—
Old master has gone to the slaveholder's rest;
He has gone where they all ought to go.

Sam.
'I heard the old doctor say the other night,
    As he passed by the dining-room door—
'Perhaps the old man may live through the night,
    But I think he will die about four.'
Young mistress sent me, at the peril of my life,
    For the parson to come down and pray,
For say she, 'Your old master is now about to die,'
    And says I, 'God speed him on his way.'

'Hang up the shovel, &c.
'At four o'clock at morn the family was called
   Around the old man's dying bed;
And oh! but I laughed to myself when I heard
   That the old man's spirit had fled.
Mr. Carlton cried, and so did I pretend;
   Young mistress very nearly went mad;
And the old parson's groans did the heavens fairly rend;
   But I tell you I felt mighty glad.

'Hang up the shovel, &c.

'We'll no more be roused by the blowing of his horn,
   Our backs no longer he will score;
He no more will feed us on cotton-seeds and corn;
   For his reign of oppression now is o'er.
He no more will hang our children on the tree,
   To be ate by the carrion crow;
He no more will send our wives to Tennessee;
   For he's gone where the slaveholders go.

'Hang up the shovel and the hoe,
Take down the fiddle and the bow,
We'll dance and sing,
And make the forest ring,
With the fiddle and the old banjo.' (133-35)

With this scene Brown created what is probably the first fictional
representation by a black author of African Americans making music
together. Many of the themes and attitudes that the slave narrative
authors expressed about the music surface in this fictional performance.
Certainly the content of the song is subversive, for the slaves celebrate
the death of a master who had reputedly treated them so well. They are
also keenly aware of the specific nature of the oppressive acts with
which Peck exploited and controlled them. Sam and his fellow slaves
express their true feelings in the call/response form, and the communal
nature of this expression is reaffirmed as they laugh and exclaim, "'Dats
de song for me'" and "'Dems dems.'" Georgiana's recognition that she
and Carlton must listen surreptitiously seems to indicate she is aware
the slaves regarded their music as exclusionary, as something reserved

for a select inner circle. She also expresses an awareness of the improvisational nature of black music. The chorus of Sam's "impromptu" song specifically identifies the slaves' acknowledgment of relief from Peck's oppression as a musical celebration in song and dance using "the fiddle and the old banjo." The proselytizing effect that Brown attempted to evoke by inserting the lyrics and suggesting the performance of a slave song in his *Narrative* is depicted in *Clotel*. Hearing the content of Sam's song, Carlton regrets that he caused Georgiana to listen, but she refuses to leave and declares, "'It is from these unguarded expressions of the feelings of the Negroes, that we should learn a lesson.'" Georgiana understands that the music means more than just singing "prettily" to the slaves and that there is a "deeper meaning" to these songs. Carlton, who had spoken against slavery to Peck, seems to turn apologist and points out to Georgiana that her father's slaves are not treated so badly. Here Brown has the young white woman articulate the lesson she has learned, the rebellious subtext that she has heard embedded in the music:

> 'Yes, yes,' answered Georgiana: 'you may place the slave where you please; you may dry up to your utmost the foundation of his feelings, the springs of his thought; you may yoke him to your labor, as an ox which liveth only to work, and worketh only to live; you may put him under any process which, without destroying his value as a slave, will debase and crush him as a rational being; you may do this, and *the idea that he was born to be free will survive it all.* It is allied to his hope of immortality; it is the ethereal part of his nature, which oppression cannot reach; it is a torch lit up in his soul by the hand of Deity, and never meant to be extinguished by the hand of man.'
> (135)

The essential message that Georgiana has extracted from Sam's song corresponds to that "first glimmering of the dehumanizing effects of slavery" that Douglass heard in the music during his time in bondage. When Carlton and Georgiana return to the house and find Sam "looking as solemn and as dignified as if he had never sung a song or laughed in his life," Carlton remarks that "I could not have believed that fellow was capable of so much deception." Like the double meaning of the lyrics which Douglass pointed out, Sam's ability to dissemble is another example of the trickster strategies developed by African Americans in order to survive the oppressive control of white society. Once again Georgiana articulates a profound lesson which she has learned through hearing Sam's song:

> Our system of slavery is one of deception; and Sam, you see, has only been a good scholar. However, he is as honest a fellow as you will find among the slave population here. If we would have them more honest, we should give them their liberty, and then the inducement to be dishonest would be gone. I have resolved that these creatures shall be free.' (136)

What Georgiana has heard in Sam's song is the sound of the jubilee. Through hearing the musical performance of her father's slaves she has come to understand that anything short of emancipation denies the essential humanity of black people.

Brown continued his ground-breaking work in the establishment of the African American literary tradition when he became the first African American writer to have a drama published.[15] *The Escape; or, A Leap for Freedom* (1858) shows further evidence that Brown felt it was important to include musical expression in his depiction of black life under slavery and to use that music as a medium to attack the system. Much of the material that had appeared in Brown's *Narrative* and *Clotel* was reworked in *The Escape*. The servant Cato is a black, vernacular figure who has many similarities to Sam in the novel. A significant correspondence between the two characters is that they express their true feelings about slavery through songs. When Cato delivers a monologue stating his intention to escape to Canada, he shows that he is merely role-playing in his life as a servant, "den I'd show 'em who I was." Cato continues by introducing a song: "Ah! dat reminds me of my song 'bout ole massa and Canada, an' I'll sing it fer yer. Dis is my moriginal hymn. It comed into my head one night when I was fass asleep under an apple tree, looking up at de moon. Now for my song: " (27-8). Following this introduction Brown inserts the lyrics to "A Song for Freedom," which he had published in *The Anti-Slavery Harp* ten years earlier.[16] Like "Jefferson's Daughter," the song attacks America's hypocrisy in maintaining slavery while professing such values as freedom and equality. The song praises the British for making Canada a place where all races are free and also condemns the alleged Christian teachings of Southern masters and the cruelties of the slave system. This song, like "Song of the Coffle Gang," has a two-fold function in Brown's text. It works as an authenticating document and also calls upon the reader (listener) to imagine a slave singing this song of protest. To reinforce both these functions, Brown includes a stage direction indicating the melody that would accompany Cato's lyrics: "Air—'*Dandy Jim.*'" Thus Brown employs a "real" song to evoke a real situation in his dramatic representation of slavery.

Cato's first act when he escapes to free territory is to question his identity: "I wonder ef dis is me? By golly, I is free as a frog. But maybe I is mistaken; maybe dis ain't me. Cato is dis you? yes, seer. Well, now it is me an' I em a free man" (44). He follows this realization of his freedom by renaming himself "Alexander Washington Napoleon Pompey Caesar." He then composes a song attacking slavery and delineating his experiences: "Let me see; I wonder ef I can't make up a song on my escape? I'll try." Brown again inserts a stage direction with the intended melody and a full set of lyrics.

AIR —'*Dearest Mae.*'

Now, freemen, listen to my song, a story I'll relate,
It happened in de valley of de ole Kentucy State:
Dey marched me out into de fiel', at every break of day,
And work me dar till late sunset, without a cent of pay.

> *Chorus.*—Dey work me all de day,
> Widout a bit of pay,
> And thought, because dey fed me well
> I would not run away.

Massa gave me his ole coat, an' thought I'd happy be,
But I had my eye on de North Star, an' thought of liberty;
Ole massa lock de door, an' den he went to sleep,
I dress myself in his bess clothes, an jump into de street.

> *Chorus.*—Dey work me all de day,
> Widout a bit of pay,
> So I took my flight, in the middle of de night,
> When de sun was gone away.

Sed I, dis chile's a freeman now, he'll be a slave no more;
I travell'd faster all dat night, dan I ever did before.
I came up to a farmer's house, jest at de break of day,

And saw a white man standin' dar, sed he, "You are a
runaway."

Chorus.—Dey work me all de day, &c.

I tole him I had left de whip an' bayin' of de hound,
To find a place where man is man, ef sich dar can be found;
Dat I had heard, in Canada, dat all mankind are free,
An' dat I was going dar in search of liberty.

Chorus.—Dey work me all de day, &c.

I've not committed any crime, why should I run away?
Oh! shame upon your laws, dat drive me off to Canada
You loudly boast of liberty, an say your state is free,
But ef I tarry in your midst, will you protect me?

Chorus.—Dey work me all de day, &c. (44-5)

Because the lyrics correspond so closely to both Cato's and Brown's
own experiences, it is quite possible that Brown composed it
specifically for *The Escape*. Brown seems to be emphasizing the
improvisational facility of black musical expression, along with the
powerfully subversive message inherent in this music. Through his
escape Cato has empowered himself, and he celebrates this act by
renaming himself with a series of names of historically renowned,
powerful generals and political leaders from white, Western culture. He
also empowers himself by testifying to his own history by reaching into
African American folk culture. Cato uses the oral tradition; he
improvises a song in the call/response pattern that tells his story and
also addresses the system that exploits and oppresses the brethren he
left behind. It is interesting to speculate if Brown actually sang the
songs he inserted into his text when he read *The Escape* to abolitionist
gatherings. For just as Cato testified to his personal history and his
resistance to slavery by composing a song, Brown made a name for
himself and attacked American racial injustice in writing his *Narrative*,
Clotel, and *The Escape*. By representing the music that was being
created by his fellow black Americans during the nineteenth century in
his autobiography and in the first novel and drama in the African
American literary tradition, Brown illustrated the importance of music
in the lives of black men and women as they struggled to gain freedom.

Martin R. Delany was another ante-bellum African American writer who recognized the importance of music in the culture of black Americans and who pioneered the representation of the music in fiction. Black music-making permeates Delany's novel *Blake; or the Huts of America* (1859-6), which recounts the adventures of Henry Blake, a.k.a. Henrico Blacus, a free black born in Cuba and kidnapped into American slavery.[17] During the first half of Delany's two-part, rambling odyssey Blake escapes from servitude and travels throughout the American South to lay the foundation for a slave rebellion and returns to Natchez to lead his family and friends to Canada. In the second part Blake goes back to Havana to rescue his African American wife who had been sold to a Cuban slave master. He eventually joins the crew of a slave ship headed for Africa and returns to Cuba to become the leader of a black revolutionary movement.[18] Delany's representation of music gives coherence to *Blake* by providing both an important link between black culture in America, Cuba and Africa and a vehicle for revolutionary, anti-slavery expression.

Throughout the first part of *Blake* music is depicted as an integral part of black life in America, often reflecting the situations which appeared in the slave narratives. When Blake's in-laws learn of an impending sale of their family members from the plantation in Natchez they ease their sorrow with "a touching lamentation" (32). The lyrics which Delany inserts at this point in the novel are an edited version of "Song of the Coffle Gang," which had appeared in Brown's *Narrative* and *Anti-Slavery Harp*. Black singers in the novel comment on events in their lives, consistently expressing the desire to break the bonds of slavery. The lyrics of two songs that are sung in connection with the escape Blake leads to Canada closely resemble the lyrics of songs that Harriet Tubman reported having sung during the Underground Railroad escapes she led.[19] The functional aspect of music in lives of slaves is illustrated by black stevedores laboring on boats along the river as they time their work routines to music. One of their songs closely resembles Stephen Foster's "Old Folks at Home"[20]:

> Way down upon the Mobile river,
> Close to Mobile bay;
> There's where my thoughts is running ever,
> All through the livelong day:
> There I've a good and fond old mother,
> Though she is a slave;

> There I've a sister and a brother,
>   Lying in their graves.
> Then in chorus joined the whole company—
> O, could I somehow a'nother,
>   Drive these tears way;
> When I think about my poor old mother
>   Down upon the Mobile bay. (100)

The insertion of songs that were familiar to both Brown and Tubman and the similarity of the stevedores' tune to Foster's testify to Delany's documentary interest in music of this time period, and the use of "real" songs provides a degree of authentification to Delany's depiction of ante-bellum black life in *Blake*. Familiarity with these same songs also illustrates the pervasiveness and communality of music in nineteenth-century African American culture.

Throughout the novel Delany emphasizes the communal nature of African American music-making with such phrases as: "Then joined in chorus the whole company" (101) or "All uniting in chorus" (143).[21] The call/response pattern of the music functions as a metaphor for the individual/communal duality that Delany feels marks the approach to the life African Americans must adopt in order to overcome slavery. Just as black men and women join together in song, Blake ultimately hopes to unite them in the effort to obtain freedom. Like Douglass who closes the tale of *his* journey to freedom with a pledge to help "my brethren in bonds," Blake refuses to allow his adventures in the South to be looked on as personal heroism. When his comrades in Natchez ask him to "tell us about yourself," Blake responds ". . . I've much to tell you; but not of myself; 'tis about our poor oppressed people everywhere I've been!" (126).

Delany's attack on the slave system includes an ironic recasting of American patriotic symbols and songs in order to illustrate the hypocrisy and duplicity of their professed values. The narrator describes the American flag over a slave prison Blake encounters in Washington, D.C.: "Conspicuously stood among the edifices; high in the breeze from the flagstaff floated defiantly the National Colors, stars as the pride of the white man, and stripes as the emblem of power over the blacks" (117). When Blake leads the party of runaway slaves toward Canada, and a white ferryman will not take them across the Arkansas River because he refuses to honor their "nigger passes," Blake responds: "'Then I have one that will pass us.' Presenting the unmistakable evidence of a shining gold eagle, at the sight of which emblem of his country's liberty, the skiffman's patriotism was at once awakened, and their right to pass as American freemen indisputable" (135).

Patriotic music is parodied along with the flag and the American eagle. Blake and his fellow black sailors on the journey to Africa revise a patriotic song in overt defiance of the white power structure. The slave ship Vulture is run by two sets of officers, one Spanish and one American, so that she can fly the colors of either country in order to circumvent British interference. Tension between the black and Spanish crewman escalates because the American captain had been overheard expressing his disapproval of the slave trade. One morning the white sailors' attention is "arrested by a merry sea song of the blacks, which they chanted with cheerful glee, and rather portentous mood and decisive air." Delany inserts lyrics which are an obvious variation of "My Country Tis Of Thee:"

> My country, the land of my birth,
>   Farewell to thy fetters and thee!
> The by-word of tyrants—the scorn of the earth,
>   A mockery to all thou shalt be!
> Hurra, for the sea and its waves!
>   Ye billows and surges, all hail!
> My brothers henceforce—for ye scorn to be SLAVES,
>   As ye toss up your crests to the gale;
> Farewell to the land of the blood-hound and chain,
>   My path is away o'er the fetterless main! (207)

Upon hearing the black sailors' tune, Royer, the American first mate, rushes to the deck "full of ardor and patriotism" and orders silence because he was "sensible that the song was a taunt by the blacks to the Americans." When they ignore his order Royer summons the Spanish and American captains to the deck. They demand to know why Royer's command had been disobeyed. Blake takes on the role of spokesman and replies that the command had been for "'Less noise'" and the singers "sung easier though it may have been more cheerfully." Blake undermines the white officer's tyranny by constructing a rhetorical attack through skillful word play based on the precise use of the dominant culture's language. He states, "My people are merry when they work," and that seamen all over the world enjoy the right to sing. The American captain dismisses Royer's concern, and at Blake's command the men return to their tune, this time focusing their revised lyrics on Cuban slavery. Wearing the mask of "merry" workers singing with "cheerful glee" these black men can openly express their defiance toward their oppressors. The performance of the song, like Blake's verbal manipulation of Royer's orders, is a manifestation of resistance through the indirection of a trickster strategy.

A few days later when Royer breaks up a group of black sailors, he comments to the captain "If I had my way, I'd keep the Negroes in their place!'" Overhearing the remark, one of the sailors began to loudly hum:

> I'm a goin' to Afraka,
> Where de white man dare not stay;
> I ketch 'im by de collar,
> Den de white man holler;
> I hit 'im on de pate,
> Den I make 'im blate!
> I seize 'im by de throat—
> Laud!—he beller like a goat! (210)

Once again black music serves as a tool of resistance to racial domination.[22] The narrator indicates that the lyrics have hit their mark: "Hastening away, Royer declared that the only place where a white man was safe and a Negro taught to know his place, was the United States; and he cared not to go, not to live anywhere else but there . . . In his own country a white man was all that he desired to be; and out of it, he was no better than a Negro" (210). Royer has clearly recognized the threat the sailor has expressed through music, the only medium through which a black living under slavery could articulate such a message, and his response illustrates the true state of freedom and equality in America. When Blake assumes the role of leader of the black revolutionary movement in Cuba he is celebrated with defiant songs calling for emancipation written by his collaborator, the poet Placido. Thus, as the novel progresses Blake intensifies his insurgent activities, and the music takes on an increasingly militant role.

With the second part of *Blake*, Delany broadens the struggle against slavery to a pan-African scope. One of the key links between the African American, Afro-Cuban and African cultures that Blake comes into contact with during his adventures is the pivotal role of music as an outlet for personal, cultural and political expression. Delany's conception of making cultural connections in the various manifestations of the African diaspora through music may have arisen from his own upbringing. His maternal grandmother, Graci, had been captured in Africa and brought to America with her betrothed, Shango, a Mandingo prince. They were freed in America because of his royal heritage, and Shango returned to Africa. Graci stayed with her daughter Pati, and Delany learned about his African heritage through his grandmother's chants and stories.[23] It is likely that the chants that Graci sang to Delany as he was growing up served as conduits of cultural values and helped to provide the foundation for the great pride he took in his African heritage and its musical manifestations throughout the diaspora.

When the slave ship in *Blake* reaches the coast of Guinea the officers deal with a Portuguese slave trader named Ludo Draco, who is married to "Zorina, a handsome native African" and has "two daughters, Angelina and Seraphina, beautiful mulatto children" (212). Blake secretly witnesses an encounter between Draco and the elder daughter, Angelina, who had recently come home from school in Portugal and learned of the brutalities involved in her father's business. Angelina becomes distraught, and upon Draco's return from finalizing a deal with the officers of the Vulture, she expresses her sorrow and protest in song: "Suddenly they were startled by a song of lamentation, the most remarkable and pathetic, in which the traffic, gains and wealth of her father, the punishment, suffering and sorrows of her mother's race, caused by him and a king unworthy to be classed with the race of her mother, were uttered in tones of scathing rebuke" (219). Draco goes to his daughter's side as her song concludes and "promised the distracted Angelina never again to traffic in human beings" (220). Angelina's "song of lamentation" is particularly effective because of the sound, the "tones of scathing rebuke," in which the singer expresses her feelings. This emphasis on an inherent meaning *in the sound* of the music echoes Douglass's comment that the "thought" in the songs of American slaves "came out—if not in the word, in the sound" (262). Clearly Delany is linking the African girl's use of music to express her rejection of slavery and the efficacy her singing has in reforming her slave trader father to the spirituals created by black men and women in response to American slavery.

The denial of any cultural heritage for enslaved blacks was a tool of oppression used by slave owners, and Delany seems to be asserting the existence of this heritage by pointing out cultural retentions, especially in music. At a gathering in Cuba celebrating Blake's new role as "Leader of the Army of Emancipation," a revolutionary ballad, composed by the poet Placido, welcomes the hero, and then the crowd witnesses a performance on an African instrument brought to the Western world by slaves:

> On this occasion Pino Golias proved himself master of the favorite instrument of his father land, the African bango. In solos of strains the sweetest Spanish guitar proved but a secondary instrument compared with the touching melodies of the pathetic bango in the hands of this Negro artiste.
>
> This instrument, heretofore neglected and despised by the better class among them, at once became the choice— and classically refined by the nearest and dearest historic reminiscences among them, by an association with the evening of the great gathering, from a seclusion of which the momentous question of immediate redemption or an endless degradation and bondage was to be forever settled. From these associations and remembrances, the Nigriton bango could thenceforth be seen in the parlors and drawing rooms of all the best families of this class of the inhabitants. (251-52)

In this description of a banjo performance Delany not only connects Afro-Cuban culture to African culture but also asserts that African-rooted cultural expression is superior to European-rooted cultural expression. In addition, within Afro-Cuban culture the display of musical artistry breaks down class distinctions which had been fostered by slave holders to prevent unified resistance to oppression. Ultimately, this musical instrument brought from Africa becomes representative of the movement to gain black emancipation in Cuba. It also seems Delany is making a connection between this performance and the banjo in African American culture, hoping to undermine the stereotyped image of the contented, banjo-strumming black musician in the minstrel tradition.

Delany provides further evidence of the link between Africa and the black cultures evolving in America and Cuba through an Epiphany celebration: "The demonstration consisted of a festival—physical, mental and religious—by the native Africans in Cuba, in honor of one of their monarchs; being identical, but more systematic, grand and imposing, with the 'Congo Dance,' formerly observed every Sabbath among the slaves of New Orleans" (299). The description that follows is credited to an eyewitness account from a "popular American literary periodical." Music is depicted as central to the festival:

> A piece of parchment stretched over a hollow log beaten with bones, or a box or gourd filled with beans or stones, rattled out of all time, comprise their instruments. The songs are quite in keeping with the instruments and performers. On this day they are allowed to use their language and their own songs, a privilege denied them on other days lest they might lay plans for a general rising. (301)

Delany introduces the borrowed description of the festival by linking the black populations of New Orleans and Havana through the retention of African, particularly music-related traditions, and in asserting that the festival functions on "physical, mental and religious" levels he emphasizes the complexity and validity of this cultural expression irrespective of Western criteria of aesthetic and social standards.[24] However, the writer of the quoted periodical piece seems to be assessing the sights and sounds he observes from this Western viewpoint. Concerning the music he states "the delicate ear is agonized by sounds proceeding from the musical instruments of Africa" (299). Yet, he also recognizes the inherent subversion expressed through the music of the slaves when he points out that African language and music are potential tools in a "general rising." He goes on to suggest: "As it is the sights, the sounds, the savage shrieks, the uncouth yells suggest very uncomfortable thoughts of Negro insurrection. . . . It would be easy on King's Day for the Negroes to free themselves, or at least to make the streets of Havana run with blood. . . ." (301). The fear of a violent black revolt the festival evokes in the anonymous "eyewitness" may have been a foreshadowing of where Delany was directing his narrative. *Blake*, as the novel exists today, breaks off at the close of Chapter 74 with the line, "'Woe be unto those devil whites, I say!'" (313), and the resolution can only be a matter of speculation until the final six chapters are found.

Even without the conclusion of the novel, it can be said with certainty that Delany was a man with a scope of vision far ahead of his time. The emblematic use of African American music in *Blake* illustrates Delany's groundbreaking articulation of a Black Nationalist perspective and anticipates many aspects of the 1960s Black Arts Movement, including the focus on music as an artistic paradigm, militant rejection of white oppression, pride in African heritage, belief in pan-African unity, and the development of a "black aesthetic" for the production of artistic/cultural expressions of these beliefs. The representation of music in *Blake* as a conduit of cultural values, a medium of resistance to slavery, and a celebration of individual and communal spiritual transcendence, testifies to the power Delany recognized in his culture's music and its influence on the roots of the tradition of African American fiction.

While white America may have only been able to perceive and accept African American music in terms of the shallow caricature of minstrel buffoonery, Brown and Delany were aware that this music was a complex and powerful cultural expression, and they included it as such in their fictional representations of ante-bellum black life. For African Americans the music was practical, helping to ease the drudgery of day to day existence. It was social, bringing folk together for creative expression and entertainment. It was political, providing an outlet for protest, rebuke and resistance. It was psychological, maintaining a link with the past, easing the burden of the present and offering hope for the future. And it was spiritual, capturing the ineffable essence of a people's soul, ensuring the survival of that soul and ultimately promising transcendence.

2.
"UPLIFTING THE RACE":
PAULINE E. HOPKINS & PAUL LAURENCE DUNBAR

The years after the Civil War brought increased exposure to the music the slaves had created. An unprecedented cultural interaction took place with the northward migration of blacks and the influx of Northerners intent on educating and improving the lot of the newly freed black men and women. Music created by the slaves, particularly the spirituals, was recognized as an important cultural phenomenon, and a number of books appeared by white writers who were enthralled by this music. Such works as *Slave Songs of the United States* (1867) by William Francis Allen, Clark Pickard Ware, and Lucy McKim Garrison, and *Army Life in a Black Regiment* (1869) by Thomas Wentworth Higginson collected and/or commented on these songs.

African American music continued to be woven into the fabric of black life and reflected the changes occurring in American society. As Eileen Southern has observed: "In keeping with his traditions, the ex-slave sang about his experiences—his new freedom, his new occupations, the strange ways of the city, current events, and his feelings of rootlessness and loneliness. Above all he sought a self-identity" (222). Slavery may have been abolished, but its legacy both in the memories of African Americans and in the treatment they received, in the South and in the North, made it clear that there would be a long, hard struggle to reach the social and economic equality seemingly promised in the principles of American democracy. Emancipation raised a host of new challenges for African Americans, providing the raw material for fiction produced by a new generation intent upon effecting social change. Just as music had been represented in the pioneering fictional efforts of Brown and Delany as a expression of protest against slavery and a means of both physically and spiritually transcending this bondage, post-Civil War African American authors, such as Pauline E. Hopkins and Paul Laurence Dunbar, incorporated music into fiction dedicated to the "uplifting of the race."

The failure of Emancipation to bring about true freedom for black Americans and the escalation of Jim Crow terrorism prompted Pauline E. Hopkins to begin writing fiction as "an humble way to raise the stigma of degradation from my race." In her Preface to her first novel, *Contending Forces: A Romance Illustrative of Negro Life North and South* (1900), Hopkins explains her decision to adopt this form:

> Fiction is of great value to any people as a preserver of manners and customs—religious, political and social. It is a record of growth and development from generation to generation. *No one will do this for us; we must ourselves develop the men and women who will faithfully portray the inmost thoughts and feelings of the Negro with all the fire and romance which lie dormant in our history*, and, as yet, unrecognized by writers of the Anglo-Saxon race. (Hopkins's emphasis) (13-14)[25]

Hopkins is asserting that blacks must assume responsibility for the presentation of themselves, certainly a call for empowerment, and her emphasis on fictional portrayal seems to echo slave narrative authors recognizing the essential and effective use of imagination to construct a sympathetic connection between writer and reader in a rhetorical attack. As Hopkins states: "It is the simple, homely tale, unassumingly told, which cements the bond of brotherhood among all classes and all complexions" (13). The fictional portrayal goes beyond any factual recitation because it enables the reader to experience "*inmost thoughts and feelings*" by appealing to emotions with "*fire and romance.*"

In *Contending Forces*, Hopkins attacks American racism at the close of the nineteenth century by linking the lives of her contemporary characters to the mob rule violence and miscegenation their ancestors endured in slavery times. Her Preface elaborates on this connection: "In these days of mob violence, when lynch-law is raising its head like a venomous monster, more particularly in the southern portion of the great republic, the retrospective mind will dwell upon the history of the past, seeking there a solution of these monstrous outbreaks under a government founded upon the greatest and brightest principles for the elevation of mankind" (14). The representation of music in *Contending Forces* strengthens the cultural ties between the ante-bellum and post-Reconstruction African American characters that Hopkins creates.

The first four chapters of the novel recount the story of Charles Monfort, a wealthy British planter from Bermuda who moves his family and slaves to North Carolina in order to manumit the slaves gradually rather than comply with British law, which was calling for immediate emancipation. Monfort hopes to wean his fortune from its dependence on slavery and prepare his slaves for freedom. He creates a kind of escrow account to recompense them for their labor. His North Carolina neighbors abhor the course he is following and suspect Mrs. Monfort of having mixed blood. A mob murders Monfort and his wife, and his sons are separated and sold into slavery. One son escapes slavery on a journey to the North and his descendants, Ma Smith and her children Will and Dora, are the focus of the remaining eighteen chapters of *Contending Forces*. The Smiths run a Boston lodging house, and the educated Will and Dora are considered members of the city's "high-toned"African American society.[26] Their civic involvement aimed at uplifting the race provides the platform for Hopkins's treatment of late nineteenth-century American racism—North and South.

The music of the slaves in Bermuda and North Carolina in the ante-bellum section of *Contending Forces* links them to the cultural heritage of Africa. In the first chapter as Monfort and his clergyman discuss the proposed move to North Carolina, Hopkins depicts the slaves coming together to make music on a Sunday afternoon:

> In the direction of the square a crowd of slaves were enjoying the time of idleness. Men were dancing with men, women with women, to the strange monotonous music of drums without tune, relics of the tom-tom in the wild African life which haunted them in dreamland. Still,

there was a pleasure for even a cultivated musical ear in
the peculiar variation of the rhythm. The scanty raiment of
gay-colored cotton stuff set off the varied complexions,
—yellow, bronze, white, the flashing eyes, the gleaming
teeth, and gave infinite variety to the scene. (26)

Hopkins presents this performance from the perspective of the two
white observers, who listen with a "cultivated musical ear" and hear the
music as "strange and monotonous" and as a relic of "the wild African
life." Yet beneath the primitivism with which these white men shade
their perception of the music Hopkins calls attention to the fact that a
sophisticated rhythmic sensibility ("pleasure in . . . the peculiar
variation of rhythm") dominates harmonic or melodic sensibility
("without tune") in African-based music-making. Hopkins further
indicates that she is aware of the music's ability to be a preserver of a
shared, cultural heritage as it allows for expression of memories ("relics
. . . which haunted them in dreamland") of their African past. The
primitivism with which the white men view the slaves is also reflected
in their giving "variety to the scene" with "flashing eyes" and
"gleaming teeth," yet in her description of the musical participants as
having "varied complexions, —yellow, bronze, white," Hopkins
foreshadows the issue of miscegenation which becomes so pivotal to
the novel's plot and illustrates that all people who share African
ancestry are brought together in the communal process of music-
making. When the Monforts are situated in North Carolina and are
ostracized by their neighbors over rumors of Monfort's plan to free his
slaves and the possibility of his wife having mixed blood, Mrs. Monfort
reminisces over the beauty of the home they left in Bermuda with her
maid and foster sister Lucy. The narrator describes the two women as
both being "born on the same day. Their relations had always been
those of inseparable friends rather than of mistress and slave" (46).
Lucy replies: "'Yas, Miss Grace' (to Lucy her mistress was always
'Miss Grace'), 'I do feel sort o' squeamish myself sometimes when I tink
of the gals all dancin' Sundays in the square; but reckon we'll git used
ter these people here arter a-while; leastwise, I hope so'" (46). For this
black woman the memory of the shared community of the Sunday
afternoon musical performances is a stark contrast to the "coldness and
reserve" with which the North Carolinians treat the Monfort household.

Communal music-making is a cultural expression that links the
enslaved blacks of Bermuda with those of United States. The opening
scene of the second chapter in *Contending Forces* focuses on the

harbor at North Carolina's Pamlico Sound, and in Hopkins's first depiction of African Americans they are joined together in song as they work on the docks:

> A band of slaves sang in a musical monotone, and kept time to the music of their song as they unloaded a barge that had just arrived:

> > Turn dat han' spike roun' an' roun',
> >   Hol' hard, honey ; hol' hard honey.
> > Brack man tote de buckra's load,
> >   Hol' hard, honey ; hol' hard, honey.

> > Neber 'fo' seed a nigger like you
> >   Hol' hard, honey ; hol' hard, honey.
> > Allers tikin' 'bout yer ol' brack Sue,
> >   Hol' hard, honey ; hol' hard, honey.

> > Ef I was an alligater what'd I do?
> >   Hol' hard, honey ; hol' hard, honey.
> > Run 'way wid ol' brack Sue,
> >   Hol' hard, honey ; hol' hard, honey.

> > Massa ketch yer, what'd he do?
> >   Hol' hard, honey ; hol' hard, honey.
> > Cut yer back an ol' brack Sue's,
> >   He, he, honey ; he, he, honey.

> > I cuss massa 'hin' de fence,
> >   Hol' hard, honey ; hol' hard, honey.
> > Massa don' hyar make no differyence,
> >   Hol' hard, honey ; hol' hard, honey.

> > Turn dat han' spike roun' an' roun',
> >   Hol' hard, honey ; hol' hard, honey.
> > Brack man tote de buckra's load,
> >   Hol' hard, honey ; hol' hard, honey. (32-33)

It is significant that the first representation of American blacks in *Contending Forces* shows them joined together in a communal work song aimed at easing the burden of enforced labor because the united efforts of the Monfort descendants and their associates to counter American racist oppression in the late nineteenth century is central to Hopkins' s design for the novel. The insertion of a full set of lyrics into the narrative functions in a similar manner to the inclusion of lyrics in both the slave narratives and *Clotel* and *Blake*. The song is not only functional in terms of easing the physical demands of slavery by providing a rhythmic timing for a work routine, but it creates an outlet for the black workers to express their communal values, their awareness of the specific nature of their exploitation and oppression, and their rejection of that condition. In addition, like the inclusion of lyrics in ante-bellum, black narrative texts, the slaves' song on the docks of Pamlico Sound calls upon the reader to imagine the sound and feeling of such a performance. When they sing that the "Brack man tote de buckra's load" they recognize that skin color is the basis for white profit made from their labor. While a "nigger" who is "Allers tinkin' 'bout yer ol brack Sue" may seem to be a playful jibe at a wistful lover, it can also be seen as an expression of concern over the constant threat of the auction block bringing about familial separation. Escape to freedom, to "Run 'way," is the preferred course of action, but this too may call for familial separation. And if a loved one is brought along, both face brutal physical punishment if they are captured. For blacks trapped in slavery survival mechanisms were developed, trickster strategies of indirect protest like cussing "massa 'hin' de fence" or masking subversive sentiments by incorporating them into the acceptable forms of work songs or spirituals. The events that these slaves sing about as the Monfort family approaches the dock also foreshadow the separation of the two Monfort boys and the vicious flogging that kills Mrs. Monfort when the mob overruns the plantation.

As the scene continues the dock workers' singing illustrates how the slaves used music to comment on the events in their day to day existence:

> As the refrain died away the bell for the noon rest
> sounded faintly in the distance, gradually drawing nearer,
> and again their rich and plaintive voices blended together
> in sweet cadences as they finished placing the heavy load
> to the satisfaction of their drivers:
> Hark, dat merry, purty bell go
> Jing-a-lingle, jing-a-lingle, jingle bell,

Jing-a-lingle, jing-a-lingle, jingle bell,
Jingle bell, jingle bell. (33)

Hopkins closes the scene with the observation: "Even so sang the children of Israel in their captivity, as they sat by the rivers of Babylon awaiting deliverance" (34). The songs of both the blacks in the American South and the Jews in Babylon were raised in protest against an unacceptable situation. The Monfort family sails directly into this "captivity" and Hopkins locates her characters in the tradition of identifying the African American struggle for freedom with the image of the "children of Israel in their captivity."[27] The implication also seems to be that the Smiths, the descendants of the Monforts in late nineteenth-century Boston, may be the "Moses" that will lead the race beyond the "stigma of degradation" to the promise of American equality.

The impulse to join together in communal music-making is carried on by the Smiths and their circle of friends. They hold regular Sunday "musical evenings or reception nights" (102) at their lodging-house. The evening described in Chapter Six includes performances of a "medley of Moody and Sankey hymns,"[28] "the duet from 'Il Trovatore,'" and "the 'Chariot Race' from 'Ben Hur' in true dramatic style" (108). It would seem from the program that the participants were attempting to live up to the lodging-house's reputation that, "You've got to be high-toned to get in there" (103), and the implication is that they are imitating the proprieties of white Bostonian society rather than being true to the folk roots of their African music-making sensibilities. Yet, one of the residents, Mrs. Ophelia Davis, an ex-slave from Louisiana who runs a laundry, comments: "'Now, I'm goin' to sing 'Suwanee River.' None o'yer high-falutin things can tech that song.'" Yet, even Mrs. Davis makes "ambitious attempts to imitate an operatic artist singing that good old-time song." The song she chooses is Stephen Foster's sentimentalized vision of the ante-bellum South, and it would seem that even Mrs. Davis feels she has to mimic white culture. At the conclusion of the song her lifelong friend, Mrs. Sarah Ann White, informs the gathering "that 'Phelia made a great impression the Sunday before at Tremont Temple":

'Phelia had no paper to see the words, —not as thet made eny matter, 'cause 'Phelia can't read nohow, —an' the gentlemen next us on the other side, he gav Phelia a paper thet *he* had. The man wanted ter be perlite. Well, 'Phelia

> was thet flattered thet she jes' let herself go, an' thet man
> never sung another note, he was *so 'sprised.* After the
> second verse 'Phelia saw the distraction she was makin',
> an' she says to me, says she:' *How's thet, Sarah Ann?'* an' I
> says to her: *'That's out o'sight, 'Phelia!'* You jes' ought ter
> seen them white folks look! they was paralyzed! Why,
> you could hear Phelia *clean* above the orgin!' (Hopkins's
> italics) (108-9)

While the program at the lodging-house, including 'Phelia's song
selection and approach, may reflect the assimilationist tendencies of
some blacks during the late nineteenth century, the description of her
Tremont Temple performance illustrates that the inherent impulses of
black music-making have been retained. Among the racially mixed
congregation 'Phelia doesn't mimic a white style of singing, but rather
proudly displays her blackness in song. She has no need of the lyric
sheet because the essence of what she does cannot be captured on the
printed page. 'Phelia, who "jes' let herself go," is using the song as a
vehicle to express her feelings of cultural pride. When she realizes after
the second verse that she has commanded the attention of the
congregation she engages her friend in a verbal exchange that reflects
the traditional call/response between black musician and audience.
Sarah Ann's vernacular response, "That's out o' sight," serves as an
exhortation to the singer to show the "white folks" the commanding
power of black musical expression.

The music's ability to act as a conduit that keeps African
Americans in touch with their cultural heritage is found in Chapter
Eight when Ma Smith hosts a church fund raiser. Although she initially
resists the suggestion that they "Get up a dance" (158) to stimulate
sales of donated ice cream because she considers dancing sinful, Ma
Smith gives in and the Smith children and their friends begin waltzing.
They decide to conclude "with the good old 'Virginy' reel":

> The dance was soon in full swing-an up-and-down, dead-
> in-earnest seeking for a good time, and a determination to
> have it if it was to be got. It was a vehement rhythmic
> thump, thump, thumpity thump, with a great stamping of
> feet and cutting of the pigeon wing. Sam had provided
> himself with the lively Jinny for a partner, and was cutting
> grotesque juba figures in the pauses of the music, to the
> delight of the company. His partner in wild vivacity, fairly

> vied with him in his efforts at doing the hoe-down and the
> heel-and-toe. Not to be outdone, the Rev. Tommy James
> and Mrs. Davis scored great hits cutting pigeon wings and
> reviving forgotten beauties of the 'walk-'round.' Tommy
> 'allowed' he hadn't enjoyed himself so much since he
> came up North. (164)

The dance in Ma Smith's parlor recalls the communal get together that
was depicted in Bermuda in the opening chapter of *Contending Forces*.
The "Virginy" reel which these late nineteenth-century African
Americans join in, puts them in touch with their African heritage. Just
as the "peculiar variation of rhythm" evoked "relics" which "haunted"
Monfort's slaves "in their dreamland," the "vehement rhythmic thump,
thump, thumpity thump" of the reel revives "forgotten beauties" for
these black Bostonians. The reel also connects them to the cultural
productions their ancestors developed in response to slavery in the
American South.

Providing a medium for communal socialization and a bond to a
cultural heritage are not the only roles that music plays for Hopkins's
characters in *Contending Forces*. When the report of another gruesome
lynching in the South reaches Boston, a meeting of the American
Colored League is held to determine the response of the African
American population. The mood of the abolitionist movement is
evoked as the meeting opens when a choir performs the "Battle Hymn
of the Republic."[29] The crowd is stirred by the performance: "In
listening to the martial strains the pulse of the vast concourse of people
was strained with excitement and expectation" (244). The first
speakers, including both white and black politicians, urge Boston's
black population to adopt an assimilationist position. The crowd
responds with "suppressed murmurs of discontent" (254). The second
position presented by Luke Sawyer, "a tall, gaunt man of very black
complexion" (254), includes a firsthand account of rape and lynching
in the South that concludes with the exhortation: "'Mr. Chairman,
gentlemen call for peace and I reply: 'Peace if possible; justice at any
rate.' Where is there peace for men like me? When the grave has closed
over me and my memories, I shall have peace. Under such conditions
as I have described, contentment, amity—call it by what name you
will—is impossible; justice alone remains to us" (262). Sawyer's
horrific tale and demand for immediate retribution is followed by a
spontaneous outburst of African American song:

> Someone at this moment began to sing that grand old
> hymn, ever new and consoling:
>> Jesus, Lover of my soul,
>> Let me to thy bosom fly,
>> While the nearer waters roll,
>> While the tempest still is nigh.' (263)

When the room quiets down Will Smith delivers the third position the
African American community can adopt: political action, self
realization through education and agitation. The two courses of action
that refuse to accept and accommodate white, racist oppression are
linked by the singing of the spiritual. While the measures advocated by
these two approaches might differ, they share the insistence on protest
and subversion against American racism that was inherent in the
spirituals. The individual black voice raised in song amidst a communal
gathering is an affirmation which identifies these African Americans
with the struggle for freedom that the spirituals traditionally
represented.[30]

For the late nineteenth-century African Americans in *Contending
Forces* music represents a link to the cultural expression of their
African *and* American past. It is an expression that is uniquely their
own, a cultural production of black men and women that was aimed
simultaneously at protesting and physically and spiritually transcending
America's refusal to make good on the basic rights that Emancipation
should have delivered.

Hopkins joined the editorial staff of the *Colored American
Magazine* in 1900, the same year in which *Contending Forces* was
published. Her next three novels, which were serialized in this
magazine, exhibit a shift away from historical romance to more popular
forms.[31] One of these magazine novels, *Of One Blood Or, the Hidden
Self*, published between November of 1902 and November of 1903,
contains a landmark representation of African American music in
fiction. The character Dianthe Lusk is a member of the renowned Fisk
Jubilee Singers and may be the first fictional "professional" black
female singer created in African American literature. With Hopkins's
move to a popular form, her drawing upon a musical group from late
nineteenth-century popular American culture is fitting, for the
appearance of a Fisk singer is appropriate to this historical moment as a
member of the Supremes might be to the 1960s or a member of En
Vogue might be to the 1990s.[32] The Fisk Jubilee Singers first made
their mark during a performance at the World Peace Jubilee in Boston

in 1872 and went on to bring the sounds of the spirituals to countless new audiences and gain worldwide recognition.[33] As W.E.B. DuBois notes in *The Souls of Black Folks* (1903): "So their songs conquered till they sang across the land and across the sea, before Queen and Kaiser, in Scotland and Ireland, Holland and Switzerland. Seven years they sang, and brought back a hundred and fifty thousand dollars to found Fisk University" (266-67). The novelty of spirituals in late nineteenth-century Boston is illustrated when Reuel Briggs, the hero of *Of One Blood*, is invited to a concert by Aubrey Livingston, a fellow medical student. Briggs inquires, "'Who gives the concert?'" His friend explains: "'Well, it's a new departure in the musical world; something Northerners know nothing of; but I who am a Southerner, born and bred, or as the vulgar have it, 'dyed in the wool,' know and understand Negro music. It is a jubilee concert given by a party of Southern colored people at Tremont Temple'" (449).

At the opening of Chapter Two Hopkins describes the mark that jubilee singers were making on late nineteenth-century America:

> A band of students from Fisk University were touring the country, and those who had been fortunate enough to listen once to their matchless untrained voices singing their heartbreaking minor music with its grand and impossible intervals and sound combinations, were eager to listen again and yet again. Wealthy and exclusive society women everywhere vied in showering benefits and patronage upon the new prodigies who had suddenly become pets of the musical world. The temple was a blaze of light, and crowded from pit to dome. It was the first appearance of the troupe in New England, therefore it was a gala night, and Boston culture was out in force. (450)

While it is easy to see that these black singers are a popular phenomenon, they are still viewed through what DuBois called the "veil," "this sense of always looking at one's self through the eyes of others, of measuring one's soul by the tape of a world that looks on in amused contempt and pity" (45). The jubilee singers may have matchless voices but nonetheless they are "untrained." Their voices and musical approach were self-developed and not the product of training overseen by some official (white) institution. The jubilee singers may be "prodigies," but they are also looked on as "pets" by "wealthy and exclusive society women" whose patronage is truly patronizing.

Hopkins does not allow her portrait of these black male and female vocalists to remain behind that veil, for as the singers take the stage the narrator remarks: "These were representatives of the people for whom God had sent the terrible scourge of blood upon the land to free from bondage." It is clear that in a land where opportunity is denied and possibility is limited, the creation of music is an avenue which the African American can choose that will allow for both social advancement and emotional expression. These representatives of the race begin with a performance of "The Lord's Prayer" that denies their role of "pets" to the wealthy and exclusive: "Stealing, rising, swelling, gathering, as it thrilled the ear, all the delights of harmony in a grand minor cadence that told of deliverance from bondage and homage to God for his wonderful aid, sweeping the awed heart with an ecstasy that was almost pain; breathing, hovering, soaring, they held the vast multitude in speechless wonder" (453). DuBois recognizes that the essence of the spirituals is a protest, a challenge and a demand for an equal share in promise of American freedom:

> The minor cadences of despair change often to triumph and calm confidence. Sometimes it is a faith in life, sometimes a faith in death, sometimes assurance of boundless justice in some fair world beyond. But whichever it is, the meaning is always clear: that sometime, somewhere, men will judge men by their souls and not by their skins. Is such a hope justified? Do the Sorrow Songs sing true? (274)

This black musical expression, because it is "untrained" and has emerged directly from African American folk culture as a response to racial exploitation and oppression, silences the witnesses from the dominant culture and empowers these representative artists.

The ensemble performance at Tremont Temple is followed by Dianthe Lusk's solo: "Scarcely waiting for a silence, a female figure rose and came slowly to the edge of the platform and stood in the blaze of lights with hands modestly clasped before her" (453). Hopkins must have known the feeling of standing before such an audience for she was a vocalist who led her "Hopkins' Colored Troubadour Quartette" for many years, and in 1882 Hopkins was described as "Boston's favorite colored soprano" in the Boston 'Daily Globe'."[34] Lusk's performance holds the audience spellbound:

> There fell a voice upon the listening ear, in celestial showers of silver that passed all conceptions, all comparison, all dreams; a voice beyond belief—a great soprano of unimaginable beauty, soaring heavenward in mighty intervals. "Go down, Moses, way down in Egypt's land, Tell ol' Pharaoh, let my people go," sang the woman in tones that awakened ringing harmonies in the heart of every listener. (453)

This voice that so transfixes the audience delivers lyrics that evoke the Chosen People/Moses typology and its inherent rejection of oppression. Beyond the actual text of "Go Down, Moses" the sound, the "tones" of Lusk's musical expression create a non-literal subtext that communicates the collective memory, the collective consciousness of the African American experience:

> Some of the women in the audience wept; there was the distinct echo of a sob in the deathly quiet which gave tribute to the power of genius. Spell-bound they sat beneath the outpoured anguish of a suffering soul. All the horror, the degradation from which a race had been delivered were in the pleading strains of the singer's voice. It strained the senses almost beyond endurance. It pictured to that self-possessed, highly-cultured New England assemblage as nothing else ever had, the awfulness of the hell from which a people had been happily plucked. (453-54)

While the people that Lusk represented may have been "happily plucked" from the hell of slavery, *Of One Blood* focuses on how the legacy of American racism continued after Emancipation and Reconstruction. True to the conventions of popular fiction, the plot of Hopkins's novel takes a series of rather sensational turns, including a medical procedure that reanimates the dead, an expedition to Africa in search of a lost civilization, and a bizarre love triangle involving Lusk and the two concert goers, Briggs and Livingston. Sending Briggs on the expedition to find the Meroe civilization allows Hopkins to link African American culture with a sophisticated African past and subvert the Anglo-Saxon world's assumption of superiority. As one of the explorers speculates early in the journey: "'Your theories may be true Professor, but if so, your discoveries will establish the primal existence of the Negro as the most ancient source of all that you value in modern life, even antedating Egypt'" (520). A parallel journey into the American past of Lusk, Briggs and Livingston brings to light a history of miscegenation and rape revealing that the three characters are "of one blood," the offspring of the union of the same Southern master and slave woman. Briggs discovers that the common lotus-lily birthmark on their chests proves that they are the long lost descendants of Meroe royalty. The Meroes express indignation at Briggs' tales of American racism and confront a white American member of the expedition:

> And yet, ye are all of one blood; descended from one
> common father. Is there ever a flock or herd without its
> black member? What more beautiful than the stain gloss
> of the raven's wing, the soft glitter of eyes of blackest tint
> or the rich black fur of your own native animals? Fair-
> haired worshippers of Mammon, do you not know that
> you have been weighed in the balance and found wanting?
> that your course is done? that Ethiopia's bondage is about
> over, her travail passed?' (585)

The Meroe leader's prediction of Ethiopia's impending release from bondage invokes Lusk's musical plea to "let my people go" and its rejection of American racism. As a royal descendant of this ancient race it is fitting that Lusk represents African Americans, who all share in the heritage of Africa's past, through musical expression because the language of the Meroes is described as "musical" and flowing with "sonorous accents " (546).

In both *Contending Forces* and *Of One Blood* Hopkins represents music as an integral part of daily African American life. The music also functions as a nexus between the culture of black men and women in America and the heritage of their African past. For a writer attempting to raise the "stigma of degradation from my race," the music-making impulses intrinsic to this heritage have created an expressive form that subverts the alleged superiority of white America. In fact, the music of African Americans stands as America's foremost cultural production. Du Bois crystallizes this assertion in *The Souls of Black Folk:*

> Little of beauty has America given the world save the
> rude grandeur God himself stamped on her bosom; the
> human spirit in this new world has expressed itself in
> vigor and ingenuity rather than in beauty. And so by

> fateful chance the Negro folk-song—the rhythmic cry of
> the slave—stands to-day not simply as the sole American
> music, but as the most beautiful expression of human
> experience born this side the seas . . . it still remains the
> singular spiritual heritage of the nation and the greatest
> gift of the Negro people. (265)

Hopkins's most significant contribution to the representation of music is the creation of the character Dianthe Lusk, for not only is she probably the first "professional" black female singer in African American fiction, but she and her fellow members of the Fisk Singers in *Of One Blood* are designated as "representatives" of their people. As the nineteenth century drew to a close a new avenue opened up for African Americans; music-making, in addition to being a mode of personal expression, became an acceptable means of earning a living. Black musicians were coming to be regarded as outstanding individuals whose talents spoke for the community and allowed them to gain fame and (relative) fortune and rise above the all too frequent drudgery of day to day black life. As the African American musical artist achieved success other barriers to racial equality in America began to fall. The inroads made through music continued to be represented in the African American fiction that detailed the progress of the race.

The emergence of music as a professional pursuit for black men and women at the turn-of-the-century is depicted in Paul Laurence Dunbar's *The Sport of the Gods* (1902). The novel is concerned with the migration of African Americans to the North and the life they discover there. When Berry Hamilton, a former slave who remained on the Oakley Plantation as a butler for twenty years after slavery, is falsely convicted and incarcerated for theft, his wife Fannie and their son Joe and daughter Kit move to New York to start a new life. For these Southern blacks, New York represents the Promised Land that "seemed to them the centre of all the glory, all the wealth, and all the freedom in the world" (77-8). It is through the character of Kitty Hamilton, who sings for the benefit of the family's church and her father's fraternal organization in the South, that Dunbar examines the entrance of African Americans into the professional world of American popular music as they pursue their dreams in the North.

When the Hamiltons arrive in New York they are immediately introduced to the black popular music that is in vogue. At their rooming house they meet William Thomas, "a decidedly dashing back-area-way Don Juan," who prophetically informs the naive family that "N' Yawk'll

give you a shakin' up 'at you won't soon forget . . . We git the best
shows here, we git the best concerts— say, now, what's the use o' my
callin' it all out? —we simply git the best of everything" (90). Thomas
also tells the family that one of their fellow boarders is a professional
musician: "There's a fellah in the house 'at plays 'Rag-time' out o' sight"
(91) and invites them to see "a good coon show" (94). When he offers
Kitty beer in front of her mother she moves to the piano to hide her
embarrassment:

> With the pretty shyness of girlhood, Kitty sang one or two
> little songs in the simple manner she knew. Her voice was
> full and rich. It delighted Mr. Thomas. I say, that's singin'
> now, I tell you,' he cried. 'You ought to have some o' the
> new songs. D' jever hear 'Baby, you got to leave'? I tell
> you, that's a hot one. I'll bring you some of 'em. Why, you
> could git a job on the stage easy with that voice o' yourn. I
> got a frien' in one o' the comp'nies an' I'll speak to him
> about you.' (94)

Thomas recognizes the natural musical abilities of this young African
American woman and quickly suggests that she apply her talent to
these "new songs." There is money to be made if she can deliver a
fashionable "hot one" like "Baby, you got to leave," a title that suggests
a theme which became common to many blues compositions. It
becomes apparent that the suggested change in material is accompanied
by a desire to introduce the innocent Kit to the sexually liberated morés
of the New York lifestyle.

When the Hamilton family attends the coon show with Thomas the
narrator of *The Sport of the Gods* begins to cast this popular urban
music produced by black artists as a debasing of their talents: "But they
could sing, and they did sing, with their voices, their bodies, their souls.
They threw themselves into it because they enjoyed and felt what that
were doing, and they gave almost a semblance of dignity to the tawdry
music and inane words" (102).[35] This comment suggests that Dunbar
finds that the natural abilities and approach these black artists bring to
the material allows them to transcend the commercial glitter of
American show business. Nevertheless, Kitty is "enchanted," and Joe is
"intoxicated." And their mother is "divided between shame at the
clothes of some of the women and delight with the music" (103).
During the second act Mrs. Hamilton tries to convince herself that it

was fitting for African Americans to be rewarded financially for the music-making talents which they derive from their folk culture:

> At first she was surprised at the enthusiasm over just such dancing as she could see any day from the loafers on the street corners down home, and then, like a good, sensible, humble woman, she came around to the idea that it was she who had always been wrong in putting too low a value on really worthy things. So she laughed and applauded with the rest, all the while trying to quiet something that was tugging to quiet at her away down in her heart. (105-6)

While the singing and dancing may be taken for granted "down home," the "tugging" which Mrs. Hamilton feels is probably the fear of the corrupting influence that show business might have on her children.

The glamour of the concert hall is not the only urban attraction which Thomas brings into the lives of the Hamilton family. He takes Joe to visit a "coloured cafe," the Banner Club. Ragtime music is an attraction, but another aspect of the club that is surely beyond the realm of Joe's experience in the South is the mixing of white and black patrons in this setting:

> Here too came sometimes the curious who wanted to see something of the other side of life. Among these, white visitors were not infrequent, —those who were young enough to be fascinated by the bizarre, and those who were old enough to know that it was all in the game. Mr. Skaggs, of the New York *Universe,* was one of the former class and a constant visitor, —he and a 'lady friend' called Maudie,' who had a penchant for dancing to 'Rag-time' melodies as only the "puffessor" of such a club can play them. (118)

Probably for the first time in African American literature, black music becomes the attraction and the backdrop for the social interaction between the races. Dunbar presents an archetypal situation in the depiction of black/white relations in northern urban life: the partying, risqué white couple who go to a black music club in pursuit of the exotic or "bizarre." As the description of the Banner Club continues the narrator pulls no punches in assessing urban nightlife: "Of course, the place was a social cesspool, generating a poisonous miasma and reeking with the stench of decayed and rotten moralities. There is no defense to be made for it. But what do you expect when false idealism and fevered ambition come face to face with catering cupidity?" (118). What aspect of the Banner Club makes it so repulsive to Dunbar's narrator? Obviously, the hedonism associated with nightlife is seen as producing "decayed and rotten moralities." Yet, the narrator's objection to this "coloured cafe" seems to go beyond a simple condemnation of the fast life. The rhetorical question which closes the description of the Banner Club seems to point out the hollowness of the dreams African Americans had of finding the promise of freedom and equal opportunity in the North. The new life is approached with "false idealism and fevered ambition" that is misdirected in pursuit of financial gain. And in calling this greed "catering," the narrator seems to be focusing on the willingness of these newly urbanized blacks to serve up anything to anyone, including whites, in order to turn a profit. The implication of the narrator's perspective is that Dunbar looks on this social interaction as a kind of prostitution that can only lead to the corruption of idealistic blacks who have left a sheltered, if restrictive, life on the plantation.

However, there seems to be a more threatening aspect to this new phenomenon of interracial socialization. Joe is fascinated with the white patrons. As Thomas fills him in on the backgrounds of Skaggs and Maudie, Joe sees the white woman is "soon dancing with one of the coloured girls who had come in" (119). The intimation here is that the possibility of miscegenation which arises in such a social meeting ground gives the narrator further cause for condemning the Banner Club. Maudie has a "penchant" for dancing to black music as played by the "puffessor," a black man. Yet, she dances with "coloured girls," because heterosexual, interracial dancing would certainly have been taboo in turn-of-the-century New York (as would its fictional portrayal). Nevertheless, the protocol of interracial relations is on Joe's mind during this scene, and he wonders if he will ever have relations with whites on a first name basis. When Thomas introduces Joe to Skaggs, the white man asserts: "'I tell you, Hamilton, there ain't an ounce of prejudice in my body. Do you believe it?'" Skaggs goes on to offer proof for this assertion:

> You see, a lot o' fellows say to me, 'What do you want to
> go down to that nigger club for?' But I say to 'em,
> 'Gentlemen, at that nigger club, as you choose to call it, I

get more inspiration that I could get at any of the greater clubs in New York.' I've often been invited to join some of the swell clubs here, but I never do it. By Jove! I'd rather come down here and fellowship right in with you fellows. I like coloured people anyway. It's natural. You see, my father had a big plantation and owned lots of slaves, —no offense, of course, but it was the custom of that time, —and I've played with little darkies ever since I remember.' (121)

Skaggs' explanation for his attraction to the Banner Club reinforces the possibility of interracial socialization leading to miscegenation. In addition to slave ownership, "the custom of that time" was for white plantation owners to have sexual relations with their female slaves and also for the "little darkies" that these relations produced to play with their white brothers and sisters. And certainly the two major motivations for the masters' sexual interest in their female slaves were greed and physical gratification. Skaggs' and Maudie's searching out black music at the Banner Club reflects another "custom" from slavery: often black men and women were required to sing and dance for the masters' entertainment. The narrator comments on Skaggs' story: "It was the same old story that the white who associates with negroes from volition usually tells to explain his taste" (121). The narrator continues by calling Skaggs a "monumental liar" and revealing that the reporter's true background was a struggle for subsistence on a Vermont farm. While Skaggs' explanation for preferring to socialize with blacks is a fabrication, he may be expressing a fantasy of miscegenation. Maudie's enthusiasm for "Rag-Time" and her dancing with a surrogate black man and Skaggs' fantasy of himself as the "massa's" son cavorting with the "darkies" are closer to self-indulgence than fellowship. The narrator's tone dismisses these "white visitors" as patronizing and insincere in their interaction with African Americans. Dunbar seems to be suggesting that the interaction between blacks and whites in the nightclubs of the turn-of-the-century North is just as demeaning and exploitative as in slavery on the plantations of the ante-bellum South.

The evening at the Banner Club continues with a performance of a number of the latest coon songs. During the performance Joe becomes enthralled with a "yellow-skinned divinity who sat at a near table, drinking whiskey straight" (125). Thomas introduces Joe to Hattie Sterling, who turns out to be one of the performers in the coon show he had attended. The relationship that develops with Hattie draws Joe into the dissolution of the sporting life. He eventually comes to ruin when he murders her in a jealous, drunken rage. Ironically, it is a relationship with another black and not the whites he meets at the Banner Club that brings about Joe's downfall.

In addition to introducing Joe to the pitfalls of urban nightlife, Hattie Sterling opens the door for Kit Hamilton's career as a musical performer. Economic opportunities are limited for blacks in New York, and although Joe has some chances, his lifestyle interferes with his ability to hold a job. Kit and her mother are in terrible financial condition, and Joe arranges for Hattie to hear his sister sing. The young girl had set her sights on the stage since the night of the coon show. Once again the narrator criticizes the popular music blacks were producing, asserting that Kit had "dropped the simple old songs she knew to practice the detestable coon ditties which the stage demanded" (130). Kit is excited at the prospect of entering the world of professional entertainment "not so much with the idea of working as with the glamour of the work she might be allowed to do"(162). And this, for a young black woman at this time, is the promise of the North, the promise of possibility. The stage is one of the only careers that would allow escape from the drudgery of domestic work or physical labor.

Hattie is impressed by both Kit's voice and appearance and tells the aspiring singer she has the ability to rise to the top. The seasoned performer also relates the hard facts of life in the entertainment business: "'The thing has to happen. Somebody's got to go down. We don't last long in this life: it soon wears us out, and when we're worn out and sung out, danced out and played out, the manager has no further use for us; so he reduces us to the ranks or kicks us out'" (163-4). She also urges Kit to avoid the mistakes that have taken a toll on her own career: "'Don't you let what I say scare you, though, Kitty. You've got a good chance, and maybe you'll have more sense than I've got, and at least save money—while you're in it'" (164). The encouragement and concern in Hattie's comments reflect a hope in the future. This is a hope that comes to mark the African American musical heritage as individual artists pass along their contributions which are absorbed into the tradition and inspire further innovation. Hattie arranges an audition for Kit with the white manager of "Martin's Blackbirds." The young singer is extremely nervous as she auditions backstage surrounded by professional entertainers: "But the courage of desperation came to her, and she struck into the song. At first her voice wavered and threatened to fail her. It must not. She choked back her fright and forced the music from her lips." To Kit's dismay Martin is laughing when she concludes. Yet, she catches a "reassuring nod and smile from Hattie Sterling, and seized on this as a last hope" (175). Martin's response illustrates one of the triumphs of African American music-making:

> 'Haw, haw, haw!' laughed Martin, 'haw, haw, haw! The little one was scared, see? She was scared, d' you understand? But did you see the grit she went at it with? Just took the bit in her teeth and got away. Haw, haw, haw! Now, that's what I like. If all you girls had that spirit, we could do something in two weeks. Try another one, girl.' Kitty's heart had suddenly grown light. She sang the second one better because something within her was singing. (176)

Martin recognizes the inner spirit, the soul, the ability to draw upon trouble and desperation and create a triumph in musical expression. His appreciation for Kitty's spirit may be in terms of his own exploitative interests, but nevertheless his reaction to her performance focuses on the power of transcendence that distinguishes African American music.

Kit goes on to become a featured performer in the company and begins "to live her own life, a life in which the chief aim was the possession of good clothes and the ability to attract the attention which she has learned to crave" (216). She goes out on the road, and as her career progresses she is subject to the rigors of stage life: "Miss Kitty Hamilton had to be very careful about her nerves and her health. She had experiences, and her voice was not as good as it used to be, and her beauty had to be aided by cosmetics" (216-17). Dunbar does not validate Kit's ability to survive and remain independent through the music profession and fails to recognize that her music-making abilities open up possibilities that would be denied to most young black women of her time. The "experiences" she has on the road may have hardened the innocent girl who sang spirituals for church functions, but her talent as a musical artist is a means of empowerment and gives her "her own life," an independence unknown to the majority of turn-of-the century African Americans, particularly women.

For all Kit's success in the North, the migration is a disaster for her brother Joe. Prior to his arrest and conviction he harasses Kit for money, and they are estranged. After his crime she distances herself from Joe so that her career will not be adversely affected. Back at the Banner Club the regulars lament Joe's fate of life imprisonment, and the narrator comments that they wished they could warn idealistic blacks that the North is no Promised Land. One aspect of the hypothetical warning presented by the narrator focuses on Southern blacks hoping to take up musical careers in the North:

> They wanted to preach to these people that good agriculture is better than bad art, —that it was better and nobler for them to sing to God across Southern fields than to dance for rowdies in the Northern halls. They wanted to dare to say that the South has its faults—no one condones them—and its disadvantages, but that even what they suffered from these was better than what awaited them in the great alleys of New York. Down there, the bodies were restrained, and they chafed; but here the soul would fester, and they would be content. This was but for an hour, for even while they explained they knew that there was no way, and that the stream of young negro life would continue to flow up from the South, dashing itself against the hard necessities of the city and breaking like waves against a rock, that, until the gods grew tired of their cruel sport, there must still be sacrifices to false ideals and unreal ambitions. (213-14)

Through his narrator's commentary Dunbar asserts that African Americans are better off remaining in the South, a message that reflects Booker T. Washington's "Atlanta Exposition Address" that urges blacks to "Cast down your buckets where you are" (219). Yet, when the exonerated Berry Hamilton retrieves his wife from New York and returns to the Oakley Plantation the life they lead is a gothic horror show. They are bound to the white man who had been their master in slavery and who had covered up the evidence of Berry's innocence and caused the breakup of their family: "Many a night thereafter they sat together with clasped hands listening to the shrieks of the madman across the yard and thinking of what he had brought to them and to himself" (255). The Hamiltons's life back in the South casts a skeptical light on the narrator's assertion about singing "across Southern fields" being "better and nobler." Dunbar's seemingly contradictory message may reflect the confusion African Americans felt when Reconstruction failed to deliver the promise of equality they felt Emancipation would bring.[36] While the narrator attempts to cling to a preference for the pastoral life, it is apparent that African Americans in *The Sport of the*

Gods are trapped between two poles, neither of which holds true to the promises of opportunity upon which America is supposedly based.[37]

The casting of these black characters as victims of a "cruel sport" of forces beyond their control situates Dunbar's novel in the tradition of American naturalism exemplified by Theodore Dreiser, who was emerging as a major literary voice at this time. Joe Hamilton's helpless descent into dissolution and violent crime might be viewed as a precursor of a naturalistic "hero" such as Clyde Griffiths in Dreiser's *An American Tragedy* (1925). Yet, despite the deterministic forces that inform the naturalism of Dreiser's novels, often a romantic stream offers an alternative, a relief from the determinism.[38] In *Sport of the Gods*, despite the narrator's disapproval of Kit Hamilton's lifestyle as a black musical artist, this new career possibility for African Americans may represent a "romantic stream," a means of liberation from the "cruel sport." When Kit's mother informs Berry of the whereabouts of his daughter, she says: "'Kit dances on de stage fu' a livin', an' Be'y, she ain't de gal she ust to be'" (247). The mother speaks despairingly of what she considers her daughter's loss of innocence, echoing the narrator's negative opinion of black music-making in the North. This deprecation of popular black music may reflect the emergence of the long-standing theme in African American culture that music that is not intended to praise the Lord is the "devil's music." But beyond the mother's (and the narrator's) perspective, there is another way of looking at this woman who is no longer "de gal she ust to be"; she is something new on the American scene. Kit Hamilton is a professional black musician, and her career, her life on the road opens up the freedom of mobility and the freedom of personal expression to her. For Kit Hamilton, music is a way out. Her life as a black musical artist provides her with at least some means of breaking free of the polarized track between the legacy of slavery on the plantations of the South and the broken promises of equal opportunity in the ghettoes of the North.

Beginning with Douglass, the black writers who have been examined all exhibited concern over how African American music was perceived by white listeners. Generally, the music that was produced by the men and women in slavery is represented as a dignified medium of cultural, political and spiritual expression. African American music-makers are depicted as having their roots within folk culture, and often when the music is divorced from this folk context, it is misunderstood or degraded. This may explain the obvious disdain the narrator of *The Sport of the Gods* has for the popular music that Kit Hamilton and her contemporaries produce at the turn-of-the-century. The music of the coon shows and the ragtime "puffessors" may be regarded as demeaning, commodified productions designed for white consumption. Although the music does seem to provide a means of individual liberation and transcendence for Kit, Dunbar apparently disdains black folk expression's movement into mainstream American culture. While many of Dunbar's dialect poems present a romanticized view of black life on Southern plantations, his poem "When Malindy Sings," which describes the performance of a spiritual by a black woman, invests the black musical artist with a transcendent power.[39] The music in "When Malindy Sings" is rooted in the folk tradition and the concern of the poem's narrator is with the perception of black music by a white listener; there is an attempt to explain to "Miss Lucy," a white witness to Malindy's performance, the powerful, spiritual aspect of the music. Kit's music is divorced from folk culture and as mere entertainment is removed from this spiritual realm. Dunbar looks upon the production of popular entertainment by blacks as a pandering to white appetites for pleasure. Even though Kit's success is as an individual, and she is not particularly concerned with voicing communal values and concerns, Dunbar fails to recognize in his own representation that artists like Kit are opening doors into mainstream American society. In a way she symbolizes the "search for self-identity" of African Americans as they carve a place for themselves in the United States of the twentieth century. Kit Hamilton is the first fictional representation of the black musicians who begin to make names for themselves in the new century and who come to be regarded as representatives paving the way for African Americans as they continue the struggle to obtain an equal share in the promise of freedom equality in America.

Notes for Chapter One

1. In Chapter 2 of *The Story of Jazz*, "From Africa to the New World," Marshall Stearns discusses Colonial restrictions on the performance of music by African slaves. Stearns indicates that in Latin-Catholic "surroundings "slaves were more free to perform their traditional music than in British-Protestant "surroundings" (16-22). Also, in Chapter 1 of *Black Culture and Black Consciousness*, "Sacred World of Black Slaves," Lawrence Levine delineates the essential components of slave songs and their development from a two way interaction with white culture (4-54).

2. Chapter 5 of Eileen Southern's *Readings in Black American Music* is a collection of slave advertisements from eighteenth-century newspapers which feature music making abilities as valuable skills of slaves being offered for sale or as distinguishing characteristics in identifying runaways (31-35).

3. Northup's description of his position in ante-bellum plantation society also anticipates the exploitation of twentieth-century black musical artists in the white dominated entertainment industry. When the black musician's art and craft has not been simply co-opted by white artists, a certain amount of renown and financial reward has been achieved, but this usually represents only a fraction of the deserved artistic recognition and profit that the various musical innovations have ultimately generated.

4. In *From Behind the Veil*, Robert Steptoe discusses how authentification in slave narratives developed into a sophisticated mechanism of authorial control (4-31).

5. As William L. Andrews has stated, African American autobiography in the nineteenth century moved toward this use of imagination in spite of white editorial insistence on strict adherence to factual recitation because black writers recognized the need "to build a bridge of sympathetic identification between the diametrical points of view of the northern white reader and the southern black fugitive" (*Free Story* 137).

6. This sharing seems to uphold Henry Louis Gates, Jr.'s assertion that "slave narratives came to resemble each other, both in their content and in their formal shape." Gates goes on to say that the narratives were produced through a "process of imitation and repetition" and eventually

became a "communal utterance, a collective tale, rather than merely an individual's autobiography" (*Classic Slave* x).

7. As Andrews asserts, by the 1850s black writers were working in an "atmosphere of heightened intellectual independence and radical self-reliance" and could no longer accept "white notions of what the reality of slavery was and how it should be represented . . . Black writers needed to take responsibility for telling the African-American story 'past, present, and future' in fresh and creative ways that would not only empower black people but apprise whites of the value of black experience to 'the original romance' of America" (Introduction 10).

8. While *Clotel* was the first novel to be written by an African American, it was published in England. Harriet E. Wilson's *Our Nig Or, Sketches From The Life Of A Free Black* (1859) was the first African American novel to be published in the United States.

9. William L. Andrews's "The Novelization of Voice in Early African American Narrative" posits that early African American fiction writers engaged in a subtle interplay of "fictive" and "natural" discourse to empower the black authorial voice.

10. According to Blyden Jackson's *A History of Afro-American Literature- Vol. 1* , the song was not original to Brown's collection, but had been printed "on both sides of the Atlantic by abolitionists" (338).

11. Bernard Bell states in *The Afro-American Novel and Its Tradition*:: "Although Jefferson is not actually portrayed, the legend of his mulatto mistress and the nobility of his works reverberate through the narrative. With caustic irony, Brown quotes the ideas expressed in the Declaration of Independence and in Jefferson's anti-slavery speeches in the Virginia legislature. The symbolic father of the nation, Jefferson is also a symbolic of the historical moral hypocrisy of the nation" (41).

12. J. Noel Heermance's *William Wells Brown and* Clotelle suggests that the "sprawling geographic structure" of the novel allows Brown to "cover the whole South" with his indictment of slavery (164-65).

13. Heermance also indicates that "Situated on the Carlton [Peck] farm, Brown can allow himself to describe in concrete detail and semi-realistic dialect those elements of Negro and poor white farm and home life which Brown had experienced in his own early years in slavery" (167-68).

14. In *The Intricate Knot* Jean Fagan Yellin asserts that the creation of the character Sam has an important significance in the

development of Afro-American literature. She calls Sam a "ironic, tough black man . . . who will reappear as the vernacular hero of black fiction" (177).

15. William Edward Farrison's *William Wells Brown: Author and Reformer* quotes a letter from Brown to William Lloyd Garrison, which appeared in *The Liberator* on March 5, 1858 stating "you will see by the handbill I send you, that I am reading my new drama, which I consider far superior to the one I gave in Lynn." The drama Brown was about to read was *The Escape*, therefore, it would seem he had written another drama which is not currently extant.

16. Except for the deletion of the third verse, "A Song for Freedom" appears in the drama almost exactly as it had in *The Anti-Slavery Harp*.

17. *Blake* was first published in book form in 1970. According to Floyd J. Miller: "Approximately eighty chapters comprise the complete novel, which appeared serially in *The Weekly Anglo-African* from November 26, 1861, until late May, 1862. . . . The complete novel contains perhaps six chapters that have not yet been uncovered" (ix).

18. In *The Intricate Knot* Yellin asserts that at times the novel loses coherence because of "Delany's inclusion of such disparate elements, coupled with his often clumsy style . . . but at its best Blake is a vigorous montage of black life at mid-century." In addition, Yellin finds "on another level the novel is a revolutionary handbook outlining the organization of a guerrilla army of black liberationists" (199).

19. See Floyd J. Miller note 4, page 315. Tubman's version of these songs appearing in: Bradford, Sarah H. *Scenes in the Life of Harriet Tubman.* Auburn: N.Y., 1869, which was republished and expanded as *Harriet Tubman: The Moses of her People* in 1886 (28 & 49-50).

20. Miller states that Delany's song "may not necessarily be a derivation" from "Old Folks at Home" because Foster was married to the daughter of a Pittsburgh physician under whom Delany had studied medicine in the 1830s, and "it is conceivable that Foster learned the song from Delany, or that both drew upon a common source" (317). Miller credits Frank A. Rollin [Whipper]. *Life and Public Service of Martin R. Delany.* Boston (1868) with this information.

21. Bernard Bell has suggested that "spirituals and work songs reinforce the theme of group solidarity" in *Blake* (53).

22. Ronald T. Takaki 's *Violence in the Black Imagination* suggests that this particular song "brings together two important themes in the

novel: black emigration to Africa and black violence against whites (96).

23. Takaki asserts that "during his childhood Martin had an intimate contact with Africa—his Mandingo grandmother (who died at the age of 107) and her chants about her homeland" (83).

24. *My Southern Home: or, The South and Its People* (Boston: A. G. Brown, 1880), William Wells Brown's reminiscences of ante-bellum slave life and observations on the post-bellum South which reworks much material from *Clotel* and *The Escape*, contains a detailed account of the New Orleans Congo Dance festival that is similar to the "borrowed" account of King's Day in *Blake* (121-25).

25. In her Introduction to *The Magazine Fiction of Pauline Hopkins* Hazel Carby asserts that Hopkins felt: "Fiction . . . could reach the many classes of citizens who never read history or biography, and thus she created fictional histories with a pedagogic function: narratives of the relations between the races that challenged racist ideologies" (xxxv).

26. The Smiths seem to be examples of what W.E.B. DuBois called the "Talented Tenth," a highly educated, elite group of African Americans who would take on the leadership in "uplifting" the masses.

27. Werner Sollors discusses "Go Down Moses" and the use of typology in the African American literary tradition in Chapter Two of *Beyond Ethnicity: Consent and Descent in American Culture*. Lawrence Levine asserts in *Black Culture and Black Consciousness* that the most pervasive image in the lyrics of the spirituals "is that of the Israelites and Moses escaping from the Pharaoh" (50).

28. The *Moody Hymnal* and *Sankey Hymnal* were collections of white Protestant hymns that were used during slavery and later into the nineteenth century. In *Blues People*, LeRoi Jones (Amiri Baraka) states that "no matter how closely a Negro spiritual might resemble superficially one of the white hymns" taken from one of these collections, "when the song was actually sung, there could be no mistake that it had been made over into an original Negro song." In fact, Jones points out that Melville Herskovits's *The Myth of the Negro Past* (1941) notes that "in a great many parts of the West Indies, all the Protestant pseudo-Christian religious songs are called 'sankeys'" (46). Therefore, the "medley of Moody and Sankey hymns" performed at Smith's musical evening could well have been rooted in the African American folk tradition.

29. Hopkins hoped "the city of Boston could be recreated as the center of black and white political agitation that it was at the height of abolitionism" (Carby Introduction xxxii).

30. The fictional representatives of Boston's black community created by Hopkins have been criticized as assimilationist depictions of African Americans. In her Afterword to *Contending Forces* Gwendolyn Brooks charges: "Pauline Hopkins had . . . a touching reliance on the dazzles and powers of anticipated integration. But she would have been remarkable indeed if, enslaved as she was by her special time and temperament, she had been forward enough to instruct blacks not to rely on goodies coming from any source save personal heart, head, hand. . . . Often doth the brainwashed slave revere the modes and idolatries of the master, and Pauline Hopkins consistently proves herself a continuing slave, despite little bursts of righteous heat, throughout *Contending Forces*. (404-5). Brooks points out the contrast between the descriptions of striking beauty that Hopkins lavishes on the light-skinned character Sappho Clark and the ordinariness of dark-skinned characters as evidence of her "enslavement" to an assimilationist perspective. However, Carby has suggested that the focus on light-skinned black characters was designed to subvert white supremacist notions rather than uphold them: "But the presence of "mixed" characters in the text did not represent an implicit desire to "lighten" blacks through blood ties with whites. Hopkins wanted to emphasize those sets of social relations and practices which were the consequence of a social system that exercised white supremacy through the act of rape." For Carby, the focus on light-skinned African American characters in *Contending Forces* "undermines the theory of total separation of the races" (*Reconstructing* 140).

31. Carby asserts that the magazine hoped to "capture both a black readership and a black advertising market." Hopkins's novels "incorporate some of the narrative formulas of the sensational fiction of dime novels and story papers" (Introduction xxxii-vi).

32. The Supremes were the premiere recording act for the Detroit-based Motown label during the 1960s. En Vogue is rap/soul/R&B/rock group from Oakland made up of four female singers who have reached tremendous levels of popular acclaim during the 1990s. The broad range of their repertoire make them representative of a wide spectrum of popular music market.

33. See Eileen Southern's *The Music of Black Americans* (227-28).

34. See Dickson Bruce, Jr.'s *Black American Writing from the Nadir* (145).

36. In *Black Magic: A Pictorial History of Black Entertainers in America* by Langston Hughes and Milton Meltzer the evolution of the "coon show" at the turn-of-the-century is descibed: "Slowly the tradition of minstrel exaggeration began to give way to a non-blackface pattern in negro musicals which incorporated large choruses of pretty girls. At first, however, these shows were not termed musicals. They were called 'coon shows' in contrast to the minstrels and Tom shows" (47-48).

36. As Bernard Bell has commented: "The narrative questions the illusion of innocence, simplicity, and harmony of life for blacks on the plantation and the popular myth of the North as a land of milk and honey" (71).

37. In *Blues, Ideology, and Afro-American Literature*, Houston Baker, Jr. states that *The Sport of the Gods* "specifically explores the proposition that a literary tradition governed by plantation and coon show images of Afro-Americans can be altered through an ironic, symbolic, fictive (blues) manipulation of such images and the tradition of which they area formative part" (137). Baker also asserts: "One's mode of explaining the novel's meaning (and, indeed, the meaning of Afro-American literary texts in general) must transcend, that is to say, a customary, sharply limiting critical strategy that yokes the analysis of works of verbal art to acts of historical interpretation" (138).

38. See Charles F. Walcutt's "Theodore Dreiser and the Divided Stream" which asserts that a "divided stream" runs through Dreiser's work; his naturalism is tempered by a romanticism.

39. Houston Baker, Jr. has asserted that in "When Malindy Sings" that "the poet raises the black American's gift of song to a cosmic and etherealized plane; Malindy's singing and the voice of God, or what is ultimately spiritual, become one" (*Black Literature* 108). According to Gayl Jones in *Liberating Voices*, Dunbar's portrait of Malindy is "glorified," yet paradoxically, she exists "in the background of the work. We never *really* see her as a complex intricate foreground personality; and there is a tension between the seen and unseen territory; to use Ellison's metaphors for being. Jones goes on to assert that the "dialect mode in the African American poetic tradition will need to be stretched and bent to move into the interior landscape and discover the true complexities of the African American voice. . . ." (21-22).

II
"Depths to Which Mere Sound Had No Business to Go"

"Hey, people, listen while I spread my news,
 I wanta tell you people all about my bad luck
blues."
                                    - Gertrude "Ma" Rainey

"Ragtime has not only influenced American music, it
has influenced American life; indeed it has saturated
American life. It has become the popular medium for
our national expression musically. And who can say
that it does not express the blare and jangle and the
surge, too, of our national spirit?"
                                    - James Weldon Johnson

"I love the life I live, I live the life I love."
                                    - Muddy Waters

"I entered the cheap café and found a colored man at
the piano, dog tired. He told me he had to play from
seven at night until seven in the morning, and rested
himself by playing with alternate hands. He told me
of his life, and it seemed to me that this poor, tired,
happy-go-lucky musician represented his race. I set it
down in notes, keeping faith with all that made the
background of that poor piano thumper."
                                    - W. C. Handy

"Hurry, hurry, hurry, take the 'A' train
To find the quickest way to get to Harlem.
     If you should take the 'A' train,
You'll find you'll get where you're going in a hurry."
                                    - Duke Ellington

"Blues tells a terrific story. It's got that suffering thing
to it and a lot of people suffer in their own way."
                                    - Albert "Budd" Johnson

1.
"THE MOST TREASURED HERITAGE OF THE AMERICAN NEGRO": JAMES WELDON JOHNSON

The tension between individual and communal expression that African American artists faced in the early part of the twentieth century is poignantly articulated in James Weldon Johnson's *The Autobiography of an Ex-Coloured Man* (1912). A pivotal work in the representation of music in the African American literary tradition, Johnson's novel is the story of a ragtime piano player whose light skin allows him to "pass" as a white man.

The Autobiography was originally published anonymously, encouraging readers to believe the text was a "real" autobiography. Johnson, like Brown and other black authors from the nineteenth century, blurred the lines between fiction and non-fiction.[1] The story of the ragtime pianist is narrated in the first person, and although the personal incidents recounted may be Johnson's fictional creations, the observations and analyses of African American music—both ragtime and spirituals—reappeared verbatim or were reworked in Johnson's landmark commentaries on African American culture, the Prefaces to *The Book of American Negro Poetry* (1922) and *The Book of American Negro Spirituals* (1925). This indicates that Johnson used the narrator to express his personal views on the music that was emerging from the black experience in America.[2] Music, for both Johnson and his narrator, is a touchstone for racial pride and a vehicle through which representative individuals can advance the status of the black race in American culture. However, there is a disparity between Johnson and his narrator. The pianist/protagonist fails to negotiate the balance between the individual and the communal with his musical abilities and reveals himself to be a selfish and spineless traitor who sells his "birthright for a mess of pottage" (211). Johnson, in his use of a narrator who decides to disappear into white American society and abandon his talent as a ragtime pianist and composer, illustrates the wasted opportunity for social advancement that the race could have attained through the efforts of the individual artist in the communal African American musical tradition.

The Autobiography opens with the narrator acknowledging that he is risking the revelation of his identity by telling his life story but that he finds "a sort of savage and diabolical desire to gather up all the little tragedies of my life, and turn them into a practical joke on society." He seems to feel that his "joke" will make amends for his abandonment of his heritage as he speaks of being "led by the same impulse which forces the un-found-out criminal to take somebody into his confidence." Yet, taunting white society with his deception is not the primary motivation for presenting his life story because the narrator proves again and again that he is a self-centered individual: "And, too I suffer a vague feeling of unsatisfaction, of regret, of almost remorse, from which I am seeking relief, and of which I shall seek in the last paragraph of this account" (3). In that paragraph the narrator addresses the abandonment of his plans to use folk sources from African American culture to forge a new musical form that will advance his race. By singling out this paragraph on the first page Johnson emphasizes the importance of the abandonment in the scheme of his novel. What prompts the narrator to reveal the details of his life is not a desire to right the wrong he has committed selfishly but to find relief from a feeling "of *almost* remorse."

Johnson's story of a black man's life has roots in the slave narratives.[3] The narrator relates that he was born in a "little Georgia town," which (like himself) remains nameless, "because there are people still living there who could be connected with this narrative" (4). He actually calls his story a "narrative," and his refusal to reveal names echoes the anonymity that Douglass and other slave narrative writers often employed to protect those left behind in the South, as well as those seeking refuge in the North. Like the slave narratives, the initial movement of the Ex-Coloured Man's story is northward. The narrator and his mother, a black servant, move north to New England when his father, a white Southern aristocrat, becomes engaged to a white woman. This situation also reflects the common trope of white males abandoning their black female lovers and children in the slave narratives and ante-bellum fiction like *Clotel*.[4]

Two aspects of his northern childhood experience that are inextricably linked to his eventual decision to pass as white are his musical education and his initiation into African American culture. The development of the narrator's skill as a pianist emphasizes his grounding in the black artistic heritage. One of the narrator's earliest memories of his life in the North is of his mother teaching him to read and, more importantly, play the piano. The Ex-Coloured Man remembers her playing "simple accompaniments to some old Southern songs which she sang. In these songs she was freer, because she played them by ear." He recalls those evenings listening to and learning the spirituals, certainly his initiation into black cultural expression, as "the happiest hours of my childhood." And his participation in those performances anticipates his facility as a ragtime pianist: "I used to stand by her side and often interrupt and annoy her by chiming in with strange harmonies which I found on either the high keys of the treble or the low keys of the bass. I remember that I had a particular fondness for the black keys" (8). His improvisational ability is apparent in these initial performances where he expands and embellishes the "simple accompaniments." Also, his "fondness for the black keys" seems symbolic of his propensity for the African American approach to music-making.

Testimony to the narrator's musical sensibilities having their roots in the African American tradition is found in his preference "not to be hampered by notes." The music teacher his mother finds him "had no small difficulty at first in pinning me down to the notes. If she played my lesson over for me, I invariably attempted to reproduce the required sounds without the slightest recourse to written characters" (9). The young pianist's attraction to playing by ear, an approach passed down to him by his mother, reflects an aspect of African American music-making that Johnson emphasizes in the Preface to *Negro Spirituals*. Johnson establishes that there are distinct differences between African and European conceptions of music, and that musicians in the European tradition have trouble playing African-derived music because "they play the notes too correctly; and do not play what is not written down" (28). Echoing the Ex-Coloured Man's aversion to "written characters," Johnson also states in the *Spirituals* Preface: "I doubt that it is possible with our present system of notation to make a fixed transcription of these peculiarities that would be absolutely true; for in their very nature they are not susceptible to fixation" (30).[5] Thus, at the earliest stages of his career as a piano player the Ex-Coloured Man is very much in tune with an African-based conception of music-making.

His piano playing abilities advance so rapidly that by the time the narrator of *The Autobiography* is twelve-years-old he gains the appellation of "infant prodigy." He says that his approach was unique for a child of this age because he did not depend on the usual trick of showing off "brilliancy of technique":

> I always tried to interpret a piece of music; I always
> played with feeling . . . . I think this was due not entirely
> to natural artistic temperament, but largely to the fact that
> I did not begin to learn piano by counting out exercises,
> but by trying to reproduce the quaint songs which my
> mother used to sing, with all their pathetic turns and
> cadences. (26-27)

The emphasis on interpretation and feeling, cornerstones of the African American approach to music-making, is attributed to his grounding in the black folk tradition, the "quaint songs," the Spirituals, which his mother learned in the American South. As he matures as a musical artist, the narrator realizes that his personal approach keeps him from becoming a good accompanist: "I have never been a really good accompanist because my ideas of interpretation were always too strongly individual. I constantly forced my *acceleraddos* and *rubatos* upon the soloist, often throwing the duet entirely out of gear" (Johnson's italics) (29). Once again the narrator asserts the individualism that marks his playing style, but he also reveals that the egotism of his approach is so extreme that the coherence of the performance suffers. His self-centered, individualistic impulses ultimately lead the pianist to abandon both his music and his race.

The Ex-Coloured Man is unaware that his piano playing exhibits characteristics of the African American music-making approach. Ironically, as a young school boy, the narrator, because of his light skin, does not even know that he is black until this is pointed out by a school official. A series of encounters serve to initiate the narrator's struggle to identify himself as an African American. The revelation of his ancestry has a devastating effect; he describes it as a "sword-thrust . . . which was years in healing" (19). The narrator's reflection on what it means to be a black man in the United States is strikingly similar to Du Bois's concept of "double consciousness": "He is forced to take his outlook on all things, not from the view-point of a citizen, or a man, or even a human being, but from the view-point of a *coloured* man" (Johnson's italics) (21). With the realization that he shares the same "status" as the other black children, the narrator withdraws into himself and "began to find company in books, and greater pleasure in music" (24).

A visit from his father has a major impact on the definition of his racial identity. His mother asks the young musician to perform a piano piece, and he plays "something in a listless, half-hearted way." But the response of his father inspires the young pianist: "My father was so enthusiastic in his praise that he touched my vanity—which was great—and more than that; he displayed that sincere appreciation which always arouses an artist to his best effort . . . I showed my gratitude by playing for him a Chopin waltz with all the feeling that was in me." The father is overjoyed and embraces his son, who remarks in his narration: "I am certain that for that moment he was proud to be my father" (35). He shows his gratitude and feels he inspires pride in his father with material chosen from the European musical tradition. The Ex-Coloured Man is puzzled by the significance of this meeting:

> The thought did not cross my mind that he was different
> from me, and even if it had, the mystery would not
> thereby have been explained; for, notwithstanding my
> changed relations with most of my school-mates, I had
> only a faint knowledge of prejudice and no idea at all how
> it ramified and affected our entire social organism. I felt,
> however, that there was something about the whole affair
> which had to be hid. (36)

The narrator sees his father (but does not reveal his identity) only one
other time in his life, many years later, fittingly at a performance of the
opera "Faust" in Paris.

While the Ex-Coloured Man does not recognize the racial
differences between himself and his father at the time of the visit, as he
matures he begins to question "my mother's and my position, and . . .
our exact relation to the world in general" (40). He is dissatisfied with
the version of American history that he learns in school.[6] He finally
finds Harriet Beecher Stowe's *Uncle Tom's Cabin*, "a book that cleared
the whole mystery . . . a book that gave me my first perspective of the
life I was entering" (41). He defends the book as "a fair and truthful
panorama of slavery," and cites as one example of Stowe's
evenhandedness: "She pictured the happy, singing, shuffling 'darky' as
well as the mother wailing for her child sold 'down river'" (42). While
he is once again drawn to the music of black folk culture, the narrator
seems unquestionably to accept the dominant culture's standard
representations of black musical artists in slavery. His reading of *Uncle
Tom's Cabin* enables the narrator to open up a dialogue with his mother
concerning their "position." She tells him of "things that had come
down to her through the "old folks" and of her love affair with his
father, who was all to them "that custom and the law would allow" (42-
3).

The Ex-Coloured Man's propensity for forms derived from African
American folk expression leads him to a fledgling sense of black pride.
At the narrator's grammar school graduation, the leading student in his
class, a dark-skinned black boy named "Shiny" is the main speaker. The
narrator wonders how it feels to stand before a predominantly white
audience and seems particularly fascinated with the concept of an
individual representing the race: "I think that solitary little black figure
standing there felt that for the particular time and place he bore the
weight and responsibility of his race; that for him to fail meant general
defeat; but he won, and nobly" (44). The oration of Wendell Phillip's
"Toussaint L'Ouverture" has a "magical" effect on the narrator:

> I felt leap within me pride that I was coloured; and I
> began to form wild dreams of bringing glory and honor to
> the Negro race. For days I could talk of nothing else with
> my mother except my ambitions to be a great man, a great
> coloured man, to reflect credit on the race and gain fame
> for myself. It was not until years after that I formulated a
> definite and feasible plan for realizing my dreams. (46)

The inspiration to become an African American leader, the "magic" that
is in Shiny's speech, reflects the narrator's affinity for the oral tradition,
and appropriately the text of that speech focuses on one of the first
black liberationist leaders in the Western hemisphere. Yet, the split
between the communal and the individual surfaces again in his dual
motivation to "reflect credit on my race" and gain personal fame. As
the Ex-Coloured Man continues his studies in high school he lives
"between my music and books," and his hero becomes Frederick
Douglass (46). When the narrator's mother dies shortly after his high
school graduation, he decides to continue his education at Atlanta
University.

The journey to the American South for the Ex-Coloured Man is
emblematic of a journey into African American culture, a symbolic
return to the black folk source. For an individual who initially looked
upon the recognition of his blackness as a "sword thrust," the descent to
Atlanta promises to initiate him into this culture so that he can bring
"glory and honour to the Negro race." Atlanta provides the narrator
with his "first sight of coloured people in large numbers." Yet, this
aspiring racial leader reacts curiously to this immersion into *his*
people:

> The unkempt appearance, the shambling, slouching gait
> and loud talk and laughter of these people aroused in me a
> feeling of almost repulsion. Only one thing about them
> awoke a feeling of interest; that was their dialect. I had
> read some Negro dialect and heard snatches of it on my
> journey down from Washington; but here I heard it in all
> of its fullness and freedom. (55-56)

Ironically, while reasserting his "interest" in the oral tradition of black
folk culture, the Ex-Coloured Man simultaneously experiences "almost
repulsion" at the folk who practice this tradition. His stay in Atlanta
turns out to be a short one, for he is robbed of his savings by a fellow
lodger in a boarding house. The narrator stows away in a Pullman
porter's closet and travels to Jacksonville, Florida.

In Florida the Ex-Coloured Man's musical education and initiation into African American culture intersect when he is introduced to ragtime music and the "cakewalk" dance. The narrator's comments on African American cultural production during this episode reappear in Johnson's *Spirituals* Preface: "It is my opinion that the coloured people of this country have done four things which refute the oft-advanced theory that they are an absolutely inferior race, which demonstrate that they have originality and artistic conception, and, what is more, the power of creating that which can influence and appeal universally." The four things include rag-time and the cakewalk, along with the Uncle Remus stories and the Jubilee songs. Typically, the Ex-Coloured Man celebrates the oral, especially musical, African American folk tradition, but also, quite typically, his praise is tempered with a note of condescension: "These are lower forms of art, but they give evidence of a power that will some day be applied to the higher forms" (87). The narrator cannot accept these cultural expressions on their own terms but rather applies Eurocentric standards of high and low culture to them.[7]

The Ex-Coloured Man finds the pulse of contemporary black musical expression when he travels to New York and comes into contact with the urban, black nightlife setting of the "Club." At the "Club," which distinctly echoes The Banner Club from *The Sport of the Gods*, the narrator is immediately drawn to the ragtime music. He is captivated by both the technical proficiency of the house pianist and the effects of this music on the listener: "It was music of a kind I had never heard before. It was music that demanded physical response, patting of the feet, drumming of the fingers, or nodding of the head in time with the beat" (98-99).

Ragtime swept America by storm in the 1890s and dominated popular musical tastes up until World War I. Considering the Ex-Coloured Man's wavering allegiance between the black and the white world, it is appropriate that he is so attracted to ragtime because as a musical style it drew heavily from both African and European musical sources. Its form and emphasis on written composition illustrate the influence of European music. However, its most dominant characteristic is its syncopated rhythm, which is African-derived.[8] Eileen Southern asserts that the earliest ragtime was "a natural outgrowth of dance-music practices of black folk." The distinctive syncopated style developed in piano music as "the left hand took over the task of stomping and patting while the right hand performed syncopated melodies" (307). Marshall Stearns explains the ragtime process as follows:

> This continual syncopation, which was easily notated, is merely the foundation. On top of this a good pianist improvises an endless variety of rhythmic suspensions, unusual accents, and between-the-beat effects. In other words, the best ragtime incorporates the horizontal rhythmic flow of all good American Negro music. It also retains its European form. The blend is a rare and sophisticated piano music that can be well played only by a very few, highly gifted virtuosos. (106)

Undoubtedly, ragtime is the result of the innovations made by black musicians as they gained access to pianos after Emancipation. Johnson reworks the narrator's description of ragtime's origin in the *Poetry* Preface:

> Ragtime music was originated by colored piano players in the questionable resorts of St. Louis, Memphis, and other Mississippi River towns. These men did not know any more about the theory of music than they did about the theory of the universe. They were guided by their natural musical instinct and talent, but above all by the Negro's extraordinary sense of rhythm. Any one who is familiar with Ragtime may note that its chief charm is not in melody, but in rhythms. These players often improvised crude, and at times, vulgar words to fit the music. This was the beginning of the Ragtime song. (12)

Even though Johnson asserts that ragtime "jes grew" or emerged naturally and anonymously from black culture, there were a number of musicians who contributed to the crystallization of the style. In a testament to the individuality that exists within communal black musical expression, the ragtime form manifested itself in African American communities throughout the country with distinct regional characteristics. Three of the foremost ragtime stylists came from diverse geographic areas: Scott Joplin, "The King of Ragtime" was based in Sedalia, Missouri; Ferdinand "Jelly Roll" Morton was from New Orleans; and Eubie Blake was from Baltimore. Each of these artists was an accomplished ragtime composer and performer who went on to extend the scope of his artistic vision beyond piano rags— something the Ex-Coloured Man eventually hopes to do but fails to accomplish when he decides to abandon black culture: Joplin wrote and produced two innovative and elaborate "ragtime operas"; Morton became a pioneer in orchestrating jazz and blues ensemble compositions; and Blake teamed with artists like Noble Sissle to write hit Broadway musicals, continuing to perform until his death at age one hundred. [9]

The "Club" and ragtime soon become central to the narrator's life in New York, and he devotes Chapter Seven to the physical description of the "Club's" interior and the activities that take place there. He says that "the walls were literally covered with photographs or lithographs of every coloured man in America who had ever 'done anything'" (104). His examples of these figures range from Frederick Douglass to famous athletes and actors, "down to the newest song and dance team." The narrator's list of accomplished African Americans begins with the first great abolitionist orator/writer and extends to current, popular African American music-makers. The implication is that the black individuals who are "doing something" of note in terms of leading the race at the time of the narration are musical artists. The narrator, however, soon reveals where his true concern lies: "The most of these photographs were autographed and, in a sense, made a really valuable collection" (104). His conception of value is not connected to pride in racial achievements but rather to terms of monetary profit from their sale.

The established black musical artists who frequent the "Club" come there to meet with their cohorts and develop their routines and only perform as special guest artists. The narrator recognizes that the "Club" is a haven for these artists who are attempting to make names for themselves in the white-dominated entertainment industry. He comes to understand what these black artists face in their struggle for success: "I often heard the younger and brighter men discussing the time when they would compel the public to recognize that they could do something more than grin and cut pigeon-wings" (105). While these black performers look to the day when they will be considered serious artists, the narrator also observes another set of regulars at the "Club" whose presence accents the genuine irony of the American racial climate. White performers who "delineated 'darky characters' . . . came to get their imitations first-hand from the Negro entertainers they saw there" (107). Even at their "home base" these black artists are subject to both co-optation and distortion from the white artists they compete against in the entertainment industry.[10]

Like these white performers who come to the "Club" to "get their imitations first-hand," the narrator frequently returns to learn the "trick" of playing ragtime:

> I took a seat at once by the side of the piano-player, and was soon lost to everything except the novel charm of the music. I watched the performer with the idea of catching

> the trick, and during one of his intermissions I took his
> place at the piano and made an attempt to *imitate* him,
> but even my quick ear and ready fingers were unequal to
> the task on first trial. (emphasis added) (112)

His attitude and approach to learning ragtime are closer to a white man
appropriating the "novel charm" of some exotic music, than to a black
man adopting and exploring a form of expression that connects him to
African American culture. He states that by continual listening and
"through my own previous training, my natural talent and
perseverance" he becomes the "best rag-time-player in New York"
(115). His specialty is applying ragtime technique to European classical
selections. His new-found celebrity as a musician leads to important
changes in his life:

> By mastering rag-time I gained several things: first of all,
> I gained the title of professor. I was known as "the
> professor" as long as I remained in that world. Then, too I
> gained the means of earning a rather fair livelihood . . .
> Through it I also gained a friend who was the means by
> which I escaped from this lower world. And, finally, I
> secured a wedge which has opened to me more doors and
> made me a welcome guest than my playing of Beethoven
> and Chopin could ever have done. (115)

The narrator's comments on his ability to play ragtime clearly focus on
his lack of communal concern and his conceited and selfish nature.
Opportunity and financial profit are his primary concern as he
condescendingly speaks of the "Club," a center for African American
culture, as a "lower world." His choice of a black approach to music-
making over "Beethoven and Chopin" is made simply because it
provides a more effective wedge that "opened to *me* more doors."

The Ex-Coloured Man explains that his piano playing, particularly
his transcriptions of "classic selections," increases the number of white
patrons who come to the "Club" for "slumming." Among them is the
friend who helps the narrator to escape the "lower world," a wealthy
white man who becomes the pianist's patron. The narrator leaves his
regular gig at the "Club" and performs exclusively for his patron and
his dinner guests: "He told me that he would give me lots of work, his
only stipulation being that I should not play any engagements such as I
had just filled for him, except by his instructions, for I was sure that I
could not be the loser by such a contract" (120). The narrator may not
have been a loser in terms of financial gain but in terms of his

independence as a black artist he enslaves himself. The pianist becomes a piece of property, for he speaks of being "'loaned' to some of his friends." The description of the musical services he renders to the patron take on the language of a slave/master relationship:

> He seemed to be some grim, mute but relentless tyrant, possessing over me a supernatural power which he used to drive me mercilessly to exhaustion. But these feelings came very rarely; besides, he paid me so liberally I could forget much. There at length grew between us a familiar and warm relationship, and I am sure he had a decided personal liking for me. On my part, I looked upon him at that time as about all a man could wish to be. (121)

Just like the stereotype of the happy darky driven "mercilessly to exhaustion" by a white "tyrant," the narrator is content with his pay, looks upon his subjugation as a "familiar and warm relationship," and finds in that tyrant an assimilationist model. Rather than using his talent to provide some kind of uplift or leadership for his race, the narrator willingly enslaves himself for personal gain.

Besides the white "slummers" and the delineators of "darky characters" who frequent the "Club," the Ex-Coloured Man describes a third group of white customers: single white women who come in search of black male escorts. And in the fictional portrayal of this phenomenon Dunbar's fear in *The Sport of the Gods* of miscegenation that might occur in the interracial urban nightclubs of the North comes to fruition. The narrator becomes involved with one of these women, a rich widow, and when her steady "very black young fellow" for whom she bought "clothes and . . . diamonds" sees the two together he draws a pistol and shoots her in the throat. Fleeing the "Club," the narrator runs into his patron and accepts an offer to travel with him to Europe as his valet.

Ironically, it is in Europe that the Ex-Coloured Man crystallizes his plan to become a African American leader through his musical abilities. The narrator continues to perform ragtime for his patron's entertainment and is perfectly content with what is basically a life of leisure until he meets a German pianist at one of his patron's soirees. The German quickly catches the narrator's "trick" and inverts it: "I sat amazed. I had been turning classic music into rag-time, a comparatively easy task; and this man had taken rag-time and made it classic. The thought came across me like a flash—It can be done, why can't I do it? From that moment my mind was made up. I clearly saw the way of carrying out the ambition I had formed when a boy" (142). Through the performance by the German the narrator revives his dream of becoming a racial leader that had been inspired by his boyhood friend Shiny's speech. He resolves to return to the heart of African American culture and include the communal in the application of his personal talents: "I made up my mind to go back into the very heart of the South, to live among the people, and drink my inspiration firsthand. I gloated over the immense amount of material I had to work with, not only modern rag-time, but also the old slave songs—material which no one had yet touched" (142-43). The patron argues against a return to America because he feels that racism there will prevent the narrator from reaching his goal. While the narrator's sense of racial pride may be genuinely stirred, his struggle over the decision to leave Europe illustrates his continued difficulty in negotiating the balance between the individual and communal in African American cultural expression: "Finally, I settled the question on purely selfish grounds, in accordance with my millionaire's philosophy. I argued that music offered me a better future than anything else I had any knowledge of, and, in opposition to friend's opinion, that I should have greater chances of attracting attention as a coloured composer than as a white one." However he adds, "But I must own that I also felt stirred by an unselfish desire to voice all the joys and sorrows, the hopes and ambitions, of the American Negro, in classic musical form" (147-48). Yet, the sincerity of this "unselfish desire" is questionable in this narrator who is so fixed on "attracting attention" that the creation of an artistic "voice" for African American culture seems to be simply an afterthought.

Back in America, the Ex-Coloured Man travels throughout the South collecting the raw material for his great cultural production, "jotting down in my note-book themes and melodies, and trying to catch the spirit of the Negro in his relatively primitive state" (173). He is eager to return to a city where he can earn a living teaching music and support himself as he composes, but at his last stop he finds a "Big meeting," a religious revival in progress and is enthralled by two itinerant preachers. One, named John Brown, "knew all the arts and tricks of oratory," and the narrator's admiration for his verbal skills reaffirms his attraction to the black oral tradition which he had felt as a young man. The other preacher was "a wonderful leader of singing, who was known as 'Singing Johnson'" (174). Much of the narrator's description of "Singing Johnson" working the meeting crowd with renditions of spirituals was incorporated into the *Poetry* Preface, indicating that the narrator's observations coincide with the author's views. The Ex-Coloured Man focuses on the call/response structure and the improvisational nature of the spirituals, elements that he seemingly hopes to emphasize in his own classical rendering of black folk materials. While he dismisses the "sentiments" of the songs as "mostly taken from the Bible," the origin of the melodies captivates the narrator:

> And so many of these songs contain more than mere melody; there is sounded in them that elusive undertone, the note in music which is not heard with the ears. I sat often with tears rolling down my cheeks and my heart melted within me. Any musical person who has never heard a Negro congregation under the spell of religious fervour sing these old songs has missed one of the most thrilling emotions which the human heart may experience. Anyone who without shedding tears can listen to Negroes sing 'Nobody knows de trouble I see, Nobody knows but Jesus' must indeed have a heart of stone. (181)

With this passage the narrator illustrates that he is in touch with that essential feeling, that nonverbal subtext, that meaning *in sound* that black writers starting with Douglass point out when describing the effect music from the African American folk source has upon listeners. He also seems to be invoking that sound in the reader's imagination in an attempt to communicate the effect the music of the "Big meeting" had upon him. He declares that "the day will come when this slave music will be the most treasured heritage of the American Negro" (182). And at this moment he does not seem merely to be attempting to appropriate or "catch the trick" but to be sharing in that heritage as he had done when his mother played him the "old Southern songs" and when he listened to Shiny's graduation oration.[11] This man who had been so ambivalent towards his race now seems as if he will be able to achieve his ambition of being a credit to himself *and* his race: "I was in that frame of mind which, in the artistic temperament, amounts to inspiration. I was now ready and anxious to get some place where I might settle down to work, and give expression to the ideas which were teaming in my head" (182).

But after leaving the "Big meeting," the Ex-Coloured Man makes one last stop, and what he encounters determines the course he chooses to follow for the remainder of his life. The night he spends in this Southern town ends the narrator's wavering between white and black culture when his anonymity allows him to pass as a white man and watch the townspeople burn a black man alive. The inspiration to draw on his African American cultural heritage and become an outstanding racial leader is immediately abandoned when he is brought face to face with the true consequences of being black in a racist society. Obviously there is no capacity for leadership in a man whose reaction to such an incident lacks even a thought of protest, let alone resistance: "A great wave of humiliation and shame swept over me. Shame that I belonged to a race that could be so dealt with; shame for my country, that it, the great example of democracy to the world, should be the only civilized, if not the only state on earth, where a human being would be burned alive. My heart turned bitter within me" (188). The Ex-Coloured Man is not outraged, not angered, over this lynching; he is merely "bitter." On the train to New York he decides to "let the world take me for what it would; that it was not necessary for me to go about with a label of inferiority pasted across my forehead." It is fitting that the motivation for this man whose narration has proved him to be vain above all else is a sense of shame:

> All the while I understood that it was not discouragement or fear or search for a larger field of action or opportunity that was driving me out of the Negro race. I knew that it was shame, unbearable shame. Shame at being identified with a people that could with impunity be treated worse than animals. For certainly the law would restrain and punish the malicious burning of animals. (190-91)

The Ex-Coloured Man ultimately cannot stand being "identified with a people;" he cannot handle being an individual tied to a community. The narrator does not have the backbone or determination to be a representative of his people. At first he describes himself being ashamed of both his race and his country, but once he arrives in New York only his blackness is rejected, and he plunges headfirst into the ultimate role for the individual divorced from the communal, the role of the white American businessman: "I had made up my mind that since I was not going to be a Negro, I would avail myself of every possible opportunity to make a white man's success; and that, if it can be summed up in any one word, means 'money'" (193). In the remainder of the closing chapter the narrator relates a Horatio Alger-like success story, along with the details of his love affair and marriage with a white woman. The couple has two children but keep the narrator's heritage a secret. When his wife dies he raises the children on his own, secure in his place as a successful white businessman.[12]

The Autobiography of an Ex-Coloured Man comes full circle when the narrator concludes by describing his being brought into contact with the songs with which his mother had initiated him into African American folk culture. He attends a benefit for the Hampton Institute, a black college, where a group of student jubilee singers "sang old songs and awoke memories that left me sad" (210). He also focuses on the presence of Booker T. Washington at this benefit because he and his colleagues are representatives of their race who "have the eternal principles of right on their side." The narrator compares himself to these racial leaders: "Beside them I feel small and selfish. I am an ordinarily successful white man who has made a little money. They are men who are making history and a race. I, too, might have taken part in a work so glorious" (211). Once again music from the African American folk tradition coupled with the aspiration to be a racial leader plunges the narrator into an ambivalent wavering over where he will locate himself in American society. He closes his text with the paragraph that he had alluded to on the opening page, the paragraph that he hopes will explain his motivation for telling his story, his attempt to seek relief from "a vague feeling of unsatisfaction, of regret, of almost remorse." The Ex-Coloured Man acknowledges that his great failure in life is his abandoning the application of his individual musical abilities to the communal traditions of African American folk culture:

> My love for my children makes me glad that I am what I
> am and keeps me from desiring to be otherwise; and yet,
> when I sometimes open a little box in which I still keep
> my fast yellowing manuscripts, the only tangible remnants
> of a vanished dream, a dead ambition, a sacrificed talent, I
> cannot repress the thought that, after all, I have chosen the
> lesser part, that I have sold my birthright for a mess of
> pottage. (211)

The anonymity under which the narrator reveals this betrayal emphasizes the continuing selfishness of this man who does not attempt to make amends but simply to seek "relief" from his personal discomfort.

With *The Autobiography of an Ex-Coloured Man* Johnson made a major contribution to the tradition of representing music in African American fiction. The novel gives testimony to his recognition that in the early years of the twentieth century music had become a field of endeavor in which black artists could make advances for themselves *and* for their race. Johnson points out the power of the music to create cultural inroads through the failure of his pianist/narrator to apply his personal talents to the communal tradition and become a representative of the African American people. The Ex-Coloured Man's sale of his "birthright," his talent as a pianist and his perceptive understanding of the African American approach to music-making, to make "a little money" is emblematic of his abandonment of his identity as an African American man. The narrator reveals himself to be a cowardly and self-centered individual, and clearly his failure to make use of his musical talent is viewed as a betrayal of the black community. Yet, in this failure Johnson makes it clear that for black artists to have a positive impact in the advancement of African Americans, they must draw upon the traditions of folk culture, particularly the music, as Johnson himself did in *The Autobiography of an Ex-Coloured Man*. Like his nineteenth-century predecessors, Johnson makes it clear that music functions in numerous roles beyond mere entertainment in African American culture. While music is an outlet for individual, creative expression that can open up opportunities and enable an artist to rise above physical limitations, it also provides a means for the uplift of the race and thus subverts the racial status quo in twentieth-century America.

2.
"THEIR JOY RUNS, BANG! INTO ECSTASY": LANGSTON HUGHES, CLAUDE MCKAY & ZORA NEALE HURSTON

The Autobiography of an Ex-Coloured Man was republished in 1927 under Johnson's name. The novel had anticipated, if not established, much of the foundation for the artistic impulses that came to fruition during what has come to be called the Harlem Renaissance, which was in full swing by the late 1920s.[13] In his introduction to the new edition Carl Van Vechten asserts the novel had not dated, and he goes on to state:

> It is simply astonishing to discover in this book, issued the year after Alexander's Ragtime Band and the same year that The Memphis Blues were published, such a statement as this:
> 'American musicians, instead of investigating rag-time, attempt to ignore it, or dismiss it with a contemptuous word. But that has always been the course of scholasticism in every branch of art. Whatever new thing the *people* like is pooh-poohed; whatever is *popular* is spoken of as not worth the while. The fact is, nothing great or enduring, especially in music, has ever sprung full-fledged and unprecedented from the brain of any master; the best that he gives to the world he gathers from the hearts of the people, and runs it through the alembic of his genius.' (xxxvii)

Van Vechten's citation of this passage from *The Autobiography of an Ex-Coloured Man* emphasizes the important role Johnson played in establishing folk culture as the wellspring of inspiration for African American artists who emerged during the Harlem Renaissance. Johnson's novel, despite his narrator's betrayal of the race, provided a paradigm for the process of applying individual talents to the communal traditions of African American culture to produce artistic works which would open doors for blacks to gain an equal share in American society. The novel itself, particularly with its focus on the African American music-making process, became a model for a number of Harlem Renaissance writers who recognized the importance of music in African American culture. Using their unique, personal approaches, writers such as Langston Hughes, Claude McKay and Zora Neale Hurston drew upon the tradition of the spirituals, ragtime and such emerging forms as blues and jazz with their inherent call/response, individual/communal duality to formulate an integral part of their fictional representations of black life in America.

The influence of Johnson's ideas concerning the relation between black folk culture and artistic production on the writers of the Harlem Renaissance can be seen in Hughes's "The Negro Artist and the Racial Mountain" (1926). A manifesto that urged black artists to be themselves, Hughes's essay rejected the notion that the creations of African Americans should be judged by white standards: "But this is the mountain standing in the way of any true Negro art in America—this urge within the race toward whiteness" (258). For Hughes, African American artists had to draw their inspiration from and celebrate the day-to-day life of black people in America. Music, playing such an integral role in that life, had a major influence in Hughes's work:

> But then there are the low-down folks, the so-called common element, and they are the majority—may the Lord be praised! The people who have their nip of gin on Saturday nights and are not too important to themselves or the community, or too well fed, or too learned to watch the lazy world go round. They live on Seventh Street in Washington or State Street in Chicago and they do not particularly care whether they are like white folks or anybody else. Their joy runs, bang! into ecstasy. Their religion soars to a shout. Work maybe a little today, rest a little tomorrow. Play awhile. Sing awhile. O, let's dance! These common people are not afraid of spirituals, as for a long time their more intellectual brethren were, and jazz is their child. They furnish a wealth of colorful, distinctive

material for any artist because they still hold their own
individuality in the face of American standardizations.
And perhaps these common people will give to the world
its truly great Negro artist, the one who is not afraid to be
himself. (259-60)

Hughes's reputation as a writer rests most solidly upon his poetry—in
which he follows his own counsel. Many of his poems, such as "The
Weary Blues," "Miss Blue'es Child," "Bound No'th Blues," "Song for
Billie Holiday" and "Dream Boogie," drew upon black folk sources,
particularly the blues, for their language, characters, themes and
form.[14]

    Certainly by the mid-1920s the blues had become what Johnson
called "whatever new thing the *people* like."[15] The advent of
commercially available phonograph recordings brought fame and
(relative) fortune, from both within and outside the black community,
to a succession of black female blues singers such as Mamie Smith,
Gertrude "Ma" Rainey and Bessie Smith. Emerging from minstrel
shows and coon shows, such as Dunbar had depicted in *The Sport of the
Gods*, these blues divas worked what developed into a vaudeville
circuit of black theaters controlled by the Theater Owners and Bookers
Association (T.O.B.A.), which, because of the exploitation and terrible
working conditions, black artists sarcastically dubbed "Tough On Black
Asses." However, despite receiving an unfair deal from the white
entertainment industry, a number of these blues artists were able to
achieve a level of recognition and independence that marked them with
distinction in the black community.

    When Hughes turned his talents to fiction with *Not Without
Laughter* (1930) a major theme in his novel focused on the emergence
of one of these blues queens. Their style of blues, which is now called
the "Classic Blues," combined elements of traditional country blues
with vaudeville and popular show music.[16] This evolution of blues
styles is illustrated in *Not Without Laughter* as the character Jimboy
Rodgers, a guitarist and singer, teaches his old-time, "country" blues to
his young sister-in-law Harriett Williams, who becomes a Classic Blues
singer, "The Princess of the Blues." Depicting the emergence of a blues
star provides Hughes with the opportunity to address the
individual/communal duality in African American artistic expression.
Unlike the traditional country blues, which were most frequently
performed by solo artists, the Classic Blues were usually performed by
a female singer with accompaniment provided by a pianist, possibly
augmented by a small instrumental combo. Nonetheless, the singer
certainly remained the dominant personality in the performance.[17]

In addition to delineating the evolution of the blues tradition and its relation to the individual/communal duality in African American culture, *Not Without Laughter* is a bildungsroman of Jimboy's son and Harrietta's nephew James "Sandy" Rodgers set in a small Kansas town and inner-city Chicago. The blues of his father and aunt, along with the spirituals of his grandmother, Aunt Hager Williams, and the jazz of what came to be called the "Territory Bands" of the American Southwest initiate Sandy into African American culture and provide him with an approach to life that will enable him to respond to and survive American racism.[18]

Not Without Laughter focuses on life in Aunt Hager's Kansas home. The old washerwoman lives with her daughter Annjee and her husband Jimboy when he is not traveling, their son Sandy, and for a time, Hager's youngest daughter Harriett, a young woman trying to establish her independence. Hager's oldest daughter Tempy, who is married to a postal worker, aspires to middle class respectability and tries to distance herself from what she considers her lower class origins. Through Aunt Hager and her family Hughes makes the common people, the people who "still hold their individuality in the face of American standardizations," the subject of his fictional representation of black life in America during the second decade of the twentieth century.

In Chapter Five, entitled "Guitar," Hughes illustrates how music that emerges from African American folk culture functions in the day-to-day lives of these common people. The chapter begins with sections of blues lyrics alternating with imagistic prose passages of Jimboy singing and playing his guitar for his family and neighbors in Aunt Hager's backyard:

> Long, lazy length resting on the kitchen-door-sill, back against the jamb, feet in the yard, fingers picking his sweet guitar, left hand holding against its finger-board the back of an old pocket-knife, sliding the knife upward, downward, getting thus weird croons and sighs from the vibrating strings:
>
> I left ma mother
> An' I cert'ly can leave you.
> Indeed I left ma mother
> An' I cert'ly can leave you,
> For I'd leave any woman
> That mistreats me like you do.

> Jimboy, remembering brown-skin mamas in Natchez,
> Shreveport, Dallas; remembering Creole women in Baton
> Rouge, Louisiana:
>> Yo' windin' an' yo' grindin'
>> Don't have no effect on me,
>> Babe, yo' windin' an' yo' grindin'
>> Don't have no 'fect on me,
>> 'Cause I can wind an' grind
>> Like a monkey round a coconut-tree! (51)

As Jimboy plays Harriett joins in, and various members of the "audience" contribute vocal commentary—both positive and negative-to the performance. The neighbors shout their approval of the impromptu blues concert, "'Wha!Wha! . . . You chillen sho can sing!'" But Aunt Hager disapproves of the "low down" nature of the blues: "'Unhuh! Bound straight fo 'de devil, that's what they is,' Hager returned calmly from her place beside the pump." This interaction between artist and audience is characteristic of the communal nature of African American musical performance.

As the chapter progresses Annjee arrives home from work and Hughes's writing shifts from an imagistic evocation of the blues performance to a more traditional prose exposition of Jimboy's relationship with his wife, particularly how the abandon with which he loses himself in the blues prevents him from giving her the special attention she desires from her man. Hughes also points out the special bond that Jimboy shares with Harriett in their love of playing the blues. In that relationship the vital process of passing traditions down to future generations is illustrated:

> Off and on for nine years, ever since he had married
> Annjee, Jimboy and Harriett had been singing together in
> the evenings. When they started, Harriett was a little girl
> with braided hair, and each time that her roving brother-
> in-law stopped in Stanton, he would amuse himself by
> teaching her the old Southern songs, the popular ragtime
> ditties, and the hundreds of varying verses of the blues
> that he would pick up in the big dirty cities of the South.
> The child, with her strong sweet voice (colored folks
> called it alto) and her racial sense of rhythm, soon learned
> to sing the songs as well as Jimboy. (54)

Hughes signals that the narrator is "in the know" with the insertion of a parenthetical aside explaining the terminology for Harriett's voice that is particular to "colored folks," and his assertion that the accomplished blues artist possesses a *racial sense of rhythm* indicates that there is an "insider" aspect to the creation of this music. The passage continues with a description of Jimboy also teaching Harriett "movements peculiar to Southern Negro dancing." The implication is that the blues and African American folk culture is not only a response to white culture but is also independent and distinct from that dominant culture. The point is hammered home with the following observation: "It was all great fun, and innocent fun except when one stopped to think, as white folks did, that some of the blues lines had, not only double, but triple meanings, and some of the dance steps required very definite movements of the hips. But neither Harriett nor Jimboy soiled their minds by thinking. It was music, good exercise—and they loved it" (54-55). The assertion that "white folks" are aware of double and triple meanings in blues lyrics gives testimony to the survival of the subversive trickster strategies found in the music of the slaves. And the reference to "very definite movements of the hips" is a manifestation of African American culture's ability to enjoy and celebrate the sensual, in contrast with the dominant culture's puritanical clinging to the rational. Yet, tricking white folks is certainly not the main concern of these blues artists; this is music made by black folks for black folks. While Harriett and Jimboy are certainly aware of the double entendre and innuendo in blues lyrics, their refusal to soil "their minds by thinking" illustrates that one of the multiple meanings inherent in the music for both the black artist and audience is that it also functions in their lives simply as their unique brand of "great fun."

The assertion that Harriett and Jimboy do not consciously think about the implications of the multiple meanings of blues lyrics may also be a reflection of an attempt by Hughes to avoid intellectualization of his depiction of the folk source of African American cultural expression. The blues as they are produced in Aunt Hager's backyard are a part of the fabric of everyday black life. The blues are a natural expression for Jimboy, and he plays them simply because it is something he loves to do. This refusal to take the music out of the realm of folk expression is apparent when a neighbor shouts his approval of Jimboy's style: "'Aw, pick it, boy,' yelled the old man. 'Can't nobody play like you.' And Jimboy remembered when he was a lad in Memphis that W. C. Handy had said: 'You ought to make your living out of that, son.' But he hadn't followed it up—too many things to see, too many places to go, too many other jobs" (57). The reference to Handy sets the historical and geographic context for Jimboy's blues style, and is particularly appropriate because Handy is credited with being the first African American musician to publish a blues composition and thus begin the transformation of the blues from an oral folk tradition.

In "Guitar" Sandy is a firsthand witness to a viable folk tradition. Watching and listening to his father teach and perform with his aunt allows the boy to become familiar with the intricacies of a particular artistic form and gain an understanding of the process of that form's evolution and its functions within the culture. Eventually Sandy himself participates in the tradition. On another occasion when Jimboy is playing his blues out in the yard Sandy asks his father to teach him :

> 'Learn me how to pick a cord, papa,' Sandy begged as he sat beside his father under the apple-tree, loaded with ripe fruit.
> 'All right, look a-here! . . . You put your thumb like this.'
> Jimboy began to explain. 'But, doggone, your fingers ain't long enough yet!'
> Still they managed to spend a half-day twanging at the old instrument, with Sandy trying to learn a simple tune. (131)

These informal performances must be considered typical of the family life in black homes like Aunt Hager's, and this process of initiation gives the blues and other forms of folk cultural expression a resonating signification of communal values in the lives of individuals who learned them in such a context.

In Chapter Eight, entitled "Dance," Sandy's initiation into black culture through music is continued. When Aunt Hager admonishes her rebellious daughter to stay home one night and watch her nephew, Harriett cannot resist a chance to attend a dance and takes the boy along on her date. "Benbow's Famous Kansas City Band," the group performing at the dance Harriett and Sandy attend, is a fictional prototype of a Territory Band.[19] Itinerant black bands, called "Territory Bands," toured the American Southwest performing a hard swinging mix of jazz and blues. Eventually the center for this unique style of African American music became Kansas City during the Depression. The Kansas City scene, with its wide open policy allowing gambling, prostitution and bootlegging, produced a stellar array of jazz innovators, including the Blue Devils, Jay McShann, the Count Basie Band, Lester Young, Charlie Parker and Big Joe Turner.

Sandy's explorations of the dance hall introduce him to world of adult sexuality. He observes his aunt and the other young men and women pairing off for each musical selection, listens to the fellows in the "GENTS" room "make fleshy remarks about the women they had danced with," and even "gallantly" shares his refreshments with a "grinning little girl" his own age. The jazz and blues played by Benbow's Band create a mood that transports the various couples from the drudgery of day-to-day existence to a realm of sensual pleasure:

> Couples began to sway languidly, melting together like candy in the sun as hips rotated effortlessly to the music. Girls snuggled pomaded heads on men's chests, or rested powdered chins on men's shoulder's, while wild young boys put both arms tightly around their partners' waists and let their hands hang down carelessly over female haunches. Bodies moved ever so easily together—ever so easily, as Benbow turned towards his musicians and cried through cupped hands: 'Aw, screech it, boys!' (96)

Hughes's descriptions of the music take its function far beyond the simple setting of a sultry background mood. In the heat of the jazz/blues performance Hughes finds the expression of the essential facts of life, the primal impulses of human sexuality. This is fitting, for it has been asserted that the term "jazz" derives from a slang expression for sexual intercourse. And so Hughes acknowledges that at its most basic level this music is all about life:

> The four black men in Benbow's wandering band were exploring depths to which mere sound had no business to go. Cruel, desolate, unadorned was their music now, like the body of a ravished woman on the sun-baked earth; violent and hard, like a giant standing over his bleeding mate in the blazing sun. The odors of bodies, the stings of flesh, and the utter emptiness of soul when all is done— these things the piano and the drums, the cornet and the twanging banjo insisted on hoarsely to a beat that made the dancers move, in that little hall, like pawns on a frenetic checker-board.
>   'Aw, play it, Mister Benbow!' somebody cried.
>   The earth rolls relentlessly, and the sun blazes for ever [sic] on the earth, breeding, breeding. But why do you insist like the earth, music? Rolling and breeding, earth and sun for ever [sic] relentlessly. But why do you insist like the sun? Like the lips of women? Like the bodies of men, relentlessly?

'Aw, play it, Mister Benbow!'
But why do you insist, music? (97-98)

The music insists because it is life affirming. The music is a survival
mechanism in African American culture. No matter how hard or unfair
life may be, it must go on. Participation in the mystery of creating
human life is essential because another generation must be produced to
continue the search for "higher ground." For a people who had been
continuously told for hundreds of years that their lives meant nothing,
the participation in that struggle gave their lives meaning. And the
music is an expression of their determination to keep on *and* enjoy
themselves in spite of the barriers placed in front of them.

The musicians who explore "depths to which mere sound has no
business to go" produce through a communal form such a perceptive
expression of the African American approach to life that they become
ritualistic representatives of the race. The individuals in Benbow's Band
hail from throughout the South, the traditional source of black folk
culture:

> These mean old weary blues coming from a little
> orchestra of four men who needed no written music
> because they couldn't have read it. Four men and a leader-
> Rattle Benbow from Galveston; Benbow's buddy, the
> drummer, from Houston; his banjoist from Birmingham;
> his cornetist from Atlanta; and the pianist, long-fingered,
> sissified [sic], a coal-black lad from New Orleans who
> had brought with him an exaggerated rag-time which he
> called jazz. (102)

Although they have become professional entertainers, these
representative artists, who are unable to read music, are still members
of the oral tradition of folk expression. The fact that Hughes located
their geographic origins in diverse black communities of the South
emphasizes that common forms and artistic language were produced
throughout African American culture. The reference to the New
Orleans pianist bringing "an exaggerated rag-time which he called jazz"
indicates that there were unique regional variations within the artistic
tradition. Yet, ultimately the five men coming together to produce
"these mean weary blues" testifies to a sharing of situations, concerns
and responses by black people all over America: "Four homeless, plug-
ugly niggers, that's all they were, playing mean old loveless blues in a
hot, crowded dance-hall in a Kansas town on Friday night. Playing the
heart out of loneliness with a wide mouthed leader, who sang

everybody's troubles until they became his own" (102). The representative role that the musician plays in African American culture is testified to by Benbow's ability to sing "everybody's troubles until they became his own."[20] While Sandy and Harriett participate in a particular dance, the implication is that the jazz/blues performance is a ritual open to countless variations in any black community.

Hughes illustrates the sacred/secular split that emerged in black music through Aunt Hager's preference for the spirituals over the "low down" blues. Ultimately he reveals that both approaches derive from the same source and serve similar functions in African American culture. Aunt Hager looks down on Jimboy as the "devil's musicianer," and she resents his teaching Harriett to sing and dance. Yet, she softens when her son-in-law turns his talent to the spirituals: "But when he took his soft-playing guitar and picked out spirituals and old-time Christian hymns on its sweet strings, Hager forgot she was his enemy, and sang and rocked with the rest of them" (34). Jimboy recognizes the connections between the two forms and musically teases his mother-in-law. She asks him to "play something kinder decent there, son, fo' you stops," and he responds by beginning to "rock and moan like an elder in the Sanctified Church, patting both feet at the same time as he played a hymn-like, lugubrious tune with a dancing overtone" (58). Jimboy, however, delivers blues lyrics to the sanctified groove: "Have you heard de latest news / A woman down in Georgia / Got her two sweet-men confused." The spirituals he hears from his grandmother teach Sandy lessons about black life in America that echo what he learns from his father's and aunt's blues. Sandy comes face-to-face with racism when he and his friends are refused entry to a new amusement park because of their skin color. Aunt Hager soothes the boy by singing a spiritual: "And Sandy, as he stood beside his grandmother on the porch, heard a great chorus out of the black past-singing generations of toil-worn Negroes, echoing Hager's voice as it deepened and grew in volume: There's a star fo' you an' me, / Stars beyond!" (214). The song brings to the boy a sense of history, a sense of tradition and a sense of hope that denies and resists the limitations of American racism.

Sandy's attitudes toward music derived from the African American folk tradition are illustrative of how he comes to view the position of his race in American society. When Aunt Hager dies and Annjee moves North in search of Jimboy, Sandy goes to live with his aunt Tempy. The music that had been so much a part of his life at Aunt Hager's is forbidden in Tempy's house:

> Blues and spirituals Tempy and her husband hated
> because they were too Negro. In their house Sandy dared
> not sing a word of *Swing Low, Sweet Chariot,* for what
> had darky slave songs to do with respectable people? And
> rag-time belonged in the Bottoms with the sinners. (It was
> ironically strange that the Bottoms should be the only
> section of Stanton where Negroes and whites mingled
> freely on equal terms.) (255-56)

Tempy's perception of black folk forms represents the "urge toward whiteness" Hughes had condemned in "The Negro Artist and the Racial Mountain." Tempy and her husband deny rather than draw upon the history and tradition of black people in America. Hughes's parenthetical aside is also significant here, for once again a black writer is acknowledging that African American music provides a meeting ground for the races. Unlike his predecessors Dunbar and Johnson, who cast this interaction between whites and blacks in a negative light, Hughes's ironic undercutting of Tempy's condemnation of black music indicates that he sees the music as a force that can promote racial tolerance and unity. Sandy's affinity for black music indicates that he has learned to take pride in his race's cultural productions, and he rejects Tempy's assimilationist training:

> Who wanted to go to high-toned people's houses, like
> the Mitchells', and look bored all the time while they put
> Caruso's Italian records on their new victrola? Even if it
> was the finest victrola owned by a Negro in Stanton, as
> they always informed you, Sandy got tired of listening to
> records in a language that none of them understood.
> 'But this is opera!' they said. Well, maybe it was, but he
> thought that his father and Harriett used to sing better.
> And they sang nicer songs. One of them was:
> > Love, O Love, O careless love—
> > Goes to your head like wine! (285-86)

Sandy's preference for the blues over opera symbolizes his cultural allegiance to African American traditions. The focusing on "language that none of them understood" in his rejection of what is considered legitimate music by white-oriented culture illustrates that Sandy has a keen awareness of orality and the existence of a black way of saying things.

The migration of African Americans to northern urban centers can be considered a "blues movement," for it is a pattern followed by

numerous black musicians and chronicled in countless songs.[21]
Jimboy, Annjee and Harriett all make this journey. When Sandy
eventually joins his mother in Chicago he quickly learns that black life
in the cities of the North is no Promised Land and that he must abandon
his high school education to work in an elevator to help his mother
make ends meet. His white employer's perception of African American
music is even more disparaging than Tempy's: "'A lot of minstrels—
that's all niggers are!' Mr. Siles had said once. 'Clowns, jazzers, just a
band of dancers—that's why they never have anything. Never be
anything but servants to the white people'" (313). Sandy's reaction to
Siles's opinion shows that he has a firm grasp on the function and value
of black musical expression, particularly in the context of a racist
society. He thinks back to his grandmother at revival meetings, to his
aunt and father performing the blues in their backyard and concludes:

> But was that why Negroes were poor, because they were
> dancers, jazzers, clowns? . . . The other way round would
> be better: dancers because of their poverty; singers
> because they suffered; laughing all the time because they
> must forget. . . . It's more like that, thought Sandy.
>   A band of dancers. . . Black dancers—captured in a
> white world. . . . Dancers of the spirit, too. Each black
> dreamer a captured dancer of the spirit. . . . Aunt Hager's
> dreams for Sandy dancing far beyond the limitations of
> their poverty, of their humble station in life, of their dark
> skins. (313)

Sandy identifies the spiritual dimension of African American music and
recognizes that this spirit is a refusal to submit to social limitation and
economic exploitation based upon racial difference.

Through his familiarity with life in Chicago's "Black Belt" Sandy
discovers that his aunt, billed as "Harrietta Williams The Princess of
the Blues," will be performing in a black vaudeville show at the
Monogram Theatre on State Street. Annjee and Sandy attend the variety
show, and Harriett's portion includes "a popular version of an old
Negro melody, refashioned with words from Broadway" and "the
familiar folk-blues." She is a resounding success as the "understanding
audience" breaks loose in "exclamations and shouts." Harriett
concludes the performance with "a dance-song which she sang in a
sparkling dress of white sequins, ending the act with a mad collection
of steps and a swift sudden whirl across the whole stage as the orchestra
joined Billy's piano in a triumphant arch of jazz" (319). Drawing upon
the folk sources she learned "down home," Harriett not only gains

success in the commercial realm of popular entertainment but participates in the evolution of the newly emerging art form of jazz.

After the show Annjee and Sandy make their way backstage and find Harriett drinking gin with the other performers. When her relatives notice the "harshness" in her voice Harriett replies, "'Smoking so much . . . Drinking, too, I guess. But a blues-singer's supposed to sing deep and hoarse, so it's all right'" (320). Rather than making a moral judgment on this aspect of the blues life, Hughes seems to be acknowledging an occupational hazard. As the reunion continues Harriett reveals that she has been through hard times but that things have improved. However, she also acknowledges that black musical artists do not have economic control of the forums that present their art and craft: "'Things are breakin' pretty good for spade acts—since Jews are not like the rest of white folks. They will give you a break if you've got some hot numbers to show 'em, whether you're colored or not. And Jews control the theatres'" (321).

The conversation finally turns to Annjee's and Sandy's lives in Chicago, and Harriett is appalled that her sister has allowed the young man to give up his education for a menial job. The singer immediately insists that she will contribute the money Sandy would have made running an elevator so that he can go back to school: "'This boy's gotta get ahead—all of us niggers are too far back in this white man's country to let any brains go to waste! Don't you realize that? . . . You and me was foolish all right, breaking mam's heart leaving school, but Sandy can't do like us. He's gotta be what his grandma Hager wanted him to be-able to help the black race, Annjee! You hear me? Help the whole race!'" (323). With this pronouncement Harriett proves that she has successfully negotiated the tension between the communal and the individual. She has used African American music to become a star, to become financially independent and transcend economic and social limitations. Yet, she has also become a representative artist who uses the resources she has acquired through the music to "'Help the whole race!'"

Hughes ends *Not Without Laughter* with a note of affirmation. On the way home from the concert Annjee and Sandy pass by a "little Southern church" where they hear the congregation singing a spiritual. The teenager remarks on the similarity to the sounds they had heard at the revivals in the South. His mother answers that "'Them old folks are still singing—even in Chicago!'" Sandy exclaims the beauty of the song, and the novel concludes with the comment, "for, vibrant and steady like a stream of living faith, their song filled the whole night: An' we'll understand it better by an' by!" (324). The African American folk tradition has been carried north with this "blues movement," and members of a new generation, like Sandy Rodgers, will continue the fight for equality by drawing upon the lessons learned from the music and other forms in that tradition.

Unlike *Not Without Laughter*, which delineated the connections between traditional folk sources of African American music and the modern forms that were emerging from twentieth-century black culture, the representation of music in Claude McKay's novel *Home to Harlem* (1928) focuses exclusively on the modern expressions of that folk culture in the context of the rapidly expanding black urban community. Although McKay had established his reputation as a poet before the novel was published, he was the first writer from the Harlem Renaissance to produce a best-selling work of fiction. Despite the popular success of *Home to Harlem*, many of the black intellectuals of the time looked down upon the work as a crude and demeaning representation of African American life.[22] The novel depicts the inner-world of lower-class black city-dwellers—the world of saloons, nightclubs, gambling halls and brothels. Cordoned off into the "Black Belt" of Harlem with little opportunity for economic advancement, the black population creates an alternative world of hedonistic pleasure.[23] The main characters in *Home to Harlem* are Jake Brown, a World War I deserter eager to return to the joys of Harlem nightlife, and his Haitian emigrant friend, Ray, an intellectual who is torn between the lofty ideals of his "formal" education and his desire to join with Jake in the street life.

Music permeates McKay's representation of this alternative world. The sounds of jazz and blues are woven into the fabric of *Home to Harlem*, evoking the spirit of these people who enjoy their lives with abandon. On his first night back in Harlem Jake is enthralled by a "little brown girl." Drinking and dancing to "a phonograph grinding out a 'blues'" with his new found love, Jake feels that his dreams of home have been fulfilled:

> Oh, to be in Harlem again after two years away. The deep-dyed color, the thickness, the closeness of it. The noises of Harlem. The sugared laughter. The honey-talk on its streets. And all night long, ragtime and "blues" playing somewhere, . . . singing somewhere, dancing somewhere! Oh the contagious fever of Harlem. Burning everywhere in dark-eyed Harlem. . . . Burning now in Jake's sweet blood. . . . (15)

The sensual imagery with which Jake conceives of Harlem places particular emphasis on sound, the laughter, the talk and particularly the music, which can be heard "all night long" throughout this city within a city. The accent on the "noises of Harlem" is appropriate because Jake and the other characters in *Home to Harlem* are the common people who emerged from the oral-based African American folk tradition in urban centers during the first two decades of the twentieth century.

While Dunbar, Johnson and Hughes had depicted the performance of black music creating a space where black and white culture would interact, McKay's working-class blacks in *Home to Harlem* prefer entertainment places like The Congo that prohibit the mixing of races:

> The Congo was a real throbbing little Africa in New York. It was an amusement place entirely for the unwashed of the Black Belt. Or, if they were washed, smells lingered telling the nature of their occupation. Pot-wrestlers, third cooks, W.C. attendants, scrub maids, dishwashers, stevedores.
>
> Girls coming from the South to try their future in New York always reached the Congo first. The Congo was African in spirit and color. No white persons were admitted there. The proprietor knew his market. He did not cater to the fast trade. 'High yallers' were scarce there. Except for such sweetmen that lived off the low-down dark trade. (29-30)

The implication of McKay's portrayal of clubs that cater solely to "the low-down dark trade" is that exclusion from socialization with the working class was based not only on race and economic class but also on the shade of black skin a person possessed. The exclusionary nature of clubs like The Congo also extends to the style of music they featured. When Jake and a friend stop by The Congo one night they hear a particular brand of the blues:

> The Congo was thick, dark-colorful, and fascinating. Drum and saxophone were fighting out the wonderful drag 'blues' that was the favorite of all the low-down dance halls. In all the better places it was banned. Rumor said it was a police ban. It was an old tune, so far as popular tunes go. But at the Congo it lived fresh and green as grass. Everybody there was giggling and wriggling to it. (36)

Linked together in the economic struggle to survive, the patrons of these "low-down dance halls" have their own music that enables them not only to thumb their noses at the propriety of those who frequent "the better places," but in the performance of this particular drag blues to flaunt their disrespect for "a police ban," which is emblematic of the authority of the dominant white culture. The fact that the white authorities may find it necessary to place restrictions on the material performed by black artists indicates their recognition of a disruptive power in the music.

The impulse to exclude whites from working class entertainment establishments may have been a reaction to the pervasive denial of admittance to blacks in white establishments, but it also may reflect a basic distrust of the motivations of these white "slummers." While "high brow" blacks may have been willing to mingle with whites because they knew there was little chance to get ahead without some kind of connections in the white world, the working class may have found these "slummers" to be insincere and condescending. To the working class blacks of *Home to Harlem* these whites were venturing into the Black Belt to amuse themselves selfishly and discard their inhibitions, rather than attempting to share in and understand African American culture. McKay creates an episode that justifies why working class blacks had more than just a patronizing attitude to resent in whites who came uptown to party. Jake flings himself back into Harlem nightlife, cruising from club to club, dancing, drinking, gambling, and he gains admittance to the highly fashionable Madame Suarez's "buffet flat," an unlicensed private club, a kind of pre-Prohibition speakeasy: "Here Jake brushed against big men of the colored sporting world and their white friends. That strange un-American world where colored meets and mingles freely and naturally with white in amusement basements, buffet flats, poker establishments" (106). Jake's travels in Europe after the war make him comfortable in different environments, and his charm enables him to fit in easily with the mixed crowd at the buffet flat. He notices three young white men who begin to frequent Madame Suarez's. They spend a great deal of money, dance with the "colored beauties" and make "lively conversation with the men." One, who plays piano, "jazzed out popular songs." The white men show up one night with two friends "when the atmosphere of Madame Suarez's was fairly bacchic and jazz music was snake-wriggling in and out and around everything and forcing everybody into amatory states and attitudes." A girl at the piano plays the "greatest ragtime song of the day. Broadway was wild about it and Harlem was crazy. All America jazzed to it." (107). The song, "about cocktails and cherries," unleashes the passion of the dancers:

> The women, carried away by the sheer rhythm of delight,
> had risen above their commercial instincts (a common
> trait of Negroes in emotional states) and abandoned
> themselves to pure voluptuous jazzing. They were
> gorgeous animals swaying there through the dance,
> punctuating it with marks of warm physical excitement.
> The atmosphere was charged with intensity and over-
> charged with currents of personal reaction. . . . Then the
> five young white men unmasked as the Vice Squad and
> killed the thing. (108)

The jazz created by this pianist takes the dancers into a different
dimension, a realm of feeling and spirit far removed from calculated
"commercial instincts" so characteristic of the predominant mindset of
white America. In allowing whites to share in the emotional release
that accompanies the intensity of the African American musical
performance, a kind of ritual communal catharsis between audience and
artist, the black patrons of the buffet flat are betrayed by these white
men, who had "posed as good fellows, regular guys looking for a good
time only in the Black Belt" (109).[24] All the patrons of the buffet flat
are arrested and fined. In addition, two white women taken in the raid
are particularly chastised by the judge, who "remarked that it was a pity
he had no power to order them whipped. For whipping was the only
punishment suitable for white women who dishonored their race by
associating with colored persons" (110). McKay is clearly pointing out
that even in supposedly cosmopolitan New York interaction between
black and white is frowned upon, and when miscegenation is merely
intimated the representatives of the white power structure are quick to
revive the brutal intolerance of slavery times.

    As the production of music shifted from a folk to a commercial
process it continued to play a communal role in African American
culture. The clubs and cabarets that fill the cityscape of *Home to
Harlem* provide the meeting ground for professional blues and jazz
artists and their audiences.[25] The development of distinctive repertoires
by these professional performers and the preservation and
commodification of selections from those repertoires in the form of
phonograph records add a new, distinctly modern dimension to black
American music.[26] The creation of a mass market that was aimed at
and almost exclusively supported by black consumers expanded the
scope of the music's communality. "Race records" of blues, jazz and
popular tunes sold in the millions, gaining widespread recognition for
the musical artists, and black listeners throughout America were living
their lives to the same recorded performances. While this phenomenon

of popular music capturing the spirit of the times was not exclusive to
the black community, it is significant because African Americans
clearly established that they were creating their *own* music that
satisfied their *own* standards. In fact, the music being made by black
artists was establishing styles and setting *the* standards for mainstream
American popular music.

Black popular song as a signifier of communality is evident in
Home to Harlem when Jake hears the same "hit" tune in the nightclubs
or on phonographs as he "jazzes" his way through the Black Belt. In the
final part of the novel McKay creates one of these popular tunes that
functions as a leitmotif for the resolution of this phase of Jake's life in
Harlem. The tune is introduced when Jake is attending a dance at Sheba
Palace, another "hall that was entirely monopolized for the amusements
of the common workaday Negroes of the Belt" (294):

> They had a new song-and-dance at the Sheba and the
> black fellows were playing it with *éclat*.
>
> > Brown gal crying on the corner
> > Yaller gal done stole her candy,
> > Buy him spats and feed him cream
> > Keep him strutting fine and dandy.
> >
> > Tell me, pa-pa, Ise you' ma-ma
> > Yaller gal can't make you fall,
> > For Ise got some loving pa-pa
> > Yaller gal ain't got atall.
>
> 'Tell me, pa-pa, Ise you' ma-ma.' The black players
> grinned and swayed and let the music go with all their
> might. The yellow in the music must have stood out in
> their imagination like a challenge, conveying a sense of
> that primitive, ancient, eternal, inexplicable antagonism in
> the color taboo of sex and society. The dark dancers
> picked up the refrain and jazzed and shouted with
> delirious joy, 'Tell me, pa-pa, Ise you' ma-ma.' The
> handful of yellow dancers in the crowd were even more
> abandoned to the spirit of the song. 'White,' 'green' of 'red'
> in place of 'yaller' might have likewise touched the same
> deep-sounding, primitive chord. . .

> Yaller gal sure wants mah pa-pa,
>   But mah chocolate turns her down,
> 'Cause he knows there ain't no loving
>   Sweeter than his loving brown.
>
> Tell me, pa-pa, Ise you' ma-ma,
>   Yaller gal can't make you fall,
> For Ise got some loving pa-pa
>   Yaller gal ain't got atall. (296-97)

"Tell me, pa-pa, Ise you' ma-ma" extols the superiority of dark skin over light skin and is thematically appropriate to the final section of *Home to Harlem* because as Jake dances to the tune with "a tall, shapely quadroon girl" he spies the "little brown" girl whom he had met on his first night back in Harlem. Often during the course of the novel he laments having lost contact with the "little brown," Felice. He literally drops the quadroon girl and rushes over to Felice, who had also given up on ever finding her lost lover, and the two quickly leave the Sheba Palace while the "Tell me, pa-pa, Ise you' ma-ma . . ." of the "black shouting chorus pursued them outside" (299). This communal shout not only marks the reunion of Jake and Felice, but also crystallizes McKay's celebration of blackness as a touchstone for racial identity.[27] For McKay, the light skin of mulattoes is a "challenge," an affront that reminds blacks of the history of racism and miscegenation in America, "that primitive, ancient, eternal, inexplicable antagonism in the color taboo of sex and society."

"Tell me, pa-pa, Ise you' ma-ma . . ." appears again and again as the relationship between Jake and Felice evolves in the last chapters of *Home to Harlem*: "Every cabaret and dancing-hall was playing it. It was the tune for the season. It had carried over from winter into spring and was still the favorite" (321). The full implications of this song as a black communal anthem are revealed at the close of the novel's final chapter as the lovers attend one last club before boarding the train for Chicago:

> Tell me, pa-pa, Ise you' ma-ma. . . .
> Jake and Felice squeezed a way in among the jazzers.
> They were all drawn together in one united mass, wriggling
> around to the same primitive, voluptuous rhythm.
>   Tell me pa-pa, Ise you' ma-ma. . . .
>   Haunting rhythm, mingling of naive wistfulness and charming gayety [sic], now sheering over into mad riotous

joy, now, like a jungle mask, strange, unfamiliar,
disturbing, now plunging headlong into the far, dim
depths of profundity and rising out as suddenly with a
simple, childish grin. And the white visitors laugh. They
see the grin only. Here are none of the well-patterned,
well-made emotions of the respectable world. A laugh
might finish a sob. A moan end in hilarity. That gorilla
type wriggling there with his hands so strangely hugging
his mate, may strangle her tonight. But he has no thought
of that now. He loves the warm wriggle and is lost in it.
Simple, raw emotions and real. They may frighten and
repel refined souls, because they are too intensely real,
just as a simple savage stands dismayed before nice
emotions that he instantly perceives as false.

Tell me, pa-pa, Ise you' ma-ma. . . . (337-38)

Like many black writers who preceded him, McKay is concerned with
the mistaken perception "white visitors" have of African American
music. They see it as mere entertainment and are oblivious to the mask
the "united mass" wears in the production of a cultural expression that
subverts the "well-patterned, well-made emotions of the respectable
world." The one-dimensional view of blacks, seeing "the grin only," is
characteristic of the white world's attempt to control through an
exclusionary focus on its conception of the orderly and rational.
Nevertheless, this world view is undermined by African American
music's ability to evoke ritualistically a spiritual realm that testifies to
the validity of the sensual and emotional aspects of life.

While the representation of music in *Home to Harlem* concentrates
on the urban African American community, McKay broadens the scope
of the music's cultural significance through the character Ray. When
Jake takes a job on the railroad he meets Ray, who is working as a
waiter on a Pullman, and the West Indian brings an awareness of the
connections between the cultures that emerged from the African
diaspora to the novel.[28] During a layover in Philadelphia Jake takes
Ray to a house party where a pianist entertains the participants with the
blues. The scene focuses on Ray's perceptions, and McKay's
description of the music clearly links the sounds created by a black
American to their African source:

The piano-player had wandered off into some dim, far-
away, ancestral source of music. Far, far away from
music-hall syncopation and jazz, he was lost in some
sensual dream of his own. No tortures, banal shrieks and

> agonies. Tum-tum. . . tum-tum. . . tum-tum. . . tum-tum. . .
> The notes were naked acute alert. Like black youth
> burning naked in the bush. Love in the deep heart of the
> jungle. . . . The sharp spring of a leopard from a leafy
> limb, the snarl of a jackal, green lizards in amorous play,
> the flight of a plumed bird, a sudden laughter of
> mischievous monkeys in their green homes. Tum-tum . . .
> tum-tum. . . tum-tum. . . tum-tum. . . . Simple-clear and
> quivering. Like a primitive dance of war or of love. . . the
> marshaling of spears or the sacred frenzy of phallic
> celebration. (196-97)

The evocation of the African jungle in the sounds of jazz was common
during the late-1920s in Harlem. During his tenure as the house band
leader at the Cotton Club, Duke Ellington supplied "jungle" tunes for
the sensational floor shows that portrayed the exotic primitivism of
Africa for the almost exclusively white audience. Ellington was aware
of what the crowd wanted and he managed to fill the bill and still turn
out incredibly inventive jazz masterpieces. Commenting on the Cotton
Club scene, Ellington once said: "Saturday night was the big night for
people to come up to Harlem. They expected the horns to blow loud
and the girls to look wild. When a girl began to wiggle and shake to the
throb of that great tom-tom Sonny Greer was beating, they thought she
was in the throes, and that the spirit of Africa was on her."[29] The
growling of muted horns and pounding drum beats are a signature
device of the Ellington band from this period. Many of Ellington's most
renowned compositions feature these "jungle" devices, including "The
Mooche," "Black and Tan Fantasy," "Black Beauty" and "Rockin' In
Rhythm."

In *Home to Harlem* McKay presents the musical evocation of
Africa as a serious cultural connection. The house party pianist's
improvisations take him on a journey back through the black American
past to a primal realm of African images, the "ancestral source of
music." The music functions as a cultural conduit. Despite the "tortures,
banal shrieks and agonies," the systematic attempts to dehumanize
blacks in slavery and lynch law segregation, the musical tradition that
evolved in America kept blacks in touch with the cultural heritage of
Africa. These "naked acute alert" notes produced by a bluesman at a
house party in Philadelphia are all about life and death, all about the
human drama of men and women of African descent all over the world.

With his second novel, *Banjo* (1929), McKay broadened the scope
of his representation of black life after World War I by examining the
cultural relationships of the various peoples that emerged from the

African Diaspora. Music plays a pivotal role in unifying the cast of black characters who come from Africa, North America, the Caribbean and Europe.[30] Set in the seamy underworld and waterfront of Marseilles, *Banjo*, like *Home to Harlem*, focuses on the black lower class. The novel, which is subtitled "A Story without A Plot," recounts the aimless existence of a group of black "beach boys" who maintain their hedonistic lifestyle by panhandling and hustling. At the center of this international group of hoboes is Lincoln Agrippa Daily, also known as "Banjo," an African American merchant seaman who decides to join the vagabond life and, as his last name implies, live day-to-day.

What sets Banjo apart from his black comrades is his ability to play and his ownership of the musical instrument after which he is nicknamed. Both Banjo and his fellow beach boys are aware he can earn money by performing on the street or in one of the numerous bistros that make up the seedy side of the city that they frequent. As he says of his beloved instrument: "'I nevah part with this, buddy, It is moh than a pal; it's mahself. . . . It ain't one or two times , but plenty, that mah steady here did make me a raise when I was right down and out'" (6).[31] However, his musical ability means much more to Banjo than just a way of making money. After a performance of "Black Bottom" to raise some funds to buy the boys wine, the West Indian Malty comments, "'Youse as good a musician as a real artist,'" and Banjo replies, "'I *is* an artist'" (8). Banjo's predilection for creative expression over money-making is apparent when McKay compares him to the white street musicians who collect money after every set of tunes: "*They* never played for fun as Banjo was prone to do. They played in a hard, unsmiling, funereal way and only for sous. Which was doubtless why their playing in general was so execrable. When Banjo turned himself loose and wild playing, he never remembered sous" (40). McKay does add that "perhaps he could afford to forget" because his girlfriend Latnah, an Indian prostitute, both collects for him and gives him money when he is in need. The accumulation of wealth is certainly not important to Banjo, as evidenced by his answer to his pal Bugsy who kids him about squandering his pay so quickly after arriving in the port: "'Muzzle you' mouf, nigger . . . The joy stuff a life ain't nevah finished for this heah strutter. When I turn mahself loose for a big wild joyful jazz a life, you can bet you' sweet life I ain't gwine nevah regretting it. Ise got moh joy stuff in mah whistle than you're got in you' whole meager-dawg body'" (24).

With his instrument as insurance that he will be able to survive, Banjo sets himself adrift in a life of carefree pleasure: "Banjo had no plan, no set purpose, no single object in coming to Marseilles. It was the port that seamen talked about—the marvelous, dangerous, attractive, big, wide-open port" (12). Yet, Banjo's musical talents soon lead him to a very definite plan and purpose. During a performance at a bistro he quits playing because the crowd noise is drowning out his music:

> Banjo put the instrument aside. It wasn't adequate for the occasion. It would need an orchestry to fix them right, he thought good-humoredly. I wouldn't mind starting one going in this burg. Gee! That's the idea. That's just what Ise gwine to do. The American darky is the performing fool of the world today. He's demanded everywhere. If I c'n only git some a these heah panhandling fellahs together, we'll show them some real nigger music. (14)

Banjo is attracted to the idea of forming an orchestra because he feels he would "be setting pretty in this heah sweet dump without worrying ovah mah wants," but it also reflects his inclination toward a communal form of musical expression. His conception of the "American darky" as the "performing fool of the world" is more a testament to the African American musician's widespread appeal and ability to set trends rather than an indication of his willingness to be a clownish entertainer. Banjo's awareness of the difference is made clear in a confrontation he has with another African American musician who arrives on the Marseilles waterfront. Banjo invites Goosey, who plays flute, to join in the orchestra, but the newcomer expresses disdain for the banjo as a black man's instrument. He claims the "banjo is bondage" and evokes the legacy of slavery.[32] When Goosey refuses to play "that black-face coon stuff," Banjo is quick to defend his instrument and the music he plays: "'Nuts on that black-face. Tha's time-past stuff. But wha' you call coon stuff is the money stuff today. That saxophone-jazzing is sure coon stuff and the American darky sure knows how to makem wheedle-whine them 'blues.' He's sure-enough the one go-getting musical fool today, yaller, and demanded all ovah the wul'" (90-91). Banjo distances himself from "black-face" and the implication of minstrel buffoonery, and he points out that the creation of jazz and blues, what Goosey calls "coon stuff," has opened new opportunities for advancement and gained world-wide recognition for black artists. While Banjo uses terms such as "nigger" and "darky" when speaking with his black comrades, he makes it clear to a group of beach boys that he will not play the servile black or tolerate racial slurs from whites: "I take life easy like you-all, but I ain't nevah gwine to lay mahself wide open to any insulting cracker of a white man. For I'll let a white man mobilize my black moon for a whipping, ef he can, foh calling me a nigger" (42).

The communal role of music in African-based cultural traditions is central to Chapter Five, entitled "Jelly Roll." The Cafe African, a new bistro opened by a Senegalese who returns to France after making money in the United States, becomes a rendezvous for the black population of Marseilles. Banjo provides the music that keeps the party rocking. The throng of blacks from around the globe love "Shake That Thing!," Banjo's version of "Jelly-Roll Blues." He does not want to "collect sous from a crowd of fellows just like himself," but he does recognize the potential for the club to be a perfect showcase for his musical project: "His plan of an orchestra filled his imagination now. Maybe he could use the Cafe African as a base to get some fellows together . . . they would start a little orchestra that would make the bar unique and popular." One afternoon Banjo finds a "cargo boat with a crew of four music-making colored boys" and brings them to perform with him at the Cafe African (47). The crowd of black bodies is transformed into a whirling, dancing blur when the band begins to "Shake That Thing!" With Banjo taking the lead, McKay once again asserts the prominence of African American music:

> The banjo dominates the other instruments; the charming, pretty sound of the ukulele, the filigree notes of the mandolin, the sensuous color of the guitar. And Banjo's face shows that he feels that his instrument is first. The Negroes and Spanish Negroids of the evenly-warm, ever-green and ever-flowing Antilles may love the rich chords of the guitar, but the banjo is preeminently the musical instrument of the American Negro. The sharp, noisy notes of the banjo belong to the American Negro's loud music of life—an affirmation of his hardy existence in the midst of the biggest, the most tumultuous civilization of modern life. (49)

For McKay, the ongoing legacy of racism must be a large part of the tumult of American life, and in describing the music that African Americans produced as an "affirmation" he, like many black writers before him, sees this unique cultural expression as a survival mechanism and mode of resistance in forging a "hardy existence."

One of the problems Banjo faces in realizing his dream of a black orchestra is the transience of the crews in a port town. He convinces Goosey, "the flute-boy," and his Nigerian guitarist friend Taloufa to join with him in a band. Taloufa teaches them a West African song, "whose music was altogether more insinuating than that of 'Shake That Thing.'" The tune is made up of simple but infectious rhythmic variations, and Goosey and Banjo find that their instruments are clashing. One of the boys suggests, "'Let Goosey play solo on the flute, and you fellows join in the chorus. The chorus is the big thing, anyway'" (96). The band agrees to the new approach: "So Goosey played the solo. And Banjo, Taloufa, and Malty took up the refrain, Bugsy, stepping with Dengel, led the boys dancing." In this performance black musicians from throughout the Diaspora create a communal call/response format that draws the audience into participation as the dancing boys form "a unique ring, doing the same simple thing, startlingly fresh in that atmosphere, with clacking of heels on the floor" (97). All the classic components of African-rooted music-making are exhibited, especially the spontaneous magic of improvisation: "It was, perhaps, the nearest that Banjo, quite unconscious of it, ever came to the aesthetic realization of his orchestra. If it had been possible to transfer him and his playing pals and dancing boys just as they were to some Metropolitan stage, he might have made a bigger thing than any of his dreams" (97).

The "orchestry" eventually drifts apart because, as Banjo says, "'Theah was so many other wonderful things in this sweet poht to take up our time'" (221). But the boys also realize that economic times are changing and scratching out a living on the beach is not as easy as it once was. Their recognition of their common cultural heritage through music and camaraderie is accompanied by the recognition that as black men they also share racist oppression and economic exploitation by whites: "Business! Prejudice and business. In Europe, Asia, Australia, Africa, America, those were the two united terrors confronting the colored man" (193). Banjo decides to leave Marseilles with a group of hedonistic, ennui-filled white British and American travelers (who could easily have come from the pages of *The Sun Also Rises*) because he feels they are "'the right folkses now to hulp me with an orchestry'" (221).[33] His departure has a strong effect on the beach boys for "his going away with his instrument left them leaderless and they fell apart" (222), which illustrates the significant role of the musician as a kind of ritual spokesperson in black communal culture. When he finds that the leader of the white group is involved with the occult, Banjo returns to Marseilles but the boys are dispersed.

The character Banjo functions not only as a leader of the beach boys but also as a role model for artistic production in the black, particularly African American, cultural tradition. McKay pursues this theme through the introduction of the character Ray from *Home to Harlem* into *Banjo*. Having worked as a merchant seaman and tramped around Europe, Ray is a fledgling writer still trying to reconcile his intellectual training with the spontaneity and sensuality of lower-class

black life. He joins the beach boys's coterie and becomes close friends
with Banjo, who reminds him of Jake. When Goosey confronts Ray
with his version of "racial uplift" that mirrored the sentiments of many
Harlem intellectuals of the time, the young writer voices his preference
for the artistic expression of black folk culture: '"But you're interested
in race—I mean race advancement, aren't you?' Goosey asked Ray.
'Sure, but right now there's nothing in the world so interesting to me as
Banjo and his orchestra'" (92). Ray's interest in black music, one of the
manifestations of the oral tradition, corresponds to his interest in
making connections between African American folk tales and African
and Caribbean folk tales. Banjo is proud of the fact that Ray is a
"writing black" and announces this fact to the boys. Goosey objects to
Ray's project to write about the beach boys because he feels black
writers should present only positive images of blacks: '"But the
crackers will use what you write against the race!"' (115). The criticism
echoes the attacks that many of the Harlem Renaissance intellectuals
leveled at McKay's novels. McKay answers his critics through Ray's
response:

> Let the crackers go fiddle themselves, and you, too. I
> think about my race as much as you. I hate to see it kicked
> around and spat on by the whites, because it is a good
> earth-loving race. I'll fight with it if there's a fight on, but
> if I am writing a story—well, it's like all of us in this place
> here, black, and brown and white, and I listen, and some
> won't. If I am a real story-teller, I won't worry about the
> differences in complexion of those who listen and those
> who don't, I'll just identify myself with those who are
> really listening and tell my story.' (115)

Hoping to break the ice, Ray tells "one of the African folk tales we
know at home" (118). When he concludes, the Senegalese recognize the
similarities with their own folk tales and are eager to tell them. The one
who begins tells a version of the tale that in the African American
tradition is called the "signifying monkey."[34] A West Indian member of
the beach boys follows this with a tale from his home. The story-telling
session continues with stories of personal exploits from Banjo and Ray,
indicating the viability of the oral tradition. Finally, in what seems to be
an attempt to justify Ray's assertion that "complexion" does not matter
in story-telling, a young Irishman tells a tale.

Banjo, with his intuitive approach to life, recognizes the
similarities between writing and music-making as forms of cultural
expression. When Ray protests that Banjo should never have to resort

to demeaning manual labor to make a living because "'You've got your banjo to work for you,'" his musician friend replies:

> 'And you got you' pen. I want you to finish that theah
> story you was telling about and read it to me. I think you'll
> make a good thing of it. Ise a nigger with a long haid on
> me. I ain't dumb like that bumpitter Goosey. I seen many
> somethings in my life. Little things getting there and
> biggity things not getting anywhere. I done seen the wul'
> setting in all pohsitions, haidways, sideways, horseways,
> backways, all ways. Ef I had some real dough I'd put it on
> you so you could have time to make good on that theah
> writing business.' (149).

For Banjo, writing, like music, can provide for the individual needs of the artist but also, from a broader perspective, seeing "the wul' setting in all pohsitions" he knows that the creation of a black way of writing is important, a "biggity thing" because it will fulfill a communal need.

The novel ends with Banjo's resolve to head out on the road. His intention to keep moving on marks him as an archetypal twentieth-century African American folk figure—the rambling blues man: "Ise a true-blue traveling-bohn nigger and I know life, and I knows how to take it nacheral. I fight when I got to and I works when I must and I lays off when I feel lazy, and I loves all the time becausen the honey-pot a life is mah middle name'" (305). Realizing that from this musician and his friends he has gained "finer nuances of the necromancy of language and the wisdom that any word may be right and magical in its proper setting" (321), Ray decides to join Banjo in his travels. To forge a black way of writing, to capture the "honey-pot a life" in words, Ray must "hold on to his intellectual acquirements" *and* draw upon the same folk source from which Banjo's music springs: "The black gifts of laughter and melody and simple sensuous feelings and responses" (322-23). Music is crucial to the development of McKay's fictional representation of post-World War I black culture. In *Banjo* it not only provides a vital link between the different peoples of the African Diaspora but also pushes McKay to look beyond the concentration on contemporary forms in *Home to Harlem* and examine the roots of the cultural tradition as artistic models.

The African American folk tradition is central to Zora Neale Hurston's work, both as an anthropologist and writer of fiction. While the novels produced by Hughes and McKay were concerned with linking this tradition with its contemporary, particularly urban, manifestations, Hurston concentrated on representing music, and folk culture in general, in the "roots" setting of the rural South.[35] Hurston knew this culture firsthand. Not only did she grow up in an all black community in south Florida, but she traveled throughout the South and in the West Indies as an anthropologist collecting folk materials independently with funding from private patrons or fellowships, as a doctoral student working under Franz Boas of Columbia University and for the Works Progress Administration's Federal Writer's Project. Many of the field recordings she made are housed in the Library of Congress' Folklife Division. Hurston accompanied folklorist Alan Lomax on a recording expedition in 1935, and in a report sent back to Washington in August of that year he called Hurston "probably the best informed person today on Western Negro folk-lore."[36] After Hurston's death in 1960 a tribute Lomax wrote in *Sing Out* magazine illustrates that she was not only a scholar and collector but also a participant in black folk culture:

> She made no brief visits with a recording machine, as most of us are forced to do. She lived in turpentine camps, traveled in the box car houses of Negro section hands, went fishing with her story tellers and took notes while laughter rocked the warm southern nights. On Saturday nights she danced in the country Jooks' and learned the steps herself, along with songs. Anyone who ever had the pleasure, as I did, of spending time with Zora, can testify that she was no reserved scientist, but a racconteur [sic], a singer and a dancer who could bring the culture of her people vividly to life. (12)

While Hurston's research and fiction may have looked to the people of the American South's black communities, she was an integral figure in the intellectual and artistic life of the Harlem Renaissance. Hurston was well aware of the contemporary manifestations of African American folk culture. In her essay "How It Feels to Be Colored Me" (1928), the description of a jazz performance functions as a cultural conduit linking Hurston to an ancestral African source. In the first half of the essay she asserts her individualism, sarcastically claiming that she is not "tragically colored" because "I am too busy sharpening my oyster knife" (153). She says that even when surrounded by white people "I remain myself." In the second half of the essay, however, she states that, "Sometimes it is the other way around." Hurston goes on to describe attending a performance by a jazz orchestra with the lone white person "in our midst." The orchestra plunges into a tune that "attacks the tonal veil with primitive fury, rending it, clawing it until it breaks through to the jungle beyond." Listening with her white companion, Hurston renders her inner reaction to the sounds of jazz:

> I follow those heathen—follow them exultingly. I dance wildly inside myself. I yell within, I whoop; I shake my assegai above my head, I hurl it true to the mark *yeeeeooww!* I am in the jungle and living in the jungle way. My face is painted red and yellow and my body is painted blue. My pulse is throbbing like a war drum. I want to slaughter something—give pain, give death to what, I do not know. But the piece ends. The men of the orchestra wipe their lips and rest their fingers. I creep back slowly to the veneer we call civilization with the last tone and find the white friend sitting motionless in his seat, smoking calmly.
> 'Good music they have here,' he remarks, drumming the table with his fingertips.
> Music. The great blobs of purple and red emotion have not touched him. He has only heard what I felt. He is far away and I see him but dimly across the ocean and the continent that have fallen between us. He is so pale with his whiteness then and I am *so* colored. (Hurston's italics) (154)

Like her sarcastic "oyster knife" dismissal of any communal concern over racial injustice, Hurston's identification with her black heritage through the jazz performance seems somewhat tongue in cheek. Her hyperbolic description of the primitivism aroused by the orchestra may have been a playful jab at the frequent use of jungle imagery to conjure an awareness of African heritage by Harlem Renaissance writers.[37] Yet, the point of representing this musical scene is essentially to link the jazz created in Harlem night clubs with its African roots. The simple statement "Music" indicates the incredulousness with which she takes in the white listener's reaction in contrast with her own. In the "tempo and narcotic harmony" Hurston hears much more than just music. She understands the emotional and sensual subtext, "the great blobs of purple and red emotion," of African American music. She understands this music captures the essence of a cultural heritage and communicates that heritage through a communal insider code.

Hurston's fictional representations of rural black life exhibit an awareness of folk expression as the backbone of African American culture. Music, verbal play and other expressive forms arise from a distinctly black mode of production but also function as responses to

American racism. She described their indirect subversion as hitting "a straight lick with a crooked stick."[38] Most of Hurston's fictional representations of African American life, however, are not concerned with the interaction with white society; she depicts the distinctive approach of black folks to their everyday lives within their own communities. Rather than producing some intellectually conceived model for racial uplift, Hurston attempted to present faithfully the rural black people of the American South as she knew them.[39]

While Hurston's use of black folk expression in her fiction may not seem to be overtly applied to the subversion of the dynamics of racial oppression in American society, she does employ these forms in response to another subjugation—the hegemony of black men over black women. The short story "Sweat" (1926), which portrays the marital relationship of Sykes and Delia Jones, illustrates Hurston's incorporation of music from the black folk tradition into the fabric of her fiction. Through her participation in black communal expression Delia gains the strength to stand up to and overcome her husband's tyranny.

A physically and psychologically abusive husband, Sykes cannot stand the fact that his wife has supported their fifteen-year marriage by washing clothes for white people. In the opening scene of the story Sykes plays on Delia's intense fear of snakes by tossing a bullwhip across her back as she sorts laundry. Within black Southern culture the bullwhip certainly evokes the legacy of slavery, and Sykes' "whipping" of Delia signifies his tyrannical enslavement of his wife. The incident triggers the beginnings of change in Delia, and for the first time she stands up to her husband. That night before going to sleep she says aloud: "'Oh well, whatever goes over the Devil's back, is got to come under his belly. Sometime or ruther, Sykes, like everybody else, is gointer reap his sowing.'" With this utterance Delia erects "a spiritual earthworks against her husband" (199).

Music derived from the African American folk tradition makes a major contribution to Delia's effort to transcend the limitations and abuse of her marriage. The attempts to drive Delia from *her home* (she bought and maintains it) intensify as he publicly flaunts an extramarital affair and culminate when he brings a rattlesnake home in a wire-covered box. Although petrified of the snake, Delia tells Sykes that she will not tolerate any further physical abuse, "'Mah cup is done run ovah.'" She also joins a church in a town four miles away so she will not have to attend the same church as her abusive and hypocritical husband. One Sunday night she drives her horse and buckboard home from her new church singing a spiritual:

She stayed to the night service—love feast—which was
very warm and full of spirit. In the emotional winds her
domestic trials were borne far and wide so that she sang
as she drove homeward,
> 'Jurden water, black an' col'
> Chills de body, not de soul
> An' Ah wantah cross Jurden in uh calm time.' (205)

When Delia reaches the porch she notices that the snake's box is quiet
and boldly asks, "Whut's de mattah, ol' satan, you ain't kickin' up yo'
racket?'" She walks on with a new hope, feeling her threats may have
convinced Sykes to end his abuse. The spiritual is emblematic of that
hope. In a communal musical performance Delia finds relief from her
"trials." For just as the bullwhip evoked the legacy of slavery, the
singing of the spiritual by this black woman brings to mind the inherent
hope and resistance this musical expression represented for the slaves.
Delia finds that Sykes has taken all but one of the matches she bought
and also senses that he has had his girlfriend in the house. This puts the
once weak and submissive wife "into a new fury" as she begins her
laundry work. She decides to leave the laundry basket in the bedroom
and sort the clothes while sitting on the bed. The hope that she had
gained through the folk idiom bolsters her spirit once more: "'An
wantah cross Jurden in uh calm time.' She was singing again. The mood
of the 'love feast' had returned" (205). As she opens the lid she finds
that Sykes has put the snake in the basket. Delia quickly grabs the lamp
and flees the house, taking refuge in the barn loft. A few hours later she
wakes to hear a drunken Sykes returning home. He enters the house
expecting the snake to be in a torpor after having bitten Delia. Having
left all the matches at his girlfriend's, Sykes struggles in the dark to
escape the snake. After he is bitten in the neck he manages to kill the
snake, and when he hears Delia approaching the house he calls to her
for help. With his face badly swollen his one good eye meets Delia's
eyes. She feels pity but leans on a tree for support and watches her
husband die: "She waited in the growing heat while she knew the cold
river was creeping up and up to extinguish that eye which must know
by now that she knew" (207). Delia, who keeps her composure
throughout this final ordeal, has been able to "cross Jurden in a calm
time." She has crossed the "black an' col'" river and found freedom
from Sykes' slavery, and he is left behind to drown in a "cold river" of
poison, fulfilling her prophecy that he would "reap his sowing." The
representation of African American music in "Sweat" not only
functions in terms of authentically portraying the cultural expressions
in the day-to-day existence of black rural folk, but is also thematically

integral to Hurston's exploration of female liberation from male
dominance in that existence. Delia draws upon a communal experience,
the "love feast," and form, the spiritual, from the African American folk
heritage in her effort to transcend the tyranny of her marriage and
achieve individual liberation.

The dual role of music as communal expression and means of
personal transcendence and liberation is amplified in Hurston's second
novel *Their Eyes Were Watching God* (1937).[40] The novel traces the
character Janie Crawford's evolution from the innocent ward of her ex-
slave grandmother through three marriages to become an independent,
self-realized woman. Her experiences with her grandmother and first
two husbands enable Janie to know how she does *not* want to live. She
withdraws into herself disappointed by the promise of love: "Things
packed up and put away in parts of her heart where he could never find
them. She was saving up feelings for some man she had never seen.
She had an inside and an outside now and suddenly she knew how not
to mix them" (68). The dominance and insensitivity of the men in her
life have forced Janie, like Delia in "Sweat," to shield her emotional
needs and desires. African American folk-derived expression plays a
role in Janie's revival as she learns to enjoy life and to be herself
through her relationship with her third husband Vergible "Tea Cake"
Woods, who is a blues singer and musician.

About fifteen-years younger than Janie, who is "around forty," Tea
Cake brings laughter and free-spirited play to her life.[41] The joy he
takes in who he is and in living life his way is certainly crystallized in
the title of the Muddy Waters' blues tune "I Love the Life I Live, I Live
the Life I Love." Music-making is one of the ways that Tea Cake
expresses his determination to enjoy life to its fullest. On his second
visit to see Janie he illustrates his awareness that she needs music in her
life and breaks down her resolution that she *should* resist his advances
through a symbolic musical performance:

> She heard somebody humming like they were feeling
> for pitch and looked towards the door. Tea Cake stood
> there mimicking the tuning of a guitar. He frowned and
> struggled with the pegs of his imaginary instrument
> watching her out of the corner of his eye with that secret
> joke playing over his face. Finally she smiled and he sung
> middle C, put his guitar under his arm and walked on back
> to where she was.
> 'Evenin", folks. Thought y'all might lak uh lil music this
> evenin' so Ah brought long mah box. "Crazy thing!' Janie
> commented, beaming out with light. (96-97)

Tea Cake's imaginary concert introduces an evening in which they play checkers, have lemonade and pound cake and slip off to go fishing in the moonlight. Janie enjoys the experience because it makes her feel "like a child breaking rules." He returns her to her youth, to where she was before Killicks and Starks force her to pack her feelings away. The next night when Janie returns from the store she finds Tea Cake waiting on her porch. After dinner Tea Cake fulfills the promise of the previous evening's imaginary performance: "Then Tea Cake went to the piano without so much as asking and began playing blues and singing, throwing grins over his shoulder. The sounds lulled Janie to soft slumber and she woke up with Tea Cake combing her hair and scratching dandruff from her scalp" (99). Tea Cake's first "real" blues performance is the vehicle that brings these two lovers together. This relationship differs from those with Killicks or Starks because Tea Cake insists that Janie recognize who she really is and become a true partner. He tells her that she does not appreciate her own beauty, and Janie admits she never gazes "in de lookin' glass." He replies "'See dat? You'se got de world in uh jug and make out you don't know it. But Ah'm glad tuh be de one tuh tell yuh'" (99). Through Tea Cake's example Janie learns to assert her independence. When her friend Phoebe questions the wisdom of marrying a younger, footloose man, Janie replies, "'Dis ain't no business proposition, and no race after property and titles. Dis is uh love game. Ah done lived Grandma's way, now Ah means tuh live mine'" (108). She also voices her realization that the marriage will succeed if they live on equal ground: "'If people's think de same they can make it all right'" (109). Janie concludes her description of her wedding plans with a line that is featured in numerous blues songs: "'Some of dese mornin's and it won't be long, you gointuh wake up callin' me and Ah'll be gone'" (110).[42] The blues lyrics that Janie quotes, which she quite possibly learned from her blues man lover, is appropriate in her voicing of the sense of self-worth and independence she has learned from him as well as her resolution to leave her established life behind and head on down the road.

Traveling to the Everglades to look for work picking crops, Tea Cake immerses Janie in the life of the working class black community. Music is integral to this communal life: "All night now the jooks clanged and clamored. Pianos living three lifetimes in one. Blues made and used right on the spot. Dancing, fighting, singing, crying, laughing, winning and losing love every hour. Work all day for money, fight all night for love. The rich black earth clinging to bodies and biting the skin like ants" (125). Hurston's description of "Blues made and used on the spot" gives testament to her awareness of the viable, ongoing process in the black folk tradition.[43] One of the first things Tea Cake does after marrying Janie is buy a new guitar, for he had sold his in order to have money to court her. Tea Cake and his guitar are even more the focus of the community than the "professional" entertainment setting of the jooks: "Tea Cake's house was a magnet, the unauthorized center of the 'job.' The way he would sit in the doorway and play his guitar made people stop and listen and maybe disappoint the jook for that night. He was always laughing and full of fun too. He kept everybody laughing in the bean field" (126). The black musician is represented as the ritual spokesperson for the community. The ritual nature of Tea Cake's position is illustrated during one of these informal gatherings at his house. A group of men join together to create a hyperbolic tale of the mythical black folk figure "Big John de Conquer."[44] One of his trickster exploits involves him "picking a guitar" and getting "all de angels doing the ring-shout" so that they are tired out and he can win a race "to Jericho and back." The verbal exchange focuses on Big John's guitar-playing skills: "Somebody tried to say that it was a mouth organ harp that John was playing, but the rest of them would not hear of that. Don't care how good anybody could play a harp, God would rather to hear a guitar. That brought them back to Tea Cake. How come he couldn't hit that box a lick or two? Well, all right now, make us know it" (149). Hurston's identification of Tea Cake and his guitar playing abilities with Big John marks him as the individual who can most poignantly express the shared feelings of the community, the one who can "make *us* know it." As in everything else he does, Tea Cake shares the communal aspect of his life with Janie: "She could listen and laugh and even talk some herself if she wanted to. She got so she could tell big stories from listening to the rest" (128). Unlike her marriage to Starks when she was not allowed to join in the tale-telling, signifying and other word play from the oral folk tradition which was part of the daily routine on the store porch, Janie joins with Tea Cake in the distinctive communal expressions of black life.

In addition to participating in African American communal life on the "muck," Janie and Tea Cake become friends with workers from the West Indies. She is attracted to their gatherings by the "subtle but compelling rhythms of the Bahaman drummers" (133).[45] Through the couple the Bahamans or "Saws" begin to associate with the "American crowd": "They quit hiding out to hold their dances when they found that their American friends didn't laugh at them as they feared. Many of the Americans learned to jump and liked it as much as the 'Saws.' So they began to hold dances night after night in the quarters, usually behind Tea Cake's house" (146). Hurston links West Indian and African American cultures through communal music-making. When one of the

"Saws" says good-bye to Janie and Tea Cake, he declares: "'If Ah never see you no mo' on earth, Ah'll meet you in Africa."[46] And with this parting, Hurston points out that the West Indian and American blacks understand that the source of the link between cultures is their shared African heritage.

When Janie and Tea Cake must flee the muck because of a hurricane he is forced to give up his role as ritual spokesperson: "Tea Cake had to throw his box away, and Janie saw how it hurt him" (153). It is during this flood that he receives the bite by the rabid dog that leads to his death. When he eventually falls ill Janie acknowledges the influence he has had on her life: "'Ah jus' know dat God snatched me out de fire through you'" (172). Janie also recognizes the importance of music in Tea Cake's expression of the approach to life which liberated her. She returns the symbol of his leadership when the undertaker prepares Tea Cake for burial: "Janie bought him a brand new guitar and put it in his hands. He would be thinking up new songs to play for her when she got there" (180). Like his mythical counterpart, Big John de Conquer, Tea Cake is equipped with a guitar to satisfy God's preference.

Upon her return to Eatonville Janie takes over Tea Cake's role and becomes a communal spokesperson. She relates her story to Phoeby and encourages her to pass it along to the townspeople: "'Ah know all dem sitters-and-talkers gointuh worry they guts into fiddle strings till dey find out whut we been talkin' 'bout. Dat's all right, Pheoby, tell 'em'" (182). Janie has come to understand the essence of Tea Cake's message about life—that each individual is responsible for living her or his own life to the fullest: "'Yo' papa and yo' mama and nobody else can't tell yuh and show yuh. Two things everybody's got tuh do fuh theyselves. They got tuh go tuh God, and they got tuh find out about livin' fuh theyselves.'" (183) Yet, with this explanation of what she learned in her travels, Janie is declaring her own independence from Tea Cake; her sense of self is not contingent upon her relationship with her man. Hurston's blues figure, a representative of the African American folk tradition, provides a model for Janie so that she can find her own voice to "tell 'em" the story within the framed narrative of *Their Eyes Were Watching God.*[47] She has been able to negotiate a balance between her individual needs and those of the community. Like Delia in "Sweat," Janie transcends the limitations of male hegemony and achieves independence and self-realization through participation in communal folk culture.

Hurston, McKay and Hughes followed Johnson's lead and looked to black folk culture, particularly music, as a source for their fictional representations of African American life. Yet, they rejected the elitism of Johnson's insistence that the folk tradition could only provide the raw materials for the production of some "higher" form of expression. They believed that the cultural productions of the black folk tradition played important roles in the African American community and were valid on their own terms. Like the character Ray in *Banjo*, Hurston, McKay and Hughes attempted to express the black experience by developing a literary tradition modeled on distinctive approaches of the oral tradition. The representation of music figured so prominently in the fiction of these writers because they hoped to emulate the distinctive spontaneity, the inherent resistance to oppression and the ineffable, life-affirming spirit of black folk expression that found their most eloquent and articulate spokesperson in the African American musician.

Notes for Chapter Two

1. In Chapter Four of *From Behind the Veil* Robert Steptoe discusses "problems created by simplistic and limited working definitions of 'fiction' and 'nonfiction'" in *The Autobiography*. Steptoe asserts that "Johnson was the first black author (we can think of) who successfully employed first-person narration in a narrative where nonfiction imposes on fiction far more than fiction (in accord with the models provided most notably by Douglass and Washington) impinges on nonfiction" (107).

2. According to Gates's Introduction to *The Autobiography* Johnson himself was a prolific and highly successful songwriter. He collaborated with his brother J. Rosamond Johnson and their friend Bob Cole to produce around two hundred musical compositions, including Broadway hits, campaign songs for Theodore Roosevelt and "Lift Every Voice and Sing," which has come to be called the "Negro National Anthem" (v-vii).

3. Steptoe discusses the "Preface" to *The Autobiography* as an "authenticating document" that functions in a manner similar to the prefaces and introductions that white abolitionists attached to the slave narratives (98).

4. Robert Steptoe finds that one of his memories from Georgia anticipates how the narrator ultimately treats his abilities as an African American music-maker. He remembers being punished for digging up "vari-coloured glass bottles stuck in the ground neck down." Steptoe says this is emblematic of placing reflective objects around graves,"an African survival in the New World," which is an "innocent yet devastating act of assault upon a considerable portion of his heritage." This foreshadows his attempt to turn black folk idioms into "classical music" (100-101).

5. In "James Weldon Johnson's Theories and Performance Practices of Afro-American Folksong" Wendell Phillips Whalum states that Johnson's writing on African American folk music goes far beyond simply providing the "stimulus for further investigation" (383).

6. The narrator rejects the official version of history which reduces events to simplistic categorization, such as 'Discovery,' 'Colonial,' 'Revolutionary,' 'Constitutional.' (40-41).

7. Johnson retains this high/low culture distinction when he repeats this section in the *Poetry* Preface. He seems to believe that while the folk provides the source for black artistic production it cannot be considered a "higher" form. Johnson further comments: "But there is

great hope for the development of this music, and that hope is the Negro himself" (20). He goes on to cite such examples as Harry T. Burleigh, Will Marion Cook and R. Nathaniel Dett, whom Eileen Southern classifies as "Black Nationalistic Composers." Southern describes their musical approach as follows: "They knew how to write music in the traditional European style and, indeed, often did so, particularly when they wanted the music to sell. But they reserved much of their creative energy for Negro-inspired composition" (*Music* 266). Thus, it would seem that Johnson, like the Ex-Coloured Man, refuses to completely abandon Eurocentric standards.

8. According to Marshall Stearns, syncopation means "accenting the normally weak beat" (105).

9. For detailed discussions of the technical aspects and development of ragtime, see Stearns, Chapter 13 and Southern, 308-29.

10. In the Ex-Coloured Man's brief overview of the development of ragtime music, which Johnson repeats in the *Poetry* Preface, he points out that the music was the cultural production of "Negro originators [who] got a few dollars" of the "small fortunes" earned by "white imitators and adulterators" (100).

11. Steptoe suggests that the narrator's tone shifts during this passage from "public" to "personal," as his descriptions of the musical interludes with his mother had been, but that as he tries to "wax eloquent" he exposes himself as "an a historically minded seer of surfaces" (120-21).

12. Sherley Anne Williams asserts in *Give Birth to Brightness* that for the Ex-Coloured Man "this retreat into passing for white is a defeat which he recognizes as his own willingness to accept the non-threatening aspects of his heritage,—Black music and the supposed Black exoticism—and his lack of psychological and physical strength to withstand the terrifying forms which racism often takes, even though these forms are also a part of the Black heritage" (140).

13. In *When Harlem Was in Vogue* David Levering Lewis dates the beginning of the Harlem Renaissance in 1919, with the return of black soldiers from World War I, and its ending in 1934 in the midst of the Great Depression (xvi). Lewis identifies Johnson as a member of what he calls "The Six," a group of intellectual leaders who acted as "midwives" to the literary production of the period. In addition to Johnson The Six included Jessie Fauset, Charles Johnson (no relation), Alain Locke, Walter White and Casper Holstein (120-21).

14. As Richard A. Long has asserted: "The creation of a body of 'blues poems' by Langston Hughes is a very important part of his overall achievement as a writer. His blues poems, at once evocations of

the life of the folk and a reflection of a musical form as well as of a musical ethos, provided him a degree of distinction as a poet shared by no other of his contemporaries" (133). For further analysis of the relationship between Hughes' poetry and the blues see the following sources: Jemie, Onwuchekwa. "Jazz, Jive, and Jam." 1976. *Langston Hughes: Modern Critical Views.* Ed. Harold Bloom. New York: Chelsea House, 1989; Johnson, Patricia A., & Walter C. Farrell, Jr. "How Langston Hughes Used The Blues." *MELUS* 6.1 (1979): 55-63; Kent, George E. "Hughes and the Afro-American Folk and Cultural Tradition." 1972. *Langston Hughes: Modern Critical Views.* Ed. Harold Bloom. New York: Chelsea House, 1989; Tracy, Steven C. *Langston Hughes & The Blues.* Urbana: U of Illinois P, 1988.

15. Lawrence Levine states that early forms of blues existed in the late part of the nineteenth century and possibly during slavery "but it was not until the twentieth century that it became one of the dominant forms of black song" (221).

16. Southern gives a brief overview of the main female Classic Blues singers (*The Music* 367-69), and Levine discusses the evolution of the style (225-26).

17. See Lawrence W. Levine for the influence of American individualism, including the teachings of Booker T. Washington, and the effects of the emergence of sound recordings on the blues as a communal folk expression (223-24).

18. As Bernard Bell has stated, music along with religion, humor and language are "cultural forms [that] enable blacks to repress and sublimate hardships as they pursue a better life for themselves and future generations" (130).

19. For a detailed analysis of the innovations of Kansas City jazz artists see Chapter 9 "Kansas City Four/Four and the Velocity of Celebration" of Albert Murray's *Stompin the Blues,*

20. In "The Blues Roots of Contemporary Afro-American Poetry" Sherley A. Williams asserts that early blues singers "helped to solidify community values and heighten community morale." She cites Michael S. Harper's liner notes to the album *John Coltrane* which allude "to the communal nature of the relationship between blues singer and blues audience when [speaking] of the audience which assumes 'we' even though the blues singer sings 'I'" (124).

21. Hazel Carby suggests in "It Jus Be's Dat Way Sometime: The Sexual Politics of Women's Blues" that the migration to urban centers may represent different things to black men and women. While the movement may have signified freedom to the men, "migration for women often meant being left behind." Carby says the female blues

singers [like Harrietta in *Not Without Laughter*] were able to articulate "the possibilities of movement" (751). Carby says the train, which was a symbol of freedom for the men, became a "contested symbol": "Being able to move both North and South the women blues singer occupied a privileged space: she could speak the desires of rural women to migrate and voice the nostalgic desires of urban women for home which was both a recognition and a warning that the city was not, in fact, the 'promised land'" (752).

22. Lewis describes the reaction to the "primitivism" of *Home to Harlem* and the comparisons made with Carl Van Vechten's *Nigger Heaven*. The librarian at Howard University called both authors "filth mongers" and DuBois said after reading McKay's novel, "I feel distinctly like taking a bath" (225-27).

23. In *Give Birth to Brightness* Willliams states that the "'jazz life'— the rowdy subculture of lower-income Black communities" is "a demi-world where music, dancing, violence and crime rage rampant. Black music becomes, in McKay and Hughes, a symbol of liberation from the stifling respectability and materialistic conventionality which have an odor of decay about them" (137).

24. Levine points to Charles Keil's *Urban Blues* for a discussion of the ritual significance of the blues performance.(234).

25. Gunter H. Lenz, in "Symbolic Space, Communal Rituals, and the Surreality of the Urban Ghetto: Harlem in Black Literature from the 1920s to the 1960s" suggests that the cabaret provides a communal space for a "community ritual" of jazz and dance. He further suggests that: "In black literature of the 1920s, cabarets are both *liminal space* ('acculturation' of Southern migrants, their 'initiation' into 'city culture,' 'socialization' of the young) *and* a *liminoid space* (suspension of the new and demanding routine of 'work,' of everyday rhythm, values, behavior; the potential, imaginative dimension of communitas in social 'reality')" (322).

26 As Levine explains: "The folk process may have been altered by the mass migrations to the cities and by the advent of mass media and commercialization, but it remained a central ingredient of Afro-American culture. This can be demonstrated further by an examination of the Negro audience. Black music was a participant activity not only for those who hollered in the fields, sang in the churches, or picked a guitar at home, but also for those who went out to listen and respond to professional entertainers" (232).

27. As David Levering Lewis has asserted: "All Renaissance writers were preoccupied with color, but McKay, to the acute distress

of Harlem's elite, was not merely obsessed with chocolate, chestnut, coffee, ebony, cream, yellow complexions, his novel (as became the quasi-Garveyite he once was) embraced antimulatto sentiments" (227).

28. McKay was born in Jamaica in 1889 and traveled to the United States to study agriculture at Kansas State College in 1914 but soon decided to move to New York (Lewis 50-51).

29. The Ellington quotation appears in Stanley Dance's liner notes to the Ellington album "Volume 2. (1928-1929) 'Hot in Harlem'" (MCA 1359). The three volumes in this series contain most of Ellington's major recordings from the 1926-31.

30. In his essay "Aimé Césaire" Amiri Baraka asserts that the Harlem Renaissance writers, particularly McKay and Hughes, had tremendous influence on Césaire and the "Negritude" poets who lived in Paris during the 1930s: "The most important book of that renaissance to these writers was Claude McKay's *Banjo*, not only because of McKay's West Indian background and because he used in this book both Europe, the Marseilles docks, and the West Indies as his setting, but also because in *Banjo* there are ideas of resistance to colonialism, and statements about black people's situation, that are presented with the clarity of fire" (327).

31. Banjo's characterization of his musical instrument as his "buddy" recalls Solomon Northup's slave narrative where he calls his fiddle "my companion—the friend of my bosom." See page 7 above.

32. Goosey's claim that "banjo is bondage" may be just the kind of stereotyping against this instrument brought from Africa to America by black musicians that Delany hoped to undermine in *Blake* when he associates it with a black liberationist movement. See page 25 above.

33. For a discussion of McKay's admiration for Hemingway's work see James R. Giles' *Claude McKay* (74-75, 93, 138-39).

34. Henry Louis Gates, Jr. adopts the "signifying monkey" tale as the overriding metaphor for his theory of African-American literary criticism in his *The Signifying Monkey*. Although he does not cite *Banjo* in his text, one of Gates's main objectives, like Ray's, is to establish the existence of a black literary tradition linking oral expression and literary expression.

35. In her conclusion to *Reconstructing Womanhood* Carby states that Hurston "felt concerned that whites just did not know who blacks were" and "chose to reconstruct figures of 'the folk' in her novels." She goes on to assert that most literary criticism "acknowledges this representation of the folk as 'the people' but does not question the historical significance of Hurston's choice" (165). Carby concludes that an established pattern depicting the "rural folk as bearers of Afro-

American history and preservers of Afro-American culture" has "effectively marginalized the fictional urban confrontation of race, class, and sexuality. . ." (174).

36. The letter from Lomax is in a Hurston file at the Library of Congress' Folklife Division. Half typed and half hand-written it is addressed to Mr. Oliver Strunk of the Music Division of the Library of Congress. The return address is given as Nassau, The Bahamas. Lomax states that the recording trip, which included himself, Hurston and New York University Professor Miss Mary Elizabeth Barnicle, had moved through Georgia and Florida. Lomax also states that although Hurston was unable to travel to the Bahamas, "up until the time she left us, she had been almost entirely responsible for the great success of our trip and for our going into the Bahamas."

37. Robert Hemenway comments that in Harlem Renaissance writing "both blacks and white became enmeshed in the cult of exotic primitivism." For whites, going to Harlem was like a "safari" to "an uptown jungle." For blacks "it was a much more serious concern, an attempt to establish a working relationship with what Locke called in *The New Negro* the 'ancestral past.'" Hemenway says of the description of the jazz performance in "How It Feels to Be Colored Me": "Her response comes not only as a function of race, differentiating her from a white companion, but also as an archetype of history" (75-76).

38. This aspect of Hurston's use of folk materials is discussed by Hemenway: "Hurston knew that black folklore did not arise from a psychologically destroyed people, that in fact it was proof of psychic health. As she put it, the folk knew how to "hit a straight lick with a crooked stick," how to devise a communicative code that could simultaneously protest the effects of racism and maintain the secrecy of that very same protest" (51).

39. As Alice Walker has stated: "Zora Neale Hurston was never afraid to let her characters be themselves, funny talk and all. She was incapable of being embarrassed by anything black people did, and so was able to write about everything with freedom and fluency" (O'Brien 200).

40. While *Their Eyes Were Watching God* was published well after the decline of what has been called the Harlem Renaissance, the novel certainly is a culmination of the work of a major figure from that historical movement.

41. In *The Signifying Monkey* Gates discusses the function of "play" in the novel. He states that "'Play' is also the text's word for the Signifyin(g) rituals that imitate 'courtship' . . . This repeated figure of play is only the thematic analogue to the text's rhetorical play, plays of

language that seem to be present essentially to reveal the complexity of black oral forms of narration" (195).

42. One of the earliest recorded usages of a variation on this line can be found in pianist/ vocalist Leroy Carr's "Shady Lane Blues" recorded in 1934. Probably the most widely known instance of this traditional line's use is in "Mean Mistreatin' Mama," which Elmore James recorded in New Orleans in 1961. James's producer Bobby Robinson took credit for composing the song.

43. Hurston speaks of this process on a Library of Congress recording she made in June of 1939 performing a number of the songs she collected. In her introduction to "Ever Been Down" she states: "It's one of those things that just go round all the jooks and whatnot, like that grows by incremental repetition again, a verse here and there. I don't suppose anybody knows just old it is or when it started" (AFS 3138 B1).

44. Levine gives a version of the tale with the character called "High John de Conqueror" and cites the WPA manuscripts, Florida File, Archive of Folk Song as his source. It is quite probable that Hurston was the collector who reported this tale.

45. In Lomax' letter he writes of hearing Bahaman music with Hurston in Florida: "Then Miss Hurston introduced us into a small community of Bahaman Negroes. We then heard our first fire-dance and for the first time, although we and other collectors had searched the South, the heavy, exciting rhythm of a drum. The dance and the songs were the closest to African I had ever heard in America." Hurston comments in her autobiography *Dust Tracks on a Road* on Bahaman music: "This music of the Bahaman Negroes was more original, dynamic and African, than American Negro songs" (60).

46. A common myth in the various cultural manifestations of the African Diaspora speaks of enslaved Africans being able to return home, usually by flight. As Gay Wilentz states in "If You Surrender to the Air: Folk Legends of Flight and Resistance in African American Literature:" "The legend of the Flying Africans is prevalent throughout the diaspora-from the coastal areas of the southern United States to the Caribbean and parts of Latin America" (22).

47. Gates's discussion of *Their Eyes Were Watching God* focuses on Hurston's interplay of first and third person narration to achieve a distinctively black American narrative voice, a "speakerly text," "a text whose rhetorical strategy is designed to represent an oral literary tradition" (181).

III
"The Only True History of the Times"

"I am tired, I am weak, I am worn.
Through the storm, through the night,
Lead me on to the light,
Take my hand precious Lord, lead me home."
                              - Thomas A. Dorsey

"I love the word jazz; it means life."
                              - Dexter Gordon

"Thundered an' lightened an' the storm begin to roll
Thousan's of people ain't got no place to go.
Den I went an ' stood upon some high ol' lonesome hill,
An' looked down on the house where I used to live."
                              - Bessie Smith

"When I think of jazz, being a jazz musician, I think
of it as being instantaneous composition, creation. I
think of it as something that never happened before
anywhere but in America because of the great
diversity of people we have here."
                              - Milt Hinton

"Tell Automatic Slim, tell razor totin' Jim,
Tell butcher knife totin' Annie, tell fast talkin' Fanny,
We gonna pitch a ball down to the union hall.
We gonna romp and tromp 'til midnight
We gonna fuss and fight 'til daylight
We gonna pitch a wang dang doodle
All night long, all night long, all night long."
                              - Willie Dixon

"When I look back on my life, I wasn't conscious of
these things, but you know everybody has a cross to
bear and mine is that I've got to make music and
please my fellow human beings. I hope things will
turn around and people will become happy. That's
why I've come back out on the street. There's nothing
greater than to have a smile and a twinkle in the eye."
                              - George "Big Nick" Nicholas

117

1.
"NOT MANY PEOPLE EVER REALLY HEAR IT": RICHARD WRIGHT, ANN PETRY & JAMES BALDWIN

While the Depression may have led to the decline of the Harlem Renaissance, during this period and continuing through the 1940s African American musicians continued to develop contemporary musical forms that derived from the folk tradition—blues, jazz and an emerging style called gospel—to unprecedented levels of both technical proficiency and emotive expression.

The blues endured as a vital and poignant artistic and cultural tradition which conveyed the essence of what it meant to be black in America—that ironic understanding of an approach to life summed up in the blues axiom "You got to laugh to keep from crying." Stylistically, the Classic Blues declined in popularity, and the traditional country blues—which encompassed wide idiomatic distinctions based on geographic regions including the Mississippi Delta, Carolina Piedmont and Texas styles—gained widespread exposure both through the field recordings made in the South and blues artists who transplanted their careers to northern urban centers. Performers such as Big Bill Broonzy, Leroy Carr, Blind Boy Fuller, Son House and Memphis Minnie Douglas were a part of this second wave of blues recording artists. The hard driving blues piano style known as "boogie-woogie" also came to the forefront during the Depression years through such musicians as Albert Ammons, Jimmy Yancey, Roosevelt Sykes and Memphis Slim (Peter Chatman).[1]

The blues artist who epitomized the virtuostic refinement and culmination of the country blues idiom was the Mississippi-born guitarist/vocalist Robert Johnson. He developed his distinctive slide guitar style by emulating the established blues men he encountered in the Delta, such as Willie Brown, Charlie Patton and Son House. Yet, he played the blues as they had never been played before; he brought a singular emotional intensity and incredible technical facility to the traditional form which allowed him to articulate a conception of a song as a complete thematic statement. Johnson captured the spirit of the rural black man attempting to fit into the rapidly urbanizing U.S. society during the years between world wars—the celebration of freewheeling mobility coupled with the realization that he must "keep movin'" or be caught up in the menace of hostility and limited possibility that was a fact of American life. Johnson's composition "Hellhound On My Trail" captures this double-edged world view:

I got to keep movin'
I've got to keep movin'
blues fallin' down like hail
blues fallin' down like hail
Ummm mmm mmm mmm
blues fallin' down like hail
blues fallin' down like hail
And the days keeps on worryin' me
there's a hellhound on my trail
hellhound on my trail
hellhound on my trail (38)

Johnson flashed across the scene like a shooting star, leaving an indelible legacy for the blues tradition. He recorded twenty-nine songs (in addition, twelve alternate takes are extant) at five sessions in Texas recording studios between November of 1936 and June of 1937. The menace of American life, that hellhound on his trail, caught up with Robert Johnson in 1938 when at age twenty-six he died of pneumonia which he contracted after a love rival poisoned him with strychnine-laced whiskey—"blues fallin' down like hail" indeed.[2]

The presence of the blues during the Depression was not only felt through the down home stylings of country blues artists, for the blues was a key ingredient in the music that captured the pulse of contemporary urban life in the U.S.A.—jazz. Even if jazz artists were performing material that did not derive from the standard twelve-bar blues form, such as ballads or popular show tunes, a "blues sensibility," an avoidance of sentimentality and an ironic awareness of the dualistic nature of life, linked them to African American folk expression. American popular culture during the 1930s and early 1940s was referred to as the "Swing Era," a name drawn from the rhythmic beat of big band jazz which was glorified in Duke Ellington's composition "It Don't Mean a Thing If It Ain't Got That Swing." The black orchestras of Ellington, Count Basie, Earl Hines, Chick Webb, Lucky Millinder, Cab Calloway and Jimmie Lunceford formed the vanguard of this musical approach, which featured highly inventive arrangements performed by brass (trumpets and trombones) and reed (saxophones and clarinets) sections propelled by a hard driving rhythm section (piano, acoustic bass, trap drums and guitar). But perhaps what is more significant in terms of African American artistic expression than the buoyant underpinning the big band rhythms and arrangements provided for dancers was the format's allowance for solo improvisation by individual band members. The bands featured outstanding musicians on each instrument who combined impeccable and innovative technique with a personal sound and style and above all the ability to imbue everything they played with that infectious, ineffable sense called *swing*. Arrangements were written with slots for soloists to improvise spontaneously on the chord changes of the composition, to "do their thing," in dialogue with the catchy rhythmic figures or "riffs" played by the sections.

Each instrument within the tradition of the jazz idiom developed a lineage of innovations and variations as unique stylists expanded this new "language" of African American musical expression. In *Stomping the Blues* Albert Murray has asserted that musicians were conscious of the evolution of each lineage and their creative responses to what had preceded them were more important than "impulse" in producing innovations: "It is thus far more a matter of imitation and variation and counterstatement than of originality. It is not so much what the blues musicians bring out of themselves on the spur of the moment as what they do with existing conventions. Sometimes they follow them by extending that which they like or accept, and sometimes by counterstating that which they reject" (126).

Jazz improvisation had found its first master in trumpeter Louis Armstrong during the 1920s; his harmonic and rhythmic innovations revolutionized modern music-making. The first musician to apply the bravura of Armstrong's brash sound and hard driving attack to the saxophone was Coleman Hawkins, whose sound and approach set the standard for saxophone stylings. The premium placed on originality by the players *within* the jazz tradition is testified to by the innovations of the tenor saxophonist Lester Young, who created a soft, airy, laid-back approach to his horn that contrasted dramatically with Hawkins's style, establishing two "schools" that future generations of saxophonists could follow and/or blend as they carved their own places in the tradition. In addition to an innovative personal approach to his horn, Young had a penchant for creating his own hipster spoken language. In an interview just prior to his death in 1959 he commented: "In my mind, the way I play, I try not to be a repeater pencil, you dig? I'm always loosening spaces, laying out, or something like that. Don't catch me like that. I'm always reaching."[3] Even though Young had secured a place for himself with a landmark style, he refused to rest on his laurels and continuously strove to articulate new ideas on his horn.

More than the public band performances, the informal gatherings of musicians known as "jam sessions" in which instrumentalists challenged each other in "cutting contests" to prove who was the most inventive and resourceful soloist were the testing grounds where jazz musicians established themselves and extended the tradition. Some of the most legendary jam sessions took place in Kansas City during the early 1930s. The competition was often unrelenting; one story tells of tenor saxophonist Ben Webster rushing to pianist Mary Lou Williams's bedroom window at four in the morning to get her to come to a club because the contest between tenor players had gone on so long all the pianists in the house were worn out. The censure for failure to perform up to standards could be devastating; another story relates how early in his career the alto saxophonist Charlie Parker was "sitting in" with the Basie band and attempted to demonstrate his personal approach to improvisation without the technical ability to execute his ideas. When Parker floundered drummer Jo Jones threw his cymbal at the saxophonist, driving him from the bandstand in humiliation and forcing him to go "woodshed" or practice until he developed his abilities up to the standards the established players demanded. While the jam session demanded that a participant contribute something new, it also insisted that the contribution be grounded in what had already been established. In the essay "Living with Music" (1955) Ralph Ellison states that he learned "something of the discipline and devotion to his art required of the artist" from the territory band jam sessions which he attended as a young man in Oklahoma:

> These jazzmen, many of them now world-famous, lived for and with music intensely. Their driving motivation was neither money nor fame, but the will to achieve the most eloquent expression of the idea-emotions through the technical mastery of their instruments (which, incidentally, some of them wore as a priest wears the cross) and the give and take, the subtle rhythmical shaping and blending of idea, tone and imagination demanded of group improvisation. The delicate balance struck between strong individual personality and the group during those early jam sessions was a marvel of social organization. I had learned too that the end of all this discipline and technical mastery was the desire to express an affirmative way of life through its musical tradition and that this tradition insisted that each artist achieve his creativity within its frame. He must learn the best of the past, and add to it his personal vision. (189)

The soloist's statement had to be crafted within the framework provided by the ensemble, and this retention of the cornerstone duality of the individual tied to the communal rooted this modern music in the African American folk heritage. These "after hours" gatherings were insider rituals that gave African American artists control over the forging of what is the most creative form of artistic expression to emerge during the twentieth century.

Blues and jazz may have been going through unparalleled creative growth during the years before World War II, but by no means did they gain wholesale acceptance in the black community. The split between the sacred and the secular in African American music continued to exist. Many blacks held steadfastly to the belief that music which did not praise the Lord was the Devil's music.[4] Even between denominations of black churches there was a division in terms of what was acceptable in terms of sacred music. After Emancipation many of the existing or newly established black churches tried to divorce themselves from a primitivism they perceived in the spirituals and adopted the more staid hymnal forms of white religions.[5] The development of Holiness, Sanctified or Pentecostal sects among lower class blacks brought the influence of secular musical styles and a reassertion of folk elements to black religious worship.[6] Call and response, improvisation and a driving, sophisticated rhythmic sensibility were the building blocks for this new church music that crystallized as a form through the compositions of pianist Thomas A. Dorsey. The storefront churches that sprang up as blacks poured into northern cities readily adopted it. Gaining his initial recognition as "Georgia Tom," a blues pianist and composer who was best known as an accompanist and music director for Ma Rainey, Dorsey began writing religious music after being inspired by a performance he heard at a black religious convention during the early 1920s. By the end of decade he was selling his songs to various churches as he traveled around the South and Midwest. Dorsey was the first person to use the term "gospel" to describe African American religious music, and he gained widespread recognition in 1930 when his composition "If You See My Saviour" was performed at the National Baptist Convention. Acknowledged as the "Father of Gospel Music," Dorsey wrote over one thousand songs. While the lyric content of his songs may have had a sacred focus, the accompanying music was certainly secular. As Dorsey described his songs: "I started putting a little of the beat into gospel that we had in jazz. I also put in what we called the riff, or repetitive (rhythmic) phrases. These songs sold three times as fast as those that went straight along on the paper without riffs or repetition."[7] Zora Neale Hurston witnessed this interchange between the sacred and the secular in the music of black religious songs while researching folklore in Florida. In a W. P. A. Federal Writer's Project manuscript written in 1938 she reported: "In recent years has come an increased popularity of the swinging type of music, even in the churches. In Jacksonville there is a jazz pianist who seldom has a free night; nearly as much of his business comes from playing for 'Sanctified' church services as for parties. Standing outside of the church it is difficult to determine just which kind of engagement he is filling at the moment."[8]

The influence of African American secular music on the formation of the gospel sound is testified to by the emergence of singer Mahalia Jackson, whose musical initiation in New Orleans included hearing the songs of the neighborhood Sanctified church, the hallmark jazz bands of her native city and the blues, particularly the records of Bessie Smith. When Jackson moved to Chicago in 1927 the mainstream black churches looked down on her rocking approach to religious songs, but during the 1930s the power of her performances that packed the city's storefront churches soon won her a devoted following. Jackson worked with Dorsey who wrote for her what became the all time most well-known gospel song "Precious Lord, Take My Hand." By the end of World War II Jackson was a national recording artist, eventually gaining international renown.

While the gospel sound certainly exhibited the crossover influences of jazz and blues, the lyrical content of this music was imbued with a message of Christian faith and hope. Thematically, gospel songs also featured lyrics with distinct differences from the sentiments expressed in their folk ancestors, the spirituals. The lyrics of gospel songs lacked the immediacy of the spirituals' lyrics and were more focused on a spiritual better day.[9] Nonetheless, the message of better days coming was perfect for the Depression era. As Dorsey commented on the popularity of the form he helped create:

> I wrote to give them something to lift them out of that Depression. They could sing at church but the singing had no life, no spirit. . . . We intended gospel to strike a happy medium for the downtrodden. This music lifted people out of the muck and mire of poverty and loneliness, of being broke, and gave them some kind of hope anyway. Make it anything but good news, it ceases to be gospel.[10]

Just as hard times pushed African American musicians toward innovative forms and new levels of creativity, black writers continued to expand the literary tradition in the years following the decline of the Harlem Renaissance. During this era, the acquisition of equal rights and opportunities was a paramount concern for African Americans that was reflected in their artistic productions. The resistance to American racism expressed in musical forms usually was not overt; the creative act of music-making during the years between the Depression and the advent of the civil rights movement often represented an implied subversion of the limitations that the dominant forces in American society imposed on blacks. As Ellison explains in the essay "Blues People" (1963):

> For the blues are not primarily concerned with civil rights or obvious political protest; they are an art form and thus a transcendence of those conditions created within the Negro community by the denial of social justice. As such they are one of the techniques through which Negroes have survived and kept their courage during that long period when many whites assumed, as some still assume, they were afraid. (257)

Thus, Robert Johnson delivering a searing slide guitar run in a Mississippi Delta juke joint or Lester Young and Herschel Evans challenging each other with chorus after chorus of saxophone improvisations in a Kansas City after-hours club or Mahalia Jackson bending and stretching the notes of a gospel hymn in a Southside Chicago Holiness church are engaged in acts of creation that are inherently but not necessarily consciously subverting the racist status quo. The overt politicizing of artistic works was a crucial question for black writers who emerged after the Harlem Renaissance. Their predecessors had established the value of African American folk culture as a touchstone for racial identity, but this new generation of writers faced a more complex task in representing black culture because of the escalation of interaction between blacks and whites. While musicians might function as ritual leaders within the black community, writers had the opportunity to reach a widespread, diverse audience with a pointed message. This chance to be a communal spokesperson invested a writer like Richard Wright with the responsibility to use his artistic form to advance a specific political agenda. Wright tailored his fiction to deliver an anti-racist message. In contrast, writers such as James Baldwin and Ralph Ellison hoped to emulate the indirect subversion that characterized much of the musical expression; the artistic method was just as important as the message (and was a mode of transcendence in itself). These two divergent approaches to depicting African American life correspond to the artistic split in the jazz tenor saxophone lineage between the Lester Young and Coleman Hawkins schools. Like saxophonists who could accept, reject, adopt or refine whatever elements they chose from either school, black writers could draw upon the art versus politics dichotomy. The variety in the fictional approaches of Ann Petry is a testament to the artistic possibilities open to African American writers as the literary tradition expanded after the Harlem Renaissance. The representation of music in the fiction of Wright, Petry, Baldwin and Ellison provides insight into these writers' perception of their art and craft and their relationship to the African American community.

The representation of music was minimal in the work of the first major writer of fiction to emerge in the generation following the Harlem Renaissance—Richard Wright. Born in the Mississippi Delta, Wright migrated to Chicago where he became a Communist.[11] In 1937 he published an essay "Blueprint for Negro Writing" that examines the interaction of race and politics in the production of literature. He rejects past African American literature, particularly the writings of the Harlem Renaissance, "the so-called Harlem school of expression," as having been "confined to humble novels, poems, and plays, prim and decorous ambassadors who went a-begging to white America":

> White America never offered these Negro writers any serious criticism. The mere fact that a Negro could write was astonishing. Nor was there any deep concern on the part of white America with the role Negro writing should play in American culture; and the role it did play grew out of accident rather than intent or design. Either it crept in through the kitchen in the form of jokes; or it was the fruits of that foul soil which was the result of a liaison between inferiority-complexed Negro "geniuses" and burnt-out white Bohemians with money. (37)

The "liaison" Wright condemns seems to be a direct reference to the patronage system that supported many of the black writers of the Harlem Renaissance. Wright asserts that this situation resulted in the production of a literature that was *not* "addressed to the Negro himself, his needs, his sufferings, his aspirations" (38). While black writers drifted away from "their people," Wright identifies the development of "a culture of the Negro which is his and has been addressed to him; a culture which has, for good or ill, helped to clarify his consciousness and create emotional attitudes which are conducive to action" (39). He designates the two sources of this culture as "the Negro church" and "the folklore of the Negro people." Although he recognizes the "revolutionary" role religion played in ante-bellum black life, Wright finds it degenerated into "an antidote for suffering and denial." However, he feels black folklore retains its validity and integrity as a form of cultural expression:

> It was, however, in a folklore molded out of rigorous and
> inhuman conditions of life that the Negro achieved his
> most indigenous and complete expression. Blues,
> spirituals, and folk tales recounted from mouth to mouth;
> the whispered words of a black mother to her daughter on
> the ways of men, to confidential wisdom of a black father
> to his black son; the swapping of sex experiences on street
> corners from boy to boy in the deepest vernacular; work
> songs sung under blazing suns-all these formed the
> channels through which racial wisdom flowed. (40)

Certainly Wright is validating the African American oral tradition and
singling out the importance of music as a cultural conduit. He goes on
to recognize the subversive nature of black folk expression, stating
these forms exhibit "those vital beginnings of a recognition of value in
life as it is *lived*, a recognition that marks the emergence of a new
culture in the shell of the old. And at the moment this process starts, at
the moment when a people begin to realize a *meaning* in their suffering,
the civilization that engenders that suffering is doomed" (Wright's
emphasis) (41). For someone who is dismissing the black literary
tradition, particularly the Harlem Renaissance, Wright's analysis of folk
culture features a surprising resemblance to Hughes's urgings in "The
Negro Artist and the Racial Mountain" and does not seem so far
removed from Hurston's concept that black folk expression could "hit a
straight lick with a crooked stick." What separates Wright from his
predecessors is that while he sees an implicit nationalism in black folk
expression which he feels black writers must embrace, he considers this
merely a preliminary step toward transcending nationalism.
Transcendence, for Wright, means that nationalism carries "the highest
possible pitch of social consciousness," and the Negro writer "is being
called upon to do no less than create values by which his race is to
struggle, live and die" (42-43). Wright found these values in Marxism:
"It is through a Marxist conception of reality and society that the
maximum degree of freedom in thought and feeling can be gained for
the Negro writer. . . it restores to the writer his lost heritage, that is, his
role as a creator of the world in which he lives, and as a creator of
himself" (44).

Wright's insistence that black literature reflect a specific political
agenda seems to be the crux of his literary feud with Hurston. The
tremendous gulf that existed between their approaches to representing
African American life is illustrated in their use of folk materials,
especially music. Wright attacked *Their Eyes Were Watching God* as
reactionary even though he admitted "her dialogue manages to catch the

psychological movements of the Negro folk-mind in their pure simplicity." He regarded Hurston's portrayal of black life to be a reiteration of the minstrel tradition: "Her characters eat and laugh and cry and work and kill; they swing like a pendulum eternally in that safe and narrow orbit in which America likes to see the Negro live: between laughter and tears." In turn, Hurston objected to what she perceived as the overt propaganda of Wright's first major work of fiction, the short story collection *Uncle Tom's Children* (1938): "The reader sees the picture of the South that the Communists have been passing around of late. A dismal, hopeless section ruled by brutish hatred and nothing else. Mr. Wright's author's solution is the solution of the PARTY—state responsibility for everything and individual responsibility for nothing."[12] In "Blueprint," however, Wright asserts that, rather than being the ultimate solution, the adoption of Marxism is only a beginning for the black writer: "No theory of life can take the place of life. After Marxism has laid bare the skeleton of society, there remains the task of the writer to plant flesh upon the bones out of his will to live." The writer must choose a negative or positive "social voice," either depicting "the horrors of capitalism encroaching upon human beings" or "the faint stirrings of a new and emerging life" (44).

In Hurston's fiction music, such as the spiritual for Delia in "Sweat" and Tea Cake's blues for Janie in *Their Eyes Were Watching God*, provides a means for the oppressed characters' transcendence. On an intellectual level Hurston perceived the cultural history and significance of these forms. On an emotional level she was aware of the deeper meaning in the sound, the soul, the feeling, the groove that the artist and audience share, making this music such a triumph of the human spirit. Wright seems to have missed or rejected the transcendent power of this emotional level as evidenced in the representation of music in *Uncle Tom's Children*.[13] Wright's insistence that the nationalist identity inherent in the folk forms themselves had to be transcended through Marxist political action is apparent in the way music informs the negative and positive social voices with which he recounts his stories.

African American music plays a role in each of the short stories that make up *Uncle Tom's Children*—a distinctly limited role—and this limitation illustrates how closely Wright follows his own blueprint. In the first story in the collection, "Big Boy Leaves Home," a black teenager must hide and be smuggled north to Chicago to escape being lynched after he kills a white man who has shot the boy's friends for trespassing. At the opening of the story four black boys are walking through the woods singing a song right out of the heart of the oral folk tradition, a dirty dozens, *"Yo mama don wear drawers . . ."* After four

lines, however, they are disappointed over the fact that they do not
know all the words to the song, "'Ah wished Ah knowed some mo lines
t tha song.' 'Me too.' 'Yeah, when yuh gits t where she hangs em out in
the hall yuh has t stop' " (17). They look for a word to rhyme with
"hall" and Big Boy suggests "quall." When his laughing friends ask
what "quall" means, Big Boy replies, "'Nigger, a *qualls* a *quall.'*" But
they do not let him off the hook and continue to demand an
explanation: "'Waal, ef a *qualls* a *quall*, what IS a *quall?'*" He responds
by repeating the original four lines and adding "'N *then she put em back
on her QUALL!* '" They greet his singing with laughter and call him
crazy. Yet, just as their knowledge of the lyrics is incomplete, Big
Boy's knowledge of the folk process is also lacking. He seems to know
that improvisation is appropriate to the form but his execution is faulty.
"Quall" does not fill the bill because it lacks the metaphorical,
onomatopoeic and rhythmical signification of such *non*-sense terms as
"boogie woogie," "rock and roll" or "ditty-wah-ditty" that are so
common in black musical vernacular. Big Boy's "quall" is not an
example of inventive word play but is simply nonsense.

As the scene continues, the boys, who are lounging about on a hot
afternoon, hear a train whistle "mournfully" in the distance. The sound
of a locomotive moving through the countryside of the American South
is certainly a blues image. Captured in countless song titles and lyrics
and evoked in the onomatopoeic effects of country blues guitarists and
harmonica players, the image of the railroad also found its way into
gospel and jazz. It is an image that resonates through African American
folk culture.[14] For Big Boy and his buddies the sound of the train
whistle triggers a litany of railroad jargon: "'There goes number fo!'
'Hittin on all six!' 'Highballin it down the line!' 'Boun fer up Noth,
Lawd, bound fer up Noth!'" (19). They join together in a chant and set
up a rhythmic accompaniment by "pounding their bare heels in the
grass." Wright inserts the lyrics to the spiritual "Dis train bound fo
Glory." Once again the boys participate in a form of communal oral
folk expression. As the song concludes "they burst out laughing,
thinking of a train bound for Glory." One of the boys comments, "'Gee,
thas a good ol song!'" Yet, the topic of the spiritual is immediately
dropped as their conversation takes a scatological turn. They accuse Big
Boy, "'NIGGER, YUH BROKE WIN!'," and the dialogue includes such
commentary as "'Yuh rotten inside!'" and "'The hen whut cackles is the
hen whut laid the egg'"(20). The abrupt shift in their conversation
indicates that folk culture does not hold any greater significance than
scatological jokes to these young men. They are not aware of why the
sound of a northward-bound train evokes a song that is "bound fo
Glory" in the tradition of African American folk culture. There is no

symbolic resonance to their performance of the song; their singing, like the jokes, simply passes the time as they idle away the hot afternoon.

Wright's representation of four black boys in the Mississippi Delta spontaneously joining together in the performance of a spiritual takes on an ironic significance because at the conclusion of the story Big Boy, like "number fo," finds himself "bound fer up Noth." Big Boy's escape in a north-bound truck driven by a friend of his family is not a conscious quest for freedom. He has no aspirations of being "bound fo Glory;" he is merely making a blind, desperate flight from a lynch mob. His fragmented knowledge of black folk culture makes Big Boy oblivious to the spirit of hope for deliverance both beyond *and* in this world which traditionally informed the spirituals. Perhaps the ambivalence with which Wright treats folk culture reflects the uncertainty of what awaits this young man when he reaches Chicago. But what seems more likely is that folk expression is an insufficient means for his characters to achieve any positive outcome in the face of racism; this result can only be reached through what Wright considers the appropriate political consciousness and action.

This perspective on African American folk expression continues to be reflected in the way music appears in the other stories in *Uncle Tom's Children*. The second story, "Down By The Riverside," takes it title from a well-known spiritual. The black religious leader of a flood-ravaged Southern town leads a family in the song to bolster their spirits. Brother Mann, the head of the family, then attempts to get his pregnant wife to an emergency hospital in a rowboat which one of his relatives has stolen. During the upstream ordeal he encounters the white owner of the boat and winds up killing him in a shoot-out. By the time Mann reaches the hospital his wife has died. Mann is forced to help in the evacuation and cannot bring himself to kill the family of the white man when he is alone with them in a rescue effort. They identify him as a murderer when they reach high ground. Mann is shot in the back fleeing from a mob of white soldiers, and his body rolls down a slope and stops "about a foot from the water's edge" (102). He is "down by the riverside" and he "ain gonna study war no mo," but his struggle has been futile and devoid of any form of transcendence. Just as in "Big Boy Leaves Home," the performance of a spiritual in "Down By The Riverside" resonates ironically through Wright's story.

"Long Black Song," the third story in the collection, begins with Sarah, a young black mother, attempting to soothe her infant by singing a traditional lullaby:

> *Go t sleep, baby*
> *Papas gone t town*

> *Go t sleep, baby*
> *The suns goin down*
> *Go t sleep, baby*
> *Yo candys in the sack*
> *Go t sleep baby*
> *Papas comin back . . .*[15]

Appropriate to Wright's representation of music the song is ineffective: "But the baby squalled louder, its wail drowning out the song" (103). In addition, the lyrical content of the musical performance, following the pattern of the two previous stories, provides an ironic commentary on the outcome of the story. As Sarah awaits the return of her husband Silas from town, a white traveling salesman arrives at the door. He is selling graphophones, and he demonstrates the machine with a recording of religious music. (Wright gives no indication if the performer is black or white.) The music softens Sarah's suspicions and reserve in dealing with the white stranger:

> A lump filled her throat. She leaned her back against a post, trembling, feeling the rise and fall of days and nights, of summer and winter; surging, ebbing, leaping about her, beyond her far out over the fields to where earth and sky lay folded in darkness. She wanted to lie down and sleep, or else leap up and shout. When the music stopped she felt herself coming back, being let down slowly. (110)

In a way this black woman is betrayed by music that promises salvation because she surrenders herself to the feelings it evokes. The white man sexually assaults her, and although she resists at first she eventually gives in to him. He departs leaving the graphophone and promising to come back the next morning to arrange a payment plan with her husband. When Silas arrives he quickly realizes what has happened. He smashes the graphophone, drives Sarah from the house and eventually kills the salesman. A lynch mob comes after Silas, and he holds them off with his rifle until they burn him to death in his house. "*Papas comin back* " does not bring the promised reward of "*candys in the sack*," but rather a tragic violence that destroys this black family. The long black song is a familiar tune, one that has been sung over and over again in the American experience: the white man exploits the black man; the white man has his way with the black woman; the white man destroys the black man when he tries to resist. For Wright, the long black song will continue to play; the lullaby will fail to soothe; the gospel tune will always betray—until the proper political response is employed.

While the first three stories in *Uncle Tom's Children* seem to reflect Wright's negative social voice, in contrast, the final two stories present "the faint stirrings of new and emerging life." The titles to both "Fire and Cloud" and "Bright and Morning Star" are taken from lyrics to songs which appear in the stories. Wright's representation of music is once again illustrative of his close adherence to his blueprint. In these stories African American music plays a positive-if limited-role in the transcendence of oppression because it corresponds with a Marxist political perspective.

In "Fire and Cloud" Reverend Taylor, the leader of a Southern black community, is being pressured to take a stand on a protest march organized by Communists. Taylor's people are in dire straits as economic hardships have forced them to the brink of starvation. The Communists are attempting to mount an inter-racial demonstration to force local authorities to provide relief and want Taylor to support their efforts publicly. The white power figures in the town, with whom Taylor has always obsequiously compromised, demand that the religious leader deter his people from participating in the march. Taylor refuses to allow the Communists to use his name but voices his support of the action to them and his church elders. When he refuses to acquiesce to the demands of the mayor and police chief to speak publicly against the demonstration Taylor is abducted and brutally beaten. This convinces him to lead his people in the demonstration. When Taylor finishes a speech that rallies the black community, one of his followers spontaneously begins to sing:

> *So the sign of the fire by night*
> *N the sign of the cloud by day*
> *A-hoverin oer*
> *Jus befo*
> *As we journey on our way. . . .* (179)

They join with the white demonstrators whom the Communists have organized: "He looked ahead and saw black and white marching; he looked behind and saw black and white marching. And still they sang" (179). Taylor, who had been forced to grovel before the mayor for so many years, demands that the white leader come to him and agree to fulfill the demand for aid. The song, which arises directly from the black common folk and unites blacks and whites, is an epiphany for the course of Taylor's future actions: "He kept his eyes on the sea of black and white faces. The song swelled louder and vibrated through him.

This is the way! he thought" (179-80). "Fire and Cloud" closes with the politicized reverend joining in with the final line of the song: "*Freedom belongs t the strong!*'"

"Bright and Morning Star" focuses on Sue, an older black woman whose two sons are Communist organizers. She sacrifices her own life in order to kill a traitor who has tricked her into revealing the identities of her sons' white and black comrades before he can turn the names over to the white racist authorities. Wright's conception that black folk culture must be embraced and then transcended in order to assume a Marxist perspective that will produce collective action is embodied in the evolution of Sue's understanding of the spirituals and religious songs that were a part of her upbringing.

Music appears in the opening of the story as Sue is ironing clothes and worrying about her sons, Sug who is in jail for his political activities and Johnny-Boy who is out "rounding up white and black Communists for a meeting":

> She was deep in the midst of her work when a song rose
> up out of the far off days of her childhood and broke
> through half-parted lips:
> *Hes the Lily of the Valley, the Bright n*
> *Mawnin Star*
> *Hes the Fairest of Ten Thousand t ma soul . . .* (182)

As Sue sings "to ease the ache of anxiety that was swelling her heart," she feels guilty and stops suddenly because she "jus cant seem t fegrit them ol songs" (183-84). She reflects on how the significance of these songs has changed for her over the years:

> She had learned them when she was a little girl living
> and working on a farm. Every Monday morning from the
> corn and cotton fields the slow strains had floated from
> her mother's lips, lonely and haunting; and later, as the
> years had filled with gall, she learned their deep meaning.
> . . . She had poured the yearning of her life into the songs,
> feeling buoyed with a faith beyond the world.
> But as she had grown older, a cold white mountain, the
> white folks and their laws, had swum into her vision and
> shattered her songs and their spell of peace. (184)

Sue did not abandon her faith; she felt her trials and tribulations were necessary to strengthen the vision in which she believed. When her boys grow to manhood they reject the vision of Christian salvation embodied in the songs and indoctrinate her into their Communist perspective: "And day by day her sons had ripped from her startled eyes her old vision, and image by image had given her a new one, different, but great and strong enough to fling her into the light of another grace" (185).

When Sue realizes that she has revealed the names to the "stool" because fear had made her faith in the new vision waver, she decides that she must act independently to protect the comrades. The imagery from the song which she has learned through participation in black folk culture is transferred to direct political action:

> Mired she was between two abandoned worlds, living, but dying without the strength of the grace that either gave. The clearer she felt it the fuller did something well up from the depths of her for release; the more urgent did she feel the need to fling into her black sky another star, another hope, one more terrible vision to give her the strength to live and act. (206)

The star that had once represented Jesus, "when she had not hoped for anything on this earth," now becomes emblematic of her efforts to protect the identity of the comrades. Knowing that the white racists will not expect resistance from a old black woman she shows "em somethin they never thought a black woman could have!" Surrounded by white men who are torturing Johnny-Boy, Sue shoots the "stool" before he can reveal the names. As they shoot her she is aware not only of successfully keeping the identities of the comrades secret but of the self-empowerment her action represents: "She yearned suddenly to talk. 'Yuh didn't git whut yuh wanted! N yuh ain gonna nevah git it! Yuh didnt kill me; Ah come here by mahsef . . .'" (215). The *"Bright n Mawnin Star"* of her song is now representative of the hope Sue sees in the movement which will live on thanks to her sacrifice: "Focused and pointed she was, buried in the depths of her star, swallowed in its peace and strength; and not feeling her flesh growing cold, cold as the air that fell from the invisible sky upon the doomed living and the dead that never dies" (215). Once again there is an insistence on Wright's part that musical expression can only provide transcendence for the black character if it goes beyond a culturally specific nationalism and embraces a Communist political agenda.

While music plays a limited role in the plots of the stories in *Uncle Tom's Children*, an examination of this limited representation provides a clear understanding of Wright's thematic and ideological concerns. As his conception of the fictional depiction of black American life evolved,

Wright rejected the short story collection. In the essay "How 'Bigger' Was Born" (1941) which discusses the experiences, influences, ideas and process that produced his most celebrated fictional effort, *Native Son* (1941), Wright calls *Uncle Tom's Children* "an awfully naïve mistake": "I found that I had written a book which even bankers' daughters could read and weep over and feel good about. I swore to myself that if I ever wrote another book, no one would weep over it; that it would be so hard and deep that they would have to face it without the consolation of tears. It was this that made me get to work in dead earnest" (xxvii). *Native Son* focuses on Bigger Thomas, a young man living in Chicago's "Black Belt" during the early years of World War II, who is so circumscribed and maimed by American racism's denial of possibility that the one act that provides him with any sense of empowerment is the killing and decapitation of a young white woman. Inevitably, Bigger is hunted, captured and condemned to execution.

In *Native Son* the representation of music is even more limited than in *Uncle Tom's Children.* Yet, the manner in which music functions (or fails to function) in Bigger's life illustrates Wright's perception of the inadequacy of African American folk expression to provide a means of transcendence. As Wright explained in "How 'Bigger' Was Born": "I had also to show what oppression had done to Bigger's relationships with his own people, how it had split him off from them, how it had baffled him; how oppression seems to hinder and stifle in the victim those very qualities of character which are so essential for an effective struggle against the oppressor" (xxvi). This split is dramatically symbolized in the representation of African American music in *Native Son*, where it functions as a source of oppression rather than transcendence.

Music is a part of day-to-day life for the Thomas family, for Mrs. Thomas sings gospel tunes as she carries out her household chores. For Bigger, however, the music his mother makes falls upon deaf ears. In the opening scene of the novel she sings a song of encouragement as she prepares breakfast:

> *Life is like a mountain railroad*
> *With an engineer that's brave*
> *We must make the run successful*
> *From the cradle to the grave. . . .* (14)

But the music certainly misses the mark with Bigger: "The song irked him and he was glad when she stopped." Later in the day when he returns home he hears her singing "*Lord, I want to be a Christian.*" Ironically, he ignores her and slips out the door with his gun, intent on committing an armed robbery. After the killing of Mary Dalton, when Bigger is fleeing the manhunt in the Black Belt, he hides in a vacant apartment. Asleep on the floor, he is roused by a "rhythmic throbbing" and springs "to his feet, his heart pounding, his ears filled with the sound of singing and shouting." Bigger discovers he is next to a storefront church whose congregation is singing the spiritual "Steal Away." As in *Uncle Tom's Children*, the lyrics of a black folk song comment ironically on the situation of Wright's character. In this song which traditionally embodied the subversive, double entendre of the slaves' lyrics, not only is the idea of stealing away to Jesus an affirmation of religious devotion and an acknowledgment of some spiritual better day, but it also signified an act of defiance against the oppressor because it functioned as a call to escape, a declaration of self-empowerment, a clarion to steal one's self away from bondage. Yet, for Bigger there is no chance of escape. In fact, this young black man is not even aware that these lyrics have implications in this world. They simply represent the naive, otherworldly optimism of his mother that repulses Bigger:

> He made sure that his gun was still intact, hearing. *Steal away, Steal away home, I ain't got long to stay here.* . . . It was dangerous to stay here, but it was also dangerous to go out. The singing filled his ears; it was complete, self-contained, and it mocked his fear and loneliness, his deep yearning for a sense of wholeness. Its fullness contrasted so sharply with his hunger, its richness with his emptiness, that he recoiled from it while answering it. Would it not have been better for him had he lived in that world the music sang of? It would have been easy to have lived in it, for it was his mother's world, humble, contrite, believing. It had a center, a core, an axis, a heart which he needed but could never have unless he laid his head upon a pillow of humility and gave up his hope of living in the world. And he would never do that. (238)

In addition to his perception of music from the black folk tradition as mere escapism, Bigger regards association with the music as demeaning. He seems well aware that for the dominant white society music and blacks are equated with minstrel tomfoolery. During their night out with Bigger, Mary and Jan express a desire to "know" more Negroes and look forward to bringing blacks into the Communist Party because "They have so much emotion!" and "They've got spirit." Mary and Jan urge Bigger to sing along on the spiritual "Swing Low Sweet Chariot":

> 'And their songs—the spirituals! Aren't they marvelous?'
> Bigger saw her turn to him. "Say, Bigger, can you sing?'
>   'I can't sing,' he said.
>   'Aw, Bigger,' she said, pouting. She tilted her head, closed her eyes and opened her mouth.
>   'Swing low, sweet chariot,
>   Coming fer to carry me home. . . .'
>   Jan joined in and Bigger smiled derisively. Hell, that ain't the tune, he thought.
>   'Come on, Bigger, and help us sing it,' Jan said.
>   'I can't sing,' he said again. (77)

Jan's and Mary's patronizing attitude and view of Bigger as some faceless representative of "a people," rather than as an individual, along with their ineptitude in performing the spiritual, confirm Bigger's suspicions about their insincerity and fuel his disdain for these new white "friends." Bigger's *refusal* to sing, for his awareness that they have the tune wrong indicates he knows the music and does not lack the ability, is emblematic of his rejection of the preconceived roles the representatives of white society, whether they be blatant racists or naive, misguided liberals, have assigned to blacks. Mary's choice of a song is ironic because the chariot that is carrying her home, the car which Bigger has been hired to chauffeur, is taking her home to her death at the hands of one of these "emotion"-filled Negroes whom she is so enthusiastic to meet.

Swing music, like the spirituals, is also viewed as a source of escapism and debasement for Bigger. When he first leaves his family's tenement at the opening of *Native Son* he feels "an urgent need to hide his growing and deepening feeling of hysteria." The popular music of the day which derived from black folk expression is among the options he considers to escape his feelings: "He longed for a stimulus powerful enough to focus his attention and drain off his energies. He wanted to run. Or listen to some swing music. Or laugh or joke. Or read a *Real Detective Story Magazine* . Or go to movie. Or visit Bessie" (30-31). Bigger and his friend Jack eventually do go to a double feature movie. Outside the theater the poster for one of the films, *Trader Horn*, depicts "black men and black women dancing against a wild background of barbaric jungle," an obviously demeaning propagation of stereotypes of Africa as primitive and cultureless that focuses on musical rhythms and dance movements. The other feature, *The Gay Woman* , which Bigger and Jack view, contains a night club scene where white couples are dancing to a swing band. Bigger projects himself into the scene:

> 'I'd like to be invited to a place like that just to find out what it feels like,' Bigger mused.
> 'Man, if them folks saw you they'd run,' Jack said. 'They'd think a gorilla broke loose from the zoo and put on a tuxedo.'
> They bent over low in their seats and giggled without restraint. (33)

These two young black men fail to recognize that the roots of their cultural heritage are being debased in the poster, *and* that the music in the supposedly sophisticated scene from white society is a co-optation of that heritage. Their indoctrination into American racism has been so thorough that they can only perceive Bigger's projected presence at a performance of this music, which ironically is an extension of the African American musical tradition, in subhuman terms.

The limited representation of music in *Native Son* illustrates Wright's conviction that only the adoption of a Marxist political consciousness could allow for any effective or viable action by a black man in America.[16] The only alternative to this consciousness was to become a Bigger Thomas or one of the variations on this "pattern." Wright looked on the role of a musician as one of these variations. As he states in "How 'Bigger' Was Born": "Still others projected their hurts and longings into more naïve and mundane forms—blues, jazz, swing—and, without intellectual guidance, tried to build up a compensatory nourishment for themselves" (xiii). Considering this opinion of African American musicians, it is not surprising that Wright wrote of the guitarist/singer Leadbelly (Hudie Ledbetter) in the *Daily Worker* in 1937: "It seems that the entire folk culture of the American Negro has found its embodiment in him." Certainly, Leadbelly's appearance at left-wing political functions would appeal to Wright.[17] But Leadbelly's incorporation of material that reflected left-wing politics into his repertoire of blues and folk songs may not have been the only appealing aspect of this black musical artist for Wright. Prior to being brought to New York by the Lomaxes to participate in the creation of the "folk music" scene, Leadbelly had been convicted and incarcerated in both Texas and Louisiana for murder. The Lomaxes used Leadbelly's violent past as part of their promotional strategy, as evidenced by the *New York Herald-Tribune* headline, "Sweet Singer of the Swamplands Here to Do a Few Tunes Between Homicides."[18] Quite possibly, Wright saw in Leadbelly both an African American musical artist who embraced and transcended folk expression with a political consciousness and a real life embodiment of the Bigger Thomas pattern. But for the Bigger Thomas Wright created in *Native Son*, music from the African American folk tradition is merely a reminder of the inferior status which the dominant culture has assigned him. The music's inability to provide transcendence or cultural connections in Wright's fictional representation of black American life is an absence that speaks louder than words.

In addition to voicing his Communist political orientation, *Native Son* reflects Wright's predilection for such "Naturalist" writers as Theodore Dreiser. In "How 'Bigger' Was Born" he states that from these writers he learned "ways and techniques of gauging meaningfully the effects of American civilization upon the personalities of people," which he adapted to create "*my* ways of apprehending the locked-in life of the Black Belt areas" (xvi).[19] The deterministic forces of American racism that circumscribe Bigger's existence render black folk forms such as music ineffectual as a means of either subversion or transcendence in Wright's fictional depiction of the Black Belt.

In the novel *The Street* (1946), Ann Petry employs many of the naturalistic elements found in *Native Son*, including a strikingly similar representation of the role of music in black culture.[20] The main character in *The Street*, Lutie Johnson, is a single mother living in Harlem during World War II. She struggles to support herself and her eight-year-old son, Bub, with a low paying civil service job. Her salary barely covers their room and board, and Lutie is constantly menaced by the threat of the "street." Like Bigger, she is trapped by economic and racial limitations and is even further marginalized because she is a single women trying to make it on her own. And ultimately, like Bigger, when Lutie is backed into a corner by these forces that seem to determine her life, she lashes out in a violent fury. Lutie differs from Bigger, however, in that she believes that she can work hard and transcend the grim realties of inner city black life. When she had worked as a live-in maid for a rich, white family in Connecticut, Lutie observed how making money was a way of life for some people and "she absorbed some of the same spirit. The belief that anybody could be rich if he wanted to and worked hard enough and figured it out carefully enough" (43). Lutie's faith in the "American Dream" is clearly articulated when she stops in a Harlem grocery store and picks up some bread as she returns from work. Walking down the street with the bread in her arms she identifies with the ultimate hard-working American icon success story, Benjamin Franklin:

> She shifted the packages into a more comfortable position
> and feeling the hard roundness of the rolls through the
> paper bag, she thought immediately of Ben Franklin and
> his loaf of bread. And grinned thinking, You and Ben
> Franklin. You ought to take one out and start eating it as
> you walk along 116th Street. Only you ought to remember
> while you eat that you're in Harlem and he was in
> Philadelphia a pretty long number of years ago. Yet she
> couldn't get rid of the feeling of self-confidence and she
> went on thinking that if Ben Franklin could live on a little
> bit of money and could prosper, then so could she. (63-
> 64)

Yet despite her efforts to get ahead, Lutie is hemmed in by the
forces of economic, racial and sexual exploitation that are facts of black
American life during World War II. The small tenement apartment that
she rents for herself and Bub in Harlem is as stifling and oppressive as
the rat-infested rooms that the Thomas family occupies in *Native Son*.
One evening, although she realizes it will ruin her carefully balanced
budget, she gives Bub money for the movies and she dresses up to go to
a local bar for a glass of beer. Her visit to the Junto Bar and Grill,
"where the light streaming from the windows and the music from its
jukebox created an oasis of warmth" (141), is an attempt to relieve the
drudgery of her day-to-day existence. Like Bigger's desire to go to the
movies or listen to swing music, Lutie looks to the bar as an escape,
and music is a key element in providing her with a means to leave the
menace of the street behind her: "The beer was incidental and
unimportant. It was the other things that the Junto offered that she
sought: the sound of laughter, the hum of talk, the sight of people and
the brilliant lights, the sparkle of the big mirror, the rhythmic music
from the juke-box" (145). As she loses herself in the bar scene, Lutie
begins to sing along with the juke-box and continues to sing after the
record ends:

> The men and women crowded at the bar stopped drinking
> to look at her. Her voice had a thin thread of sadness
> running through it that made the song important, that
> made it tell a story that wasn't in the words-a story of
> despair, of loneliness, of frustration. It was a story that all
> of them knew by heart and had always known because
> they had learned it soon after they were born and would
> go on adding to it until the day they died. (148)

Petry describes the music that Lutie makes in terms of a non-literal meaning in sound, a concept that can be traced back to Douglass's description of the spirituals in the mid-nineteenth century. But the story in Lutie's song is not one of hope or transcendence or resistance but one of despair. She speaks for her people but her song is not a affirmation of a cultural heritage; it is a recitation of a stifling, deterministic legacy.

Yet, Lutie's spontaneous expression of bitter sadness ironically leads to a potentially positive opportunity. She is overheard by a pianist/band leader, Boots Smith, who offers to let her audition for his big band which works regularly at a nearby dance hall, the Casino. She quickly seizes on the possibility of a singing job as a way out of life on the street: "But if she could sing-work hard at it, study, really get somewhere, it would give direction to her life-she would know where she was going" (160). Lutie, who has no professional experience and has developed her skill by singing along with the radio, is not concerned with artistic creativity or communal expression or spiritual transcendence. Like practical, hard-working Ben Franklin, she sees the position of vocalist with Smith's band as purely and simply a job.

At the audition Lutie immerses herself in the performance and the music carries her away from her circumscribed life. While it may be on a material level, it would seem that the music does have some transcendent power for this struggling black woman: "Though she sang the words of the song, it was of something entirely different that she was thinking and putting into the music: she was leaving the street with its dark hallways, its mean, shabby rooms . . . She and Bub were getting out and away, and they would never be back" (222). Even though the band members have been skeptical of Lutie, they acknowledge her performance with deep bows: "She was filled with triumph at the sight, for she knew that this absurd, preposterous bowing was their way of telling her they were accepting her on merit as a singer, not because she was Boots' newest girl friend" (222). The band members may take the creative aspect of music-making seriously, but Lutie quickly realizes that for the black patrons of the Casino, as it is for herself, music is merely an escape: "It doesn't make much difference who sings or whether they sing badly or well, because nobody really listens. They're making love or quarreling or drinking or dancing" (224). Nevertheless, Lutie leaves the Casino after that first night uplifted with the thought that singing will enable her to earn the extra money she needs to start a new life for Bub and herself.

Lutie's dream of getting away from the street through her musical abilities is quickly shattered when she learns that Boots has no intention of paying her. The pianist never had the power to hire and pay her; he is controlled by the white man, Junto, who owns both the Casino and the neighborhood bar where Lutie's singing first catches Boot's attention. Junto is attracted to Lutie and he wants to keep her from becoming financially independent so that he can control her and use her for sexual gratification. Although Boots himself is attracted to Lutie, he refuses to cross Junto: "There weren't many places a colored band could play and Junto could fix it so he couldn't find a spot from here to the coast. He had other bands sewed up, and all he had to do was refuse to send an outfit to places stupid enough to hire Boots's band. Junto could put a squeeze on a place so easy it wasn't funny" (264).

In *The Street* the jazz artist is no communal spokesperson or ritual leader; Boots Smith is a white man's puppet looking out for his own financial well-being. At one time music-making had been important to Smith but with the hard times of the Depression he scuffled to earn a living playing the piano, often either in dives that jeopardized him with the threat of violence or trouble with the law or in clubs where he resented the demeaning treatment he received from white customers. He took a job as a Pullman porter and swore never to touch the piano again. Nonetheless, one night when he stopped in Junto's bar he forgot his vow and began playing an old piano. Junto heard him and offered him a job at the Casino but it seems that music-making has become simply an alternative to waiting on white people in a Pullman car:

> It had been okay from the night he had started playing the piano. He had built the orchestra slowly, and Junto had been pleased and revealed his pleasure by paying him a salary that had now grown to the point where he could afford to buy anything in the world he wanted. No. Lutie Johnson wasn't that important to him. He wasn't in love with her, and even if he had been she didn't weigh enough to balance the things he would lose. (273-74)

After walking out on Boots, Lutie makes another attempt at becoming a singer. She answers an advertisement from a talent agency and the white man who auditions her recognizes her ability. Yet, she is once again subjected to sexual harassment when the booking agent proposes, "If you and me can get together a coupla nights a week in Harlem, those lessons won't cost you a cent" (321). As she storms out in anger Lutie thinks of white masters raiding slave quarters "for a likely wench any hour of the day or night" (322). As she rides back uptown on the subway she thinks of all the instances of sexual, racial and economic exploitation that have imprisoned her and wishes the train "would go faster, make more noise, rock more wildly, because the tumultuous anger in her could only be quelled by violence" (322). Her thoughts on the train ride foreshadow the violent act that closes the novel. She gives up the pursuit of a singing career and resigns herself to the tedium her civil service job when a financial crisis forces her to call Boots Smith. The musician promises to help her but when they meet he says she must have sex with Junto for the money. Lutie explodes in a blind rage and crushes the pianist's skull with an iron candlestick. As she flees to Chicago she contemplates the course her life has taken: "Lutie tried to figure out by what twists and turns of fate she had landed on this train. Her mind balked at the task. All she could think was, It was that street. It was that god-damned street" (436). For Lutie Johnson, music derived from the African American folk tradition is impotent as a means of transcendence over that deterministic symbol of urban black life-he street. Her attempt to use her music-making skills to find some financial relief eventually seals her fate. Boots's selling of his soul to a white man and his betrayal of Lutie is emblematic of the failure of black music as an effective tool in the resistance and subversion of racial, economic and sexual oppression and exploitation. In the naturalistic realm Petry creates in *The Street* Lutie Johnson's murder of her would-be musical mentor is a ritual enactment of this failure.

The World War II time frame for *The Street* was at the heart of the career of the preeminent female jazz vocalist of all time-Billie Holiday.[21] Throughout her life Holiday faced many of the same trials and tribulations that dogged Lutie Johnson. She was the victim of sexual abuse by a series of lovers and husbands. She was humiliated by American racism. When she toured as the only black member of clarinetist Artie Shaw's big band Holiday often had to stay backstage or sit in the kitchen while the rest of the musicians socialized in the club; Shaw also had a white female singer on tour to perform Holiday's material in clubs that would not allow a black woman on stage with whites. She earned a decent living but never saw the kind of financial remuneration that white imitators of her innovative style received. Additionally, she succumbed to a major occupational hazard of the jazz life—substance abuse—that ruined her health and gave legal authorities an excuse to harass her continuously .

Yet despite all these burdens weighing her down, Holiday placed the impulse to create music—jazz and blues—first and foremost in her life. She was keenly aware of the African American musical tradition, both in terms of her place in the lineage and the shared tropes of the idiom. As she explains in her autobiography *Lady Sings the Blues* (1956): "Unless it was the records of Bessie Smith and Louis Armstrong I heard as a kid, I don't know of anybody who actually

influenced my singing, then or now. I always wanted Bessie's big sound
and Pops' feeling" (39). Holiday also placed a premium on
individuality, originality and spontaneity: "No two people on earth are
alike, and it's got to be that way in music or it isn't music . . . I can't
stand to sing the same song the same way two nights in succession, let
alone two years or ten years. If you can then it ain't music, it's close-
order drill or exercise or yodeling or something, not music" (48).[22]

Without formal musical training Holiday created a relaxed yet
swinging style that won the respect of the leading jazz artists of her
lifetime; she was considered a member of the band rather than a singer
being backed up by accompanists. She channeled the pain and
frustration as well as the joy and free spiritedness of her personal life
into the songs she sang and touched the souls of her listeners. A man
may have hurt her deeply, both emotionally and physically, but when
she sang "My Man" or "Billie's Blues" or "Don't Explain," she
transformed the experience into an artistic triumph. Holiday did not
submit to American racism and in 1939 she boldly made one of the first
social protest recordings with "Strange Fruit." During a 1956 television
interview when reporter Mike Wallace asked her why so many jazz
artists died at an early age (Holiday passed away three years later at age
forty-four), she replied: "We try to live one hundred days in one day.
And we try to please so many people and we try to—Like myself. I
want to bend this note and bend that note, and sing this way and sing
that way and get all the feeling and eat all the good foods and travel all
over in one day and you can't do it."[23]

There is a striking contrast between the role that music played in
Billie Holiday's life and Petry's representation of music in Lutie
Johnson's life in *The Street*. Unlike Lutie, Holiday did not despair and
surrender to fate but clung to her music as an affirmation of her lust for
life. For Holiday, engagement in the African American music-making
process was a source of fulfillment; creative expression was her
motivation. Hardship dogged her throughout her career, but both she
and the musicians knew that the triumph of her artistry was genuine.
For Lutie, there is no creative engagement; she is solely interested in
the paycheck she can acquire through her singing. And in a white-
controlled music industry Lutie is looked on as little more than a sexual
plaything. Petry's representation of the distinctly limited role African
American music played in Lutie Johnson's life seems to be a conscious
strategy appropriately evoking the naturalistic perspective of *The Street*.

While the approach Billie Holiday took to music-making may not
have informed Petry's representation of a black female singer in *The
Street*, Petry's own approach to the creative process reflects Holiday's
refusal "to sing the same song the same way two nights in succession."

Petry also rejects repetition in her explorations of fiction: "I always want to do something different from what I have done before; I don't want to repeat myself. If I belong to a certain tradition, I don't want to belong, because my writing would be very boring if I always wrote in a particular style" (160).

The short story "Solo on the Drums" (1947) testifies to Petry's predilection for varying her stylistic approach. In a dramatically different representation of music than found in *The Street*, the story centers on a single performance by Kid Jones, the star drummer of a big band. Unlike Lutie Johnson and Boots Smith, this black jazz man uses music-making as an outlet for personal catharsis and a voice for communal expression. Through the solo, the best he has ever played, Kid Jones is able to channel creatively the rage and pain he experiences after having been abandoned by his wife for another band member.

The representation of music in "Solo on the Drums" goes beyond simply providing Petry with subject matter for a thematic exploration of the black experience in America. The story breaks new fictional ground because music actually informs Petry's compositional approach and structure.[24] Petry's language emulates a jazz drum solo through the staccato repetition of words and phrases, for example: "He wanted to cover his ears with his hands because he kept hearing a voice that whispered the same thing over and over again. The voice was trapped somewhere under the roof—caught and held there by the trumpet. 'I'm leaving I'm leaving I'm leaving'" (237). The repetition, particularly the recollection of the "voice" and the words it delivers, does not only appear within the passage but shows up in variations throughout the story. Petry also approximates instrumental jazz technique by fleshing out the information concerning Kid's situation through this use of repeated variations. Like a jazz artist improvising on a basic theme, new ideas enter the narrative, drawing the listener into the creative process.[25] By the conclusion of the story the quotation that the recalled voice delivers is expanded to: "'I'm leaving it's the guy who plays the piano I'm in love with the Marquis of Brund he plays such sweet piano I'm leaving leaving leaving—'" (241-42).

The story that is revealed through this jazz-like structure is an archetypal blues situation that is exemplified by guitarist/singer "Hound Dog" Taylor's "Wild About You, Baby":

> Well, I'm leaving this morning and I really don't want to go,
> Yes, I'm leaving this morning and I really don't want to go,
> Well, you got somebody and you don't want me no more.
> Ain't that a pity, oh ain't that a cryin' shame,

Ain't that a pity, oh ain't that a cryin' shame.
Well now, the woman I love, She in love with another man.[26]

Like the blues singer's "I" that is heard by the black audience as "we,"
"Solo on the Drums" is an individual's story that speaks for the
community.[27] The opening of the story focuses on the marquee of a
theater in Times Square on which Kid Jones's name is featured beneath
the name of the jazz orchestra. Kid is singled out as a communal
leader: "The people who pushed their way through the crowded street
looked up at it and recognized it and smiled" (235). He has excelled
and achieved recognition in one of the few fields of endeavor open to
an African American. Yet, on the day of the performance this star
musician is concentrating upon himself, trying to understand why his
wife has abandoned him. He glances in the dressing room mirror
looking for some change: "He frowned. Because he felt that the things
that were eating him up inside ought to show. But they didn't" (236).
Once Kid is on stage, however, his interior examination is carried out in
public in a communal context. He may be the featured soloist but he
remains a member of a group. As the band begins to play, "he made a
mental note of the fact that the boys were working together as smoothly
as though each one had been oiled" (236). Kid looks on the band
members, including himself, as parts of a machine. He is not the only
player capable of expressing shared emotions, and as one of the
trumpeters takes the first solo Kid hears a reiteration of the morning
encounter with his wife: "And now—well, he felt as though he were
floating up and up and up on that long blue note of the trumpet. He half
closed his eyes and rode up on it. It was that whispering voice, making
him shiver. Hating it and not being able to do anything about it. 'I'm
leaving it's the guy who plays the piano I'm in love with him and I'm
leaving now today'" (237).

When it is time for his solo the spotlight falls on Kid Jones, and he
engages the piano player in a musical duel. At first the piano is "a little
more insistent than the drums," but as the performance progresses "the
drums slowly dominated the piano" (238). The music becomes a battle
between the two love rivals: "When he hit the drums again it was with
the thought that he was fighting with the piano player. He was choking
the Marquis of Brund. He was putting a knife in clean between his ribs.
He was slitting his throat with a straight blade. Take my woman. Take
your life" (168). The musical exchange between the drummer and the
pianist lends a visceral resonance to the concept of a jazz competition
as a "cutting contest." Yet, even as Kid symbolically vents his personal
rage on the pianist, a communal significance arises from the solo:

> The drums took him away from them, took him back, and
> back, and back, in time and space. He built up an illusion.
> He was sending out the news. Grandma died. The
> foreigner in the litter has an old disease and will not
> recover. The man from across the bigwater is sleeping
> with the chief's daughter. Kill. Kill. Kill. The war goes
> well with the men with the bad smell and the loud laugh.
> It goes badly with the chiefs with the round heads and the
> peacock's walk. (239)

The music becomes a conduit that joins a black American jazz artist to
his African roots, to the talking drums of his ancestors. Aside from
establishing the existence of a cultural tradition, the scenario that the
solo brings to Kid's mind evokes the slave trade and the betrayal of
Africans by other Africans, which corresponds to the betrayal of the
drummer by his fellow band member. The disruption of the lives of the
black people who experienced the "Middle Passage" is a legacy that has
passed down through the generations of African Americans. Kid Jones's
thoughts return to his wife's words and the Marquis of Brund and then
shift to the preceding generation and his father's abandonment of his
mother. Finally, he zeroes in on the drums: "He forgot the theater,
forgot everything but the drums. He was welded to the drums, sucked
inside them. All of him. His pulse beat. His heart beat. He had become
part of the drums. They had become part of him," and his emotions are
translated into and communicated in a non-literal story in pure sound:

> Again and again he filled the theater with a sound of
> thunder. The sound seemed to come not from the drums
> but from deep inside himself; it was a sound that was
> being wrenched out of him—a violent, raging, roaring
> sound. As it issued from him he thought, this is the story
> of my love, this is the story of my hate, this is all there is
> left of me. And the sound echoed and re-echoed far up
> under the roof of the theater. (239-40)

Kid comes to an important recognition when he concludes : "He was
still himself. Kid Jones. Master of the Drums. Greatest drummer in the
world." He also knows that this solo has been his crowning
achievement. He has been able to channel the negativity of his wife's
abandonment into a creative triumph. Yet, he also understands that he
has commodified his artistry, that he is "selling himself a little at a
time," and with this performance he has "sold all of himself—not just a
piece" (241). He is a consummate artist and he has invested his soul in

his performance, yet he is also aware that often in America jazz is regarded merely as entertainment. As Kid bows repeatedly he feels "like one of those things you pull the string and it jerks, goes through the motion of dancing. Pull it gain and it kicks," and his thoughts return to his wife's words. With the puppet imagery Petry seems to be questioning whether the musician has achieved a genuine transcendence over his personal anguish with the solo. Nonetheless, at the close of the story he looks across the stage in defiance at the pianist, "Then he stood up and bowed again. And again" (241-42). While the painful situation still exists in his life, "Solo on the Drums" closes with Kid acknowledging the audience's appreciation of his artistic triumph. The final "again" implies that he will also play again, and it will not be a futile, puppet-like repetition because his ritual killing of the pianist has enabled the drummer to avoid an act of physical violence that for a black man in America is ultimately self-destructive.[28]

While the failure of black folk-derived forms such as music to provide transcendence over racism and economic exploitation in *Uncle Tom's Children* and *Native Son* illustrates Wright's adherence to a clearly defined political agenda, the contrasting representation of music in *The Street* and "Solo on the Drums" indicates that Petry is not only conscious of different perspectives towards this creative form within African American culture but is also aware of its potential as a model in the construction of a literary vision of black life in America. In the naturalistic realm of *The Street* it is appropriate that transcendence through music fails; in "Solo on the Drums," with its effective use of jazz/blues paradigms, it is appropriate that transcendence through music is achieved. Political and social criticism or "protest" are present in Petry's fiction but they are not the primary objectives.

The issue of art versus protest is central to the early work of James Baldwin and is clearly articulated in the essay "Many Thousands Gone" (1951).[29] Baldwin specifically takes Wright's fictional vision of African American life to task because of a "failure to convey any sense of Negro life as a continuing and complex group reality" (39). In essence Baldwin is asserting that Wright has set Bigger adrift in a Black Belt where there is no sense of community or heritage and that this is an inaccurate representation constructed solely to hammer home a political point. The essay opens with the assertion that: "It is only in his music, which Americans are able to admire because a protective sentimentality limits their understanding of it, that the Negro in America has been able to tell his story. It is a story which otherwise has yet to be told and which no American is prepared to hear" (24). Once again an African American writer describes the music in terms of telling a collective story. There is a cultural history imbedded in the sounds, rhythms and lyrical and technical tropes developed by black music-makers. Mainstream America has been able to accept the story in music because as a medium it taps into the emotions more directly (and often seductively) than writing. Baldwin states that America has conceived of blacks purely in the "social arena" and not as "personal or human, " and this "dehumanization" is evidenced in the "protest" approach to the fictional representation of black life in America. He states that novels such as *Native Son* have "led us all to believe that in Negro life there exists no tradition, no field of manners, no possibility of ritual or intercourse, such as may, for example, sustain the Jew even after he has left his father's house" (35-36). It would seem that in challenging the preeminent African American novelist of the day, Baldwin, the young black writer, is setting the goal of representing the humanity of his race by creating fiction with a sense of "continuing and complex group reality."

In his essay "The Discovery of What It Means to Be an American" (1959), Baldwin discusses his early expatriate experiences in Europe. He credits African American music as a key to his discovery of a sense of racial identity. Moving from Paris to a small Swiss village, Baldwin describes accepting his role "in the extraordinary drama which is America":

> There, in that absolutely alabaster landscape, armed with two Bessie Smith records and a typewriter, I began to try to re-create the life that I had first known as a child and from which I had spent so many years in flight.
> It was Bessie Smith, through her tone and her cadence, who helped me to dig back to the way I myself must have spoken when I was a pickaninny, and to remember the things I had heard and seen and felt. I had buried them very deep. I had never listened to Bessie Smith in America (in the same way that, for years, I would not touch watermelon), but in Europe she helped to reconcile me to being a 'nigger.' (5)

The possessions that Baldwin brings, a typewriter and two blues records, as he plunges into a world of sheer whiteness with the hopes of defining what it means to be an American—a black American—are emblematic of the influence of music, a form from the oral folk tradition, in the attempt to forge an African American literary tradition.

Music appears in much of the fiction that Baldwin produced, but it is in the short story "Sonny's Blues" (1948) that Baldwin most effectively explores the role of music in African American culture.[30]

The story's narrator, a Harlem math teacher, comes to a reconciliation with his brother Sonny, a jazz pianist and recovering heroin addict, after attending a performance at a Greenwich Village jazz club. And it is through witnessing his brother play the blues that the narrator gains insight into the collective nature of African American life.

For Sonny, music means everything. As the narrator senses when he describes his brother's incessant practicing as a teenager: "Sonny was at that piano playing for his life" (125). While the narrator has attempted to ignore his own position as a black man in America, Sonny is aware of how severely his possibilities are limited. The menace of American racism is so overwhelming that Sonny succumbs to the quick fix of drugs in order to insulate himself enough to play. He tries to explain to the narrator: "'It's not so much to *play*. It's to *stand* it, to be able to make it at all. On any level . . . In order to keep from shaking to pieces'" (131). Ultimately, jazz, a distinctly African American form that allows for a premium of personal expression, is the avenue Sonny hopes to follow in overcoming the limitations that are imposed upon him. As he reveals the background of his relationship with his brother, the narrator recalls a conversation during World War II when Sonny first expressed his ambition to be a jazz musician. The exchange illustrates the narrator's disaffection with African American culture. When the teenage Sonny says he is going to be a musician his brother assumes his intention is to be a "concert pianist" and "play classical music," and his immediate concern is not with the creative process but with the question of being able to earn a living. Sonny's reply indicates he would like to avoid categorization, but he clearly spells out his ambition: "'I mean I'll have a lot of studying to do, and I'll have to study *everything*, but I mean, I want to play *with* —jazz musicians . . . I want to play jazz'" (Baldwin's italics). By stating that he wants to play "*with*" jazz musicians Sonny seems to be communicating his need to be engaged in a communal process. The narrator, who had always thought of jazz musicians as "good time people," discloses how far removed he is from understanding Sonny's desire to play jazz: "Well, the word had never sounded as heavy, as real, as it sounded that afternoon in Sonny's mouth" (120). He asks Sonny if he means music like Louis Armstrong plays but the younger man rejects the suggestion as "old-time, down home crap." Finally, the narrator asks Sonny to explain his interest in jazz:

> 'Well. look, Sonny, I'm sorry, don't get mad. I just don't altogether get it, that's all. Name somebody-you know, a jazz musician you admire.'
> 'Bird.'

'Who?'

'Bird! Charlie Parker! Don't they teach you nothing in the goddamn army?'

I lit a cigarette. I was surprised and then a little amused to discover that I was trembling. 'I've been out of touch,' I said. 'You'll have to be patient with me. Now. Who's this Parker character?'

'He's just one of the greatest musicians alive,' said Sonny, sullenly, his hands in is pockets, his back to me. 'Maybe *the* greatest,' he added, bitterly, 'that's probably why *you* never heard of him.' (Baldwin's italics) (120-1)

Despite Sonny's obvious enthusiasm for the creative aspect of the music-making process, the older brother cannot help but ask, "'Doesn't all this take time? Can you make a living at it?'" The aspiring jazz artist answers that it does take time and he can earn a living, adding in exasperation: "'But what I don't seem to be able to make you understand is that it's the only thing I *want* to do.'" Rejecting the narrator's notion that "'people can't always do exactly what they want to do,'" Sonny argues, "'I think people *ought* to do what they want to do, what else are they alive for?'" (121-2). In a world where he is circumscribed by racial oppression and economic exploitation jazz represents possibility to this young black man, the possibility of expressing himself on his own terms.

Sonny's citation of alto saxophonist Charlie Parker, nicknamed "Yardbird" or "Bird," as his musical role model indicates that the young pianist wants to pursue a style of jazz which came to be called "bebop." Parker, along with trumpeter Dizzy Gillespie, guitarist Charlie Christian, pianists Thelonious Monk and Bud Powell and drummers Kenny Clarke and Max Roach, pioneered this revolutionary approach to jazz improvisation at jam sessions that took place in after-hours Harlem clubs during the early 1940s. Technically, bebop is marked by sophisticated harmonic variations on basic chord changes, a rhythmic sense that tends to lag behind the beat, odd variations in song pattern construction and the use of unusual intervals (abrupt shifts from high to low notes) in melodies.[31] The sounds of bebop often reflected the chaos of a modern world in the midst of an awesomely destructive war. To the young lions of bop the sounds this approach produced made perfect sense; to most others, bop sounded like it came from outer space when compared with the solos of the swing era stylists. This tendency to sound a bit "off" or slightly "out there" was intentional on the part of these young players. They wanted to make the music exclusionary, something in which only a select inner circle could participate. The odd chord changes and breakneck tempos functioned as insider codes, preventing players that were not "hip" from getting on the bandstand. The bebopers rejected the role of entertainers that the big band swing players filled. They were also disgruntled that swinging jazz had been co-opted by white players and watered down to "swing," literally whitewashing all reference to its roots in a black musical tradition. These modern jazz men did not want to provide background music for dancers; they wanted to be *listened to* and accepted as musical *artists*. And bebop epitomized the concept of possibility; musicians like Parker and his colleagues could improvise on a simple riff ad infinitum.

Bebop was not simply an approach to music-making; it was an approach to life. Bop artists had their own style of dress, a way of carrying themselves, a manner of talking, an attitude that thumbed its nose at conventional, mainstream American life. As the narrator of "Sonny's Blues" begins to understand more about his brother he notices this attitude in the pianist's walk: "He has a slow, loping walk, something like the way Harlem hipsters walk, only he's imposed on this his own halfbeat" (130). Sonny's rejection of both Armstrong's style of jazz and his brother's emphasis on earning a living is accurate in light of his identification with the bebop lifestyle.

The narrator tries to ignore the realities of black inner-city life and the toll they take on his people, especially his brother. He blocks out Sonny's existence and tries to lead a "normal" American life with his high school teaching job and his nuclear family until he experiences a personal tragedy. With the death of his young daughter the narrator reaches out and attempts to understand Sonny's pain: "My trouble made his real" (127). Sonny comes to stay with his brother's family after being released from a drug rehabilitation center, and the narrator begins to examine their relationship. The narrator takes a major step toward understanding Sonny and his impulse to play jazz when they engage in a conversation after witnessing a street-corner gospel music performance. Fittingly, Sonny is out on the street absorbing the gospel sounds, while the narrator is up in his apartment, taking in the performance through the window. The revival scene is a familiar one to the narrator, and he describes the details in a jaded tone, skeptical that anyone will find any kind of redemption in the song. Yet, he continues to follow the performance closely and is able to see something that had previously escaped him: "As the singing filled the air the watching, listening faces underwent a change, the eyes focusing on something within; the music seemed to soothe a poison out of them; and time seemed, nearly, to fall away from the sullen, belligerent, battered faces, as though they were fleeing back to their first condition, while dreaming of their last" (129). He recognizes the music's ability to bring

some, if transitory, transcendence to the lives of these beleaguered
street people. As he continues to survey the scene he sees Sonny on the
edge of the crowd, and it is at this point that he notices Sonny's hipster
walk, commenting "I had never really noticed it before." Like the street
singers, Sonny is seen in a new light by the narrator.

The gospel group continues to sing as Sonny enters the apartment
and there is an attempt to reach out by both brothers. The narrator
offers Sonny a beer and they both comment on the performance going
on in the street below. Almost immediately Sonny invites his brother to
come hear him play that night in a Greenwich Village jazz club, and the
narrator senses that he "couldn't possibly say No." Sonny tries to
explain his involvement with heroin, and although the narrator feels
almost impelled to voice his objections, he once again follows his
senses: "And something told me that I should curb my tongue, that
Sonny was doing his best to talk, that I should listen" (131). When the
pianist discusses the inevitability of human suffering and his
paradoxical refusal to accept it the narrator understands how deeply he
has failed his brother: "I realized. . . there stood between us, forever,
beyond the power of time of forgiveness, the fact that I had held
silence—so long!—when he had needed human speech to help him"
(132). Afraid that it will sound like "empty words and lies," the
narrator can only make a promise to himself never to fail Sonny again.

Sonny proves that he can overcome the boundary of that silence
through his ability to express himself in the non-verbal language of
jazz. What the brother perceives as impossible finds possibility in
Sonny's improvisations on the blues. In the jazz club Sonny is no longer
simply the narrator's problem-plagued brother. His music-making
abilities mark him with distinction; he is a communal leader:

> And it turned out that everyone at the bar knew Sonny, or
> almost everyone; some were musicians, working there, or
> nearby, or not working, some were simply hangers-on,
> and some were there to hear Sonny play. I was introduced
> to all of them and they were all very polite to me. Yet, it
> was clear that, for them, I was only Sonny's brother. Here,
> I was in Sonny's world. Or, rather: his kingdom. Here, it
> was not even a question that his veins bore royal blood.
> (136)

The jazz club is an alternative community, a safe haven where all those
who come join in a surrogate kinship, and Sonny's ability to play jazz
marks him as an honored celebrant in the forthcoming ritual drama. The
leader of the band is an older black bass player named Creole, who

functions as a father-figure for both Sonny and his brother. After escorting the narrator to a table, "Then-being funny and being, also, extremely ceremonious-Creole took Sonny by the arm and led him to the piano" (137). Sonny, who has not played the piano for over a year, is also "funny" and "ceremonious" as he "put both hands to his heart and bowed from the waist" (137). The ritual nature of the performance is emphasized by the "ceremonious" gestures of the musicians, and the fact that they are also "funny" is a reflection of the dualistic nature of the blues sensibility. Just before the performance begins the narrator inserts a commentary on the music-making process:

> All I know about music is that not many people really ever hear it. And even then, on the rare occasions when something opens within, and the music enters, what we mainly hear, or hear corroborated, are personal, private, vanishing evocations. But the man who creates the music is hearing something else, is dealing with the roar rising from the void and imposing order on it as it hits the air. What is evoked in him, then, is of another order, more terrible because it has no words, and triumphant, too, for that same reason. And his triumph, when he triumphs, is ours. (137)

The narrator shows that he is conscious of the duality of the blues and the representative role the musician plays in black culture. It seems that this introduction to the jazz session is made with hindsight because prior to accompanying Sonny to the club the narrator had exhibited almost no knowledge of music and the creative process. Although earlier in the day when he was observing the street corner gospel performance he had recognized the potential for music to act as an anodyne, the narrator could only have come to understand the deeper significance of these sounds—made by artists whom he had once thought of as "good-time people"—through watching and listening to Sonny interact with his fellow jazz musicians.[32] As he describes the music the narrator reveals that it is through this performance that he acquires the understanding of his brother and the music that is presented in the narrative: "I never before thought of how awful the relationship must be between the musician and his instrument. He has to fill it, this instrument, with the breath of life, his own" (138).

Sonny's need for human communication finds its fulfillment in the jazz performance; he is "having a dialogue" in music with Creole. The musical exchanges are described in terms of human speech: "the piano stammered"; "Creole answered"; "the drums talked back"; "the horn

insisted." Sonny's playing is tenuous in the first set but with the second
set, "they all came together again, and Sonny was part of the family
again." Sonny finds his place within the community once more and can
now express his individual story. But before he does this Creole asserts
himself one more time, ensuring that musicians and audience alike are
aware of the musical context: the sounds being created are rooted in the
African American experience:

> Then Creole stepped forward to remind them that what
> they were playing was the blues. He hit something in all
> of them, he hit something in me, myself, and the music
> tightened and deepened, apprehension began to beat the
> air. Creole began to tell us what the blues were all about.
> They were not about anything very new. He and his boys
> were up there keeping it new, at the risk of ruin,
> destruction, madness, and death, in order to find new
> ways to make us listen. For, while the tale of how we
> suffer, and how we are delighted, and how we may
> triumph is never new, it always must be heard. There isn't
> any other tale to tell, it's the only light we've got in all this
> darkness. (139).

Creole reiterates the paradox of the blues: life is painful, suffering is
inevitable, but you must go on. And within this context Sonny is ready
to play *his* blues. He can tell a story about his "trouble in mind" and
create a triumph so that all can see that he has refused to give up, that
there is possibility even in the darkest moments:

> I seemed to hear with what burning he had made it his,
> with what burning we had yet to make it ours, how we
> could cease lamenting. Freedom lurked around us and I
> understood, at last, that he could help us to be free if we
> would listen, that he would never be free until we did.
> Yet, there was no battle in his face now. I heard what he
> had gone through, and would continue to go through until
> he came to rest in earth. He had made it his: that long line,
> of which we knew only Mama and Daddy. (140)

With his creation of this blues Sonny has taken his place as a ritual
spokesperson for the community. The creation of a blues from "what he
had gone through" frees Sonny from his suffering, and his
transcendence acts as a model for his listeners, assuring them that the
lament is not the only response to the battle of life, that the possibility

of triumph also exists. In addition, the narrator recognizes that the form his brother has chosen is distinctly African American; Sonny's blues captures "that long line" of generations of black men and women in America, perpetuating a heritage by telling the collective stories of trials ultimately transformed into triumphs: "And he was giving it back, as everything must be given back, so that, passing through death, it can live forever." Yet, the transitory nature of this transcendence also becomes apparent: "And I was yet aware that this was only a moment, that the world waited outside, as hungry as a tiger, and that trouble stretched above us, longer than the sky." The narrator sees that the approach to life captured in the blues sensibility and the possibility inherent in jazz improvisation must be continuously renewed because the tide of trouble faced by human beings can never be completely stemmed. The acknowledgment of this condition places a tremendous burden on the black musician because the creation of the representative ritual performance is an ongoing process. At the conclusion of this momentous blues drama the narrator buys drinks for the band. After Sonny sips from his "Scotch and milk" he places the glass on top of his piano to begin the next set and the process begins again. The narrator focuses on Sonny's drink as he concludes the story with the assertion: "For me, then, as they began to play again, it glowed and shook above my brother's head like the very cup of trembling" (141). The Biblical "cup of trembling," which was symbolic of the Chosen People's suffering, was to be passed to those who had inflicted the suffering.[33] Sonny continues to drink from the "cup" because he knows (and his brother understands) that the African American struggle for freedom goes on and as a black musician he must create new ways to tell the story in the blues.[34]

The "tradition," the "field of manners" and "the possibility of ritual or intercourse" that Baldwin misses in *Native Son* are realized in the jazz performance that closes "Sonny's Blues." Like Bigger Thomas, Sonny is filled with pain and rage over the position to which he has been relegated in America. But he is able to keep channeling those emotions into a musical creativity that provides transcendence for himself and the community he represents, rather than into a violent, self-destructive nihilism. In his essay "Notes of a Native Son" (1955) Baldwin acknowledges inheriting this same nihilistic sense of alienation from his father: "He had lived and died in an intolerable bitterness of spirit and it frightened me, as we drove him to the graveyard through those unquiet streets, to see how powerful and overflowing this bitterness could be and to realize that this bitterness now was mine" (88). Realizing "this bitterness was folly" and that hatred "never failed to destroy the man who hated," Baldwin resolves to fight injustice but "to keep my own heart free of hatred and despair" (113-14). Like Sonny "playing for his life," the young Baldwin[35] was writing for his life, channeling his rage into the creative process. In "Sonny's Blues" the jazz musician functions as a model for the African American artist that Baldwin aspired to be, the artist that he describes in "Many Thousands Gone" as having a "discernible relationship to himself, to his own life, to his own people" (34).

2.
"THE BROTHER DOES NOT [DOES] SING": RALPH ELLISON

By the early 1950s the blues styles which had been carried north with the migration of African Americans had undergone a major metamorphosis. Electrification modernized traditional forms and blasted them into the frenzy of life in urban American. Chicago's South Side was the hotbed of this musical activity, and the king bee of the down home-rooted, electric urban blues was the guitarist/singer Muddy Waters (McKinley Morganfield).[36] Born near Clarksdale, Mississippi to sharecropper parents in 1915, Waters recognized early on that playing the blues could provide him with a ticket out of the drudgery of farm labor. He consciously modeled his blues approach on local stars Son House and Robert Johnson and was recorded for the Library of Congress by Alan Lomax in 1941 in the pre-Civil War, cypress log slave cabin in which he had lived since childhood. When the blues man arrived in Chicago in 1943 he worked in a paper factory and performed on the side as a solo, acoustic act. But Waters soon pioneered new musical frontiers when he switched to electric guitar and began building a band. The electrified band format was in part a necessity because the working class clubs that would hire down home stylists, often called "buckets of blood," were invariably rough and rowdy and loud. But the new blues that Waters and his contemporaries, including Howlin' Wolf (Chester Burnett), Elmore James, Sonny Boy Williamson (Rice Miller), Little Walter Jacobs and Willie Dixon, were forging with searing slide guitar runs, wailing harmonicas and driving dance rhythms expressed the pulse and intensity of inner city life.

Black men and women had come north in search of change and had left behind the complacency and laid-back demeanor of the rural life. The civil rights movement was beginning to take shape and many of these emigrants were angry with the discovery that life in the North contained the same injustices they had experienced in the South. Yet, the urban scene gave them greater mobility and opportunity and a sense of having broken with a setting inextricably linked to slavery. The feeling of unrest and independence, particularly for black males, was articulated in the bravura and braggadocio of Waters' lyrics. He literally spells out this macho defiance in his line "I spell M-A-N, I'm a man!"[37]

The style of electric blues that Waters created declined in popularity with the majority of the black audience by the mid-1950s, and a smoother style which came to be called Rhythm & Blues performed by such artists as Bobby "Blue" Bland and B. B. King, along with the early rock and roll of Chuck Berry, Little Richard (Penniman) and Fats Domino, came to dominate black popular tastes. However, the down home Chicago blues maintained a loyal following and enjoyed a resurgence as it provided the foundation for the blues-influenced rock of the 1960s.

What is most significant about the innovations of Waters and his contemporaries is that they were able to create something vital and modern that remained firmly rooted in the African American folk tradition. Muddy Waters's Chicago-style blues featured the same basic form and many of the same guitar riffs and lyrical tropes found in the Delta-style blues of Robert Johnson and Son House, but the surge of electricity transformed these blues into something that had never been heard of before. This transformation was not simply in terms of volume; the electric blues signaled a new amplified *conception* of a traditional form. More raucous, more powerful, more intense, Muddy Waters and his contemporaries played these new blues with a sensibility that reflected the new and complex experiences that made up life in urban America during the mid-twentieth century.

This same process of transforming and amplifying the conception of folk expressions was engaged in by Ralph Ellison in the writing of the novel *Invisible Man* (1952). Ellison drew on the forms from the African American folk tradition, especially music, which he integrated into a sophisticated literary technique derived from careful study and absorption of the European and American tradition of the novel[38] to create an innovative work of African American fiction that reflected the complexities and contradictions of modern American existence. An examination of the ways in which music informs this long and complex work can shed light on Ellison's method and purpose.[39]

The premium Ellison placed on both folklore and literary technique in *Invisible Man* brings the intention of his fictional representation of African American life into conflict with Wright's attempt to use writing as a forum for a political agenda.[40] In the essay "The World and the Jug" (1963-64) Ellison asserts that the intentions of artistic production are much broader in scope than specific ideological concerns: "I believe that true novels, even when pessimistic and bitter, arise out of the

impulse to celebrate human life and therefore are ritualistic and
ceremonial at their core. Thus they would preserve as they destroy,
affirm as they reject" (114).[41] The essential paradoxes Ellison finds in
the purpose of the novel explain why folk-derived forms such as the
blues provide an appropriate artistic model for *Invisible Man*: "My goal
was not to escape, or hold back, but to work through; to transcend as
the blues transcend the painful conditions with which they deal" (137).
In order to achieve his goal Ellison used his literary craftsmanship to
integrate folk forms into his fiction.[42] Ellison's use of folklore in
Invisible Man, especially traditionally based musical forms, is essential
to the understanding of his compositional approach and thematic
concerns.

Jazz improvisation is a model for Ellison's compositional approach
to *Invisible Man*. As he explains in his 1981 introduction to the novel,
"I knew that I could draw upon the rich culture of the folk tale as well
as that of the novel, and that being uncertain of my skill I would have to
improvise upon my materials in the manner of a jazz musician putting a
musical theme through a wild star-burst of metamorphosis" (xxii-
xxiii).[43] His admiration for the dynamics that comprise the creation of
jazz is illustrated in the essay "The Charlie Christian Story" (1958):

> There is a cruel contradiction implicit in the art form
> itself. For true jazz is an art of individual assertion within
> and against the group. Each true jazz moment (as distinct
> from the uninspired commercial performance) springs
> from a contest in which each artist challenges all the rest;
> each solo flight, or improvisation, represents (like the
> successive canvases of a painter) a definition of his
> identity: as individual, as member of the collectivity and
> as a link in the chain of tradition. Thus, because jazz finds
> its very life in an endless improvisation upon traditional
> materials, the jazzman must lose his identity even as he
> finds it. (234)

In its insistence on constant reinvention, jazz (like the novel for Ellison)
preserves as it destroys, affirms as it rejects.[44] This process is an
appropriate paradigm for the composition of *Invisible Man* because the
Prologue sets up the themes or riffs that will be improvised on in
various forms throughout the text. The movement of reversal resounds
throughout the Prologue in images of light and darkness, sleep and
awakening and, most importantly, visibility and invisibility.[45] Like the
jazz improviser, the narrator of *Invisible Man* is constantly redefining

his identity, and invisibility is the key for him in understanding this process. The narrator realizes that as a black man in America he is invisible; people fail to acknowledge his humanity: "I am invisible, understand, simply because people refuse to see me" (3). The recognition of this invisibility invests the narrator with the same sense of possibility that Ellison sees in the jazz soloist's "endless variations upon traditional materials." His invisibility is ultimately liberating: If people don't even know that he's there, why shouldn't he envision endless possibilities for his identity? Through the experiences he narrates following the Prologue the Invisible Man shows how he came to a fundamental understanding of human existence: "that (by contradiction, I mean) is how the world moves: Not like an arrow, but a boomerang. (Beware of those who speak of the *spiral* of history; they are preparing a boomerang. Keep a steel helmet handy.)" (6). The narrator learns that the only thing definite in life is that change is inevitable. Even history is not fixed; just as the possibilities for self-perception are countless, there are multiple perspectives from which events can be viewed. The world that Ellison presents in *Invisible Man* is non-linear and non-exclusionary.

The essential duality that Ellison identifies in the blues makes this folk form a fitting model for the expression of life's boomeranging reversals, the contradictions by which the world moves. Ellison identifies this double-edged point of view in his classic definition of the blues in the essay "Richard Wright's Blues" (1958):

> The blues is an impulse to keep the painful details and episodes of a brutal experience alive in one's aching consciousness, to finger its jagged grain, and to transcend it, not by the consolation of philosophy but by squeezing from it a near-tragic, near-comic lyricism. As a form, the blues is an autobiographical chronicle of personal catastrophe expressed lyrically. (78-9)[46]

Although Ellison is describing what he feels Wright accomplished with his autobiography *Black Boy*, he could easily have been outlining exactly what the Invisible Man constructs with the narration of his life.[47] The Invisible Man, like Muddy Waters, makes the classic blues movement from the rural South to a black enclave in a Northern urban center. Also, like Waters, he draws upon traditional folk sources to forge a sense of identity, to "make a name for himself," and produces an autobiographical expression that captures the drive, the intensity and the contradictions of the tumultuous and alien world of inner city America.

While African American music informs the compositional approach and structure of *Invisible Man,* it also functions within the narrative as a touchstone for racial identity. The narrator's journey toward understanding his invisibility and the boomeranging nature of the world is punctuated by encounters with blues, jazz, spirituals, gospel and other forms of black folk-derived expression.[48] These encounters contain important lessons for the narrator, although often he only grasps their significance with the hindsight that he displays in the Prologue and Epilogue.[49] Because music is the most articulate, poignant and powerful form of African American folk-derived expression, the narrator's "musical encounters" are particularly significant conveyors of knowledge. An examination of some of the key episodes in which the Invisible Man comes into contact with folk-derived music illustrates how he arrives at the perspectives on his identity and the world that are presented in the Prologue and Epilogue.

The visit with the sharecropper Jim Trueblood is one of the Invisible Man's most important musical encounters. The narrator thinks he is amusing Mr. Norton, the wealthy white trustee of his college, when he drives him past Trueblood's cabin. And when Norton insists on meeting the sharecropper and hearing the story of how he has impregnated both his wife and his daughter, the narrator is annoyed and embarrassed. The Invisible Man blames his expulsion from college on the story because it upsets Norton and causes his physical collapse. The narrator fails to recognize that the story contains the essence of the blues process, the ability to find triumph in tragedy. As he comments after Trueblood concludes: "Something was going on which I didn't get" (68). Driving toward the cabin of the sharecropper, the narrator illustrates his alienation from his own culture with his dismissal of Trueblood's folk artistry. Ironically, the narrator's attempt to assimilate into white culture is marked by such intense self-loathing that he cannot understand the awe the white visitors to the campus experience when Trueblood's group sings:

> He was also a good tenor singer, and sometimes when special white guests visited the school he was brought up along with the members of a country quartet to sing what the officials called 'their primitive spirituals' when we assembled in the chapel on Sunday evenings. We were embarrassed by the earthy harmonies they sang, but since the visitors were awed we dared not laugh at the crude, high, plaintively animal sounds Jim Trueblood made as he led the quartet. (47)

The narrator obviously considers himself too sophisticated to take the "primitive" expression seriously and cannot understand why this distinguished white man would be interested in the sharecropper's disgrace. In painful detail Trueblood relates the story of incest with his daughter to a mesmerized Norton and an increasingly uncomfortable Invisible Man. The daughter had been sleeping with her parents because their cabin was cold. Trueblood became sexually aroused through a dream and without realizing whom he was holding, began having intercourse with the girl. The aftermath of his sexual act is extremely painful to Trueblood. He cannot help thinking about "how I'm guilty and how I ain't guilty." Not only must he face his violently outraged wife, his daughter and the local community, but, more importantly, he also must face himself. Trueblood overcomes the horror of the situation in which he finds himself through the spontaneous creation of a blues:

> Finally, one night, way early in the mornin', I looks up and sees the stars and I starts singin'. I don't mean to, I didn't think 'bout it, just start singin'. I don't know what it was, some kinda church song, I guess. All I know is I *ends up* singin' the blues. I sings me some blues that night ain't never been sang before, and while I'm singin' them blues I makes up my mind that I ain't nobody but myself and ain't nothin' I can do but let whatever is gonna happen, happen. I made up my mind that I was goin' back home and face Kate; yeah, and face Mary Lou too. (Ellison's italics) (66)

He has expressed himself in a communal form but these blues are uniquely his own. Trueblood's act of blues creation has provided him with the ability to transcend "the painful details and episodes of a brutal experience." He also realizes that he must be himself—something that takes the Invisible Man the whole length of his narrative to figure out. In his assertion that he is guilty but not guilty Trueblood expresses an awareness of the dualistic nature of the world. And he also gives the narrator a perfect example of an ironic boomeranging reversal; ostracized by the black community, he becomes the recipient of help from the white community. Through a seemingly disastrous act, life, in many ways, improves for Trueblood and his family: "But what I don't understand is how I done the worse thing a man can do in his own family and 'stead of things gettin' bad, they got better" (68). Throughout Trueblood's story the Invisible Man is "torn between humiliation and fascination." At the conclusion he comments: "But now as the voice ended I sat looking down at Mr. Norton's feet. Out in the yard a woman's hoarse contralto intoned a hymn" (68). Whoever may be singing the hymn—possibly Trueblood's daughter or his wife—is using a form from African American folk culture to respond with resiliency to the tragic situation while the subservient narrator can only look at a white man's feet. [50]

The Invisible Man's introduction to the boomeranging nature of life through the blues continues when he encounters Peter Wheatstraw on a Harlem street. Intent on finding a job that will enable him to return to the college, the narrator heads off one morning and runs into Wheatstraw singing as he pushes a cart filled with discarded blueprints:

> It was a blues, and I walked along behind him remembering the times that I had heard such singing at home. It seemed that here some memories slipped around my life at the campus and went far back to things I had long ago shut out of my mind. There was no escaping such reminders.
> *She's got feet like a monkey*
> *Legs like a frog—Lawd, Lawd!*
> *But when she starts to loving me*
> *I holler Whoooo, God-dog!*
> *Cause I loves my baabay,*
> *Better than I do myself . . . '* (172-73)

Once again the Invisible Man tries to distance himself from African American folk culture; the campus represents his ticket away from that culture and into the world of Mr. Norton. Wheatstraw is the ultimate representative of black folk culture, a blues man whose language is filled with allusions to traditional trickster figures, boasts, ritual greetings, HooDoo, and even "greasy greens." Claiming to be a piano player and calling himself "the Devil's only son-in-law," Wheatstraw is modeled on the St. Louis-based blues singer/pianist/ guitarist Peetie Wheatstraw (1905-1941). The real life Wheatstraw billed himself as "the Devil's Son-in-Law" and "the High Sheriff from Hell," and created a mythical public persona that featured a swaggering braggadocio in the face of all odds and adverse conditions.[51] The blues lines Ellison's Wheatstraw sings are from the Count Basie/Jimmy Rushing tune "Boogie Woogie (I May Be Wrong)." Having heard Trueblood speak of the folk blues he created in the rural South, it is fitting that the narrator hears a swinging jazz variation on the form in Harlem. The opening line of the tune (which the narrator does not relate in the text) embodies Wheatstraw's survival instincts and the contradiction by which the world moves: "I may be wrong but I won't be wrong always." Of course, at this point in his blues journey the narrator is oblivious to the concept of boomeranging. This becomes clear when they discuss the load of blueprints Wheatstraw has salvaged from the trash:

> 'You have quite a lot,' I said.
> 'Yeah, this ain't all neither. I got a coupla loads. There's a day's work right here in this stuff. Folks is always making plans and changing 'em.'
> ' Yes, that's right,' I said, thinking of my letters, but that's a mistake. You have to stick to the plan.'
> He looked at me, suddenly grave. 'You kinda young, daddy-o,' he said. (175)

Wheatstraw recognizes the narrator's naiveté, his inability to grasp the necessity to improvise and adapt in a chaotic world. He tries to communicate the necessity of employing folk forms to survive, but the narrator has forgotten how to reply to the ritual wordplay that he had learned "back of school." The blues man departs intoning the essential duality of his approach to life, "I'll teach you some good bad habits. You'll need 'em. Good luck" (176). As Wheatstraw moves down the street he returns to the song:

> I strode along, hearing the cartman's song become a lonesome, broad-toned whistle now that flowered at the end of each phrase into a tremulous, blue-toned chord. And in its flutter and swoop I heard the sound of a railroad train highballing it, lonely across the lonely night. He was the Devil's son-in-law, all right, and he was a man who could whistle a three-toned chord . . . God damn, I thought, they're a hell of a people! And I didn't know whether it was pride or disgust that suddenly flashed over me. (177)

The Invisible Man possesses a keen insight into Wheatstraw's folk expression. Not only does he identify the appropriate imagery that the blues evoke, but he is able to make a technical analysis of the song's harmonic structure. Yet, he is ambivalent at best about the value of this knowledge, failing to see that it is the key to his survival. While the blues man knows that "All it takes to get along in this here man's town is a little shit, grit and mother-wit. And man, I was bawn will all three," the Invisible Man thinks he will find his place in the world by denying African American folk culture and returning to the campus education that is typified by his promise to Mr. Norton to read Ralph Waldo Emerson.[52]

Another example of Ellison's "blues riffing" on themes such as the individual/communal relationship and the dualistic nature of life can be found in the narrator's encounter with Mary Rambo, the woman who runs a Harlem boarding house. After a factory accident and the hospital's attempt to erase all sense of identity in the Invisible Man, Mary takes him in and tries to restore his sense of self-worth. She embodies the communal spirit and hopes to inspire him to become "a credit to the race." Mary is well aware of the duality of the blues sensibility: "'I'm in New York, but New York ain't in me'" (255). She clearly articulates the blues process of creating triumph from troubles: "'It's just hard times you going through . . . Everybody worth his salt has his hard times, and when you git to be somebody you'll see these here very same hard times helped you a heap.'" The narrator may not understand the full significance of Mary's approach to life, but he is aware that she is more than just a "friend": "She was something more-a force, a stable, familiar force like something out of my past which kept me from whirling off into some unknown which I dared not face" (258). What Mary does is keep the narrator in touch with his cultural heritage. When he is first trying to convince the narrator to become a spokesman for the Brotherhood's "scientific" approach to life Brother Jack dismisses people like Mary as "'The old one, they're agrarian types, you know. Being ground up by industrial conditions. Thrown on the dump heaps and cast aside'" (290). But the narrator recognizes that Mary with her transcendent blues sensibility is a survivor: "She was far from dead, or of being ground to bits by New York. Hell, she knew very well how to live here, much better than I was with my college training" (295). Nevertheless, when he returns to Mary's after refusing Jack's offer the narrator feels guilty because he is deeply in debt to Mary. He realizes his selfishness in not even checking out an opportunity that might, as Mary paraphrases Mahalia Jackson's song, "'move us all on up a little higher'" (255). Finally, it is through hearing Mary sing a Bessie Smith blues that the Invisible Man gains the motivation to call Jack about the job: "Then from down the hall I could hear Mary singing, her voice clear and untroubled, though she sang a troubled song. It was the 'Back Water Blues.' I lay listening as the sound flowed to and around me, bringing me a calm sense of my indebtedness. When it faded I got up and put on my coat" (297). This blues tells the story of Southern townspeople driven from their homes by rising flood waters. Like the eviction on the street in Harlem that triggers the narrator's meeting with Brother Jack, "Backwater Blues" is a story of dispossession and a community in crisis.[53] Although he identifies the essential contradiction of the "untroubled" voice singing a "troubled song," the narrator is still unable to grasp the implications this has on how he should live his life. As Mary asks him the following morning when he is preparing to move out and work for the Brotherhood: "'Why don't folks act according to what they know?'"(320). The Invisible Man drinks a cup of coffee with Mary before leaving, and she sees that he finds it bitter and comments: "'Guess I'll have to get some better filters . . . These I got just lets through the grounds along with the coffee, the good with the bad. I don't know though, even with the best of filters you apt to find a ground or two at the bottom of your cup'" (323). Mary continues to explain the contradiction by which the world moves, and as the Invisible Man heads out the door she is "singing something sad and serene" (327). Ironically, he hears Mary's last communication of his cultural heritage in the sound of African American music as he is contemplating his new identity—the paper with the name that has been chosen for him by his new white employer.[54]

In addition to jazz and blues, spirituals and gospel music play a role in guiding the narrator of *Invisible Man* toward the definition of his identity, his relationship to the African American community and America as a whole.[55] A gospel song accents the message of an influential conversation the narrator has when he is chief spokesman for the Harlem District of the Brotherhood. Disturbed by an anonymous letter warning him that his successes are creating enemies among his colleagues, the Invisible Man calls in Brother Tarp, an older black member, to sound him out about the warning. When the narrator had been given the assignment Tarp brought him a poster of Frederick Douglass. His choice of a role model for the young spokesman is in contrast with Jack's suggestion that the narrator "shall be the new Booker T. Washington," for the former advocated agitation while the latter advocated assimilation as the approach blacks should take in defining their role in American society. The Douglass poster comes to represent an emerging perspective for the narrator: "For now I had begun to believe, despite all the talk of science around me, that there was a magic in spoken words" (381). Even though he may not realize it, Tarp's gift of the Douglass poster enables the narrator to begin reconnecting with the oral tradition of his folk heritage.

The conversation with Tarp following the receipt of the anonymous letter crystallizes this sense of belonging to a cultural heritage. Tarp attempts to encourage the narrator in the concrete actions he has taken to benefit the Harlem community. He narrates his story of an unjust imprisonment in the South and his escape from a chain gang, a story that reflects Douglass's *Narrative*. He gives the narrator the link from the leg chain that he cut through to make his escape. "I saw him place his hand on the desk. 'Brother,' he said, calling me 'Brother' for the first time, 'I want you to take it. I guess it's a kind of luck piece. Anyway, it's the one I filed to get away'" (388). Tarp's description of the chain link, a brutal reminder of his humiliation and bondage, as a "luck piece" is another example of the narrator being instructed in the essential duality of human existence. With this encounter the narrator exhibits growth toward the perspective he reaches in the Prologue and Epilogue. He looks on Tarp's gift of the chain link like a watch that has been passed along from father to son because he senses "the overtones of unstated seriousness and solemnity of the paternal gesture which at once joined him with his ancestors, marked a high point of his present, and promised a concreteness to his nebulous and chaotic future" (390). Not only does the gift literally link the narrator to a communal past but it also gives him a glimpse that the world is chaotic and, as he eventually discovers, "not like an arrow, but a boomerang." As he contemplates the significance of his encounter with Tarp, the narrator hears the sound of a gospel song:

> I could feel the air from the window hot against my neck
> now as through the smell of morning coffee I heard a
> throaty voice singing with a mixture of laughter and
> solemnity:
> > *Don't come early in the morning*
> > *Neither in the heat of the day*
> > *But come in the sweet cool of the*
> > *Evening and wash my sins away . . .*
> A whole series of memories started to well up, but I threw
> them off. There was no time for memory, for all its
> images were of times passed. (390)

Once again the narrator recognizes the duality of African American musical expression. And even though he has yet to comprehend that in the boomeranging movement of life the key to moving forward is found in "times passed," he says that the encounter with Tarp "restored my perspective." This restoration which takes place as the Invisible Man hears black sacred music echoes Douglass's restored perspective of himself as a man, the "first glimmering conception of the dehumanizing character of slavery" which he heard in the spirituals. When the Brotherhood revises its strategy for Harlem and insists that the narrator abandon his "agitation" for the black community he finds that Tarp has disappeared and that the Douglass poster is also gone. However, the chain link remains with the Invisible Man as a reminder of the lesson Tarp has passed along.[56]

The performance of the spiritual "There's Many a Thousand Gone" at the funeral of Brother Tod Clifton has a tremendous impact on the narrator's journey toward the definition of his self-identity and his relation to his cultural heritage. Clifton, who had been shot down by police for resisting arrest, had been engaged in act of ironic self-parody by selling paper Sambo puppets after learning that the black membership has been betrayed by the Brotherhood's revised Harlem strategy. The narrator cannot reach Jack and the Brotherhood committee for instructions on how to react to the slaying and decides to organize a large funeral in order to revive black support for the Brotherhood. As the funeral procession assembles in an uptown park an old man spontaneously breaks into "There's Many a Thousand Gone" and is joined in a duet by a euphonium player. It immediately puts the narrator in touch with his heritage: "It was a song from the past, the past of the campus and the still earlier past of home" (452). He also recognizes his previous inability to draw upon the past to establish a course of action: "It was as though the song had been there all the time and he knew it and aroused it; and I knew that I had known it too and had failed to release it out of vague, nameless shame or fear" (453). When the crowd consisting of people from diverse backgrounds joins in, the narrator understands that the folk expression has "touched upon something deeper than protest, or religion":

> And yet all were touched; the song had aroused all. It was not the words, for they were all the same old slave-borne words; it was as though he'd changed the emotion beneath the words while yet the old longing, resigned, transcendent emotion still sounded above, now deepened by that something for which the theory of Brotherhood had given me no name. (453)

Although he still rejects the past, the "same old slave-borne words," and fails to recognize the protest, the subversion, the resistance to oppression inherent in the lyrics, he does respond to "that something," the ineffable feeling, the emotion, that is so poignantly articulated in African American music. The performance of the spiritual influences the approach of his speech; he eulogizes Clifton as a friend, as an individual black man and as a member of the community. At the conclusion of the speech the narrator feels he has failed because, "I had let it get away from me, had been unable to bring in the political issues" (459). When he is called before the committee to be reprimanded for valorizing someone they consider a traitor the narrator begins to exhibit his emerging sense of self-identity by defending the funeral plans based on "personal responsibility." He also shows that he is beginning to reject the committee's linear, exclusionary views when he dismisses their pat assessment of Clifton as a traitor and asserts "he was jam-full of contradictions" (467).[57] During this committee meeting the Invisible Man discovers the true nature of the role the Brotherhood expects him to play. They conceive of him as a paid performer, the living embodiment of Clifton's minstrel puppet. He asserts "'there's nothing like isolating a man to make him think,'" and Jack snaps back that "'you were not hired to think. Had you forgotten that? If so, listen to me: You were not hired to think'" (469).

The one encounter with African American music outside of black culture that occurs in *Invisible Man* should have alerted the narrator to the fact that the Brotherhood is not hiring him to think and regards him as little more than a mouthpiece it can manipulate. On the night that he first joins the Brotherhood the narrator is taken to a party, and the first warning of the Brotherhood's intention to exploit him comes as he hears a "series of rich arpeggios sound on the piano." At the same time he overhears the hostess Emma ask Jack "'But don't you think he should be a little blacker?'" Jack's replies "'We're not interested in his looks but in his voice'" (303). He wonders if she wants a "black-face comedian" or if she "wants to see me sweat coal tar, ink, shoe polish, graphite. What was I, a man or a natural resource?" Nevertheless, he decides that Jack is the one who is doing the hiring and assumes he is interested in both the sound *and* content of the oratorical abilities that the narrator had exhibited earlier in the day at the eviction. But what is not made clear is that the Brotherhood is not interested in him as a man who can contribute something to the cause; in fact, Jack does think of the Invisible Man as a "natural resource." Yet, Jack cloaks his agenda for the narrator in the promise he will be the new Booker T. Washington, "the true interpreter of the people."

After Jack settles "business" matters with the Invisible Man they head into the large room where a group of members is gathered around the piano "singing folk songs with more volume than melody." Ironically, one of these brothers is also interested in the narrator's voice. Echoing Jack's earlier assertion "'We've been waiting for you for months,'" the man at the piano says, "'You're just who we need. We been looking for you.'" When the brother asks the narrator to sing he sends Jack into a rage:

> 'How about a spiritual, Brother? Or one of those real
> good ole Negro work songs? Like this: *Ah went to*

> *Atlanta-nevah been there befo'* , ' he sang, his arms held
> out from his body like a penguin's wings, glass in one
> hand, cigar in the other. *'White man sleep in a feather bed,*
> *Nigguh sleep on the flo'* . . . Ha! Ha! How about it,
> Brother?'
>   'The brother *does not sing!* ' Brother Jack roared
> staccato.
>   'Nonsense, *all* colored people sing.'
>   'This is an outrageous example of unconscious racial
> chauvinism!' Jack said.
>   'Nonsense, I *like* their singing,' the broad man said
> doggedly.
>   'The brother *does not sing!* ' Brother Jack cried, his face
> turning a deep purple. (Ellison's italics) (312)

The man insists that Jack let "*him* say whether he can sing or not" and
calls on the narrator to "git hot! *Go Down, Moses* ." As the man is led
out of the room drunkenly singing "St. Louis Blues" everyone stares at
the narrator as though he is responsible for the incident. He begins to
laugh hysterically, exclaiming such comments as, "'He hit me in the
face with a yard of chitterlings!'" and "'He threw a hog maw.'" Soon the
whole room joins in the laughter. Even though it hurts he plays the
"black-face comedian" in order to relieve this white "audience" of its
discomfort: "I fought against the painful laughter, and as I calmed I saw
them looking at me with a sort of embarrassed gratitude." A woman
approaches him and apologizes, "'*I* would never ask our colored
brothers to sing, even though I love to hear them. Because I know that
it would be a very backward thing.'" He says that he is "puzzled" after
her comments and wonders if she truly understands the resentment
blacks feel at the assumption that they are "all entertainers and natural
singers." But he is also disturbed by the "mutual laughter" and wonders,
"Shouldn't there be some way for us to be asked to sing? Shouldn't the
short man have the right to make a mistake without his motives being
considered consciously or unconsciously malicious? After all, *he* was
singing , or trying to. What if I asked *him* to sing?" (314). The narrator
senses that the issue is more complex than the Brotherhood's
undeviating stance that the request is "backward," yet he still has not
come to understand the contradictory nature of the world and simply
decides "whatever she meant, she's nice and I like her." By the end of
the evening he naively decides that these white folks "were different"
from those who had exploited and oppressed his family in the South.
     This scene in which the brother asks the Invisible Man to sing
along on a spiritual indicates that Ellison is, as Henry Louis Gates, Jr.

calls it, "Signifyin(g)" on the scene where Jan and Mary are encouraging Bigger Thomas to join in on "Swing Low Sweet Chariot" in *Native Son*.[58] In both instances the stereotypical assumption that musical ability is endemic to African Americans is made by drunken whites who are members of organizations dedicated to uplifting the working class. Both Bigger and the Invisible Man recognize the demeaning nature of the assumption. The reaction of each character in these musical encounters is indicative of the disparate approaches each author takes to the fictional representation of African American life. Bigger refuses to participate and withdraws into himself, simmering with a rage that will explode in an act of violence that will lead him unswervingly to his annihilation. The Invisible Man, who at first naively overlooks the incident, eventually comes to understand the betrayal by the Brotherhood and is able to use what Mary Rambo called his "hard times" so he can "git to be somebody" to define his own identity as a black man in America. When Jack bluntly tells him at the meeting that he has not been hired to think, it becomes clear that the narrator is not a man but a natural resource being exploited by the Brotherhood. As Jack and the other brothers attack him for taking "personal responsibility" for Clifton's funeral and for asserting that he knows and feels the "political consciousness of Harlem," the narrator comes to the critical understanding that Jack's insistence on blind adherence to discipline means that "He doesn't even see me" (475). It is a major breakthrough for the narrator's self-conception and world view because he begins to see the possibility that arises from being invisible. Unlike Bigger, the Invisible Man is able to contain his rage; he looks at Jack "carefully now with some of the red spots fading and with the feeling that I was just awakening from a dream. I had boomeranged around" (476). He has taken a major step forward in shedding the naiveté that prevented him from seeing that Jack's interest in his voice for making speeches was essentially the same as the drunken brother's interest in his voice for singing "Go Down, Moses."

While the Invisible Man is unable to grasp the full significance of his encounters with African American music, he almost always senses at the time he hears the music that there is more going on than he is capable of decoding. Invisible Man is drawn to the sound of blues, jazz, gospel and spirituals, feeling that there is a message to be found somewhere beneath the music's surface. The nature of this message begins to become apparent to the narrator after Tod Clifton's death. As he rides back uptown on the subway he begins to question if the Brotherhood's conception of history actually includes the African Americans for whom he is supposed to be the chief spokesman. He begins to realize that the Brotherhood's version of history is just that—a version: "All things, it is said, are duly recorded—all things of importance, that is. But not quite, for actually it is only the known, the seen, the heard and only those events that the recorder regards as important that are put down, those lies his keepers keep their power by" (439). Emerging onto 125th Street, the narrator sees the black men, women and children of Harlem as *his* people for the first time: "They'd been there all along, but somehow I'd missed them." And he realizes that "They were outside the groove of history," the linear, exclusionary groove that the Brotherhood insisted was history. As he walks along the street he understands that a culture with an oral tradition— "we who write no novels, histories or other books"—records its history in forms that are not recognized by the keepers of power:

> I moved with the crowd, the sweat pouring off me, listening to the grinding roar of traffic, the growing sound of a record shop loudspeaker blaring a languid blues. I stopped. Was this all that would be recorded? Was this the only true history of the times, a mood blared by trumpets, trombones, saxophones and drums, a song with turgid, inadequate words? (443)

The history of African Americans is preserved in their music; the shared emotions and experiences of the culture are passed along and expressed in sound. The narrator, however, sees (hears?) that a literary culture maintains power by establishing a "permanent" version of history through written documentation.[59]

The Invisible Man's most fully realized expression of the perception that meaning is embedded in the sound of African American music are his encounters with the jazz recordings of Louis Armstrong in the Prologue and Epilogue. Inside his manhole the narrator's emphasis on sheer sound is apparent when he says that he would like to have five phonographs so he could "hear five recordings of Louis Armstrong playing and singing 'What Did I Do to Be so Black and Blue' —all at the same time." He claims "when I have music I want to *feel* its vibration, not with my ear but with my whole body" (8). He wants to immerse himself in the sound of Armstrong's jazz because it is a part of the very fabric of his existence. The Invisible Man identifies with Armstrong "because he's made poetry out of being invisible. I think it must be because he's unaware that he *is* invisible. And my own grasp of invisibility aids me to understand his music" (8). The jazz man represents possibility, not only through musical improvisation, but in his ability to define and redefine his public persona. His life is a testament to possibility; a young black man emerging from a New

Orleans waif's home, Armstrong applied his personal talent to a traditional idiom and wound up laying the foundation for one of the most creative forms of modern artistic expression. After conquering the jazz world he went on establish himself as a genuine icon of American popular culture. He is the ultimate trickster figure, the musical genius who wins mass appeal behind a comic mask. As Ellison describes him in "Change the Joke and Slip the Yoke" (1958): "Armstrong's clownish license and intoxicating powers are almost Elizabethan; he takes liberties with kings, queens and presidents; emphasizes the physicality of his music with sweat, spittle and facial contortions; he performs the magical feat of making romantic melody issue from a throat of gravel" (52). On the recording of the Fats Waller's "What Did I Do to Be so Black and Blue" Armstrong proves himself to be a fitting representative of life's boomeranging contradictions. The lyrics are a pathetic lament on the bruised state of existence of a black man in America:

> How will it end?
> Ain't got a friend.
> My only sin is in my skin.
> What did I do to be so black and blue?

Yet, for the Invisible Man when "Louis bends that military instrument into a beam of lyrical sound" triumph emerges from tragedy. The Invisible Man is also attracted to the impeccable and irresistible timing of Armstrong's sense of swing:

> Invisibility, let me explain, gives one a slightly different sense of time, you're never quite on the beat. Sometimes you're ahead and sometimes behind. Instead of the swift and imperceptible flowing of time, you are aware of its nodes, those points where time stands still or from which it leaps ahead. And you slip into the breaks and look around. That's what you hear vaguely in Louis' music. (8)

In the jazz improviser's refusal to adhere strictly to the beat the narrator finds a correspondence to his own rejection of a linear conception of history. Time, like history, does not move forward in an undeviating, incremental path.

Invisibility means questioning what seems fixed, looking below surface appearances, and the narrator applies this "new way of listening" to the Armstrong recording. As with so many of his other encounters with African American music, he is drawn to the sound, but this time with the awareness of his invisibility he is able to uncover the hidden message: "The unheard sounds came through, and each melodic line existed of itself; stood out clearly from all the rest, said its piece, and waited patiently for the other voices to speak. That night I found myself hearing not only in time, but in space as well. I not only entered the music but descended, like Dante, into its depths" (8-9). His dreamlike descent carries him through three levels: he hears an old woman singing a spiritual; he sees a beautiful, ivory-colored girl on a slave auction block; he hears a sermon on the "Blackness of Blackness." What the Invisible Man finds embedded in the sound of this jazz performance is a descent into the roots of the black experience in America. On the third level in the call/response of the sermon he learns that "*Black will make you . . . . or black will un-make you.*" It was the blackness of their skin that was used as an excuse to "unmake" Africans as human beings and "make" them into slaves. And it was the blackness of their skin that allowed slaves to "unmake" their subhuman status by bonding together for survival to "make" African Americans. As he moves from the sermon the narrator meets the old slave woman and learns that her sons are the product of a sexual union with her master. She quite possibly was the girl on the auction block "*pleading in a voice like my mother's as she stood before a group of slaveowners who bid for her naked body* ." In his identification of his own mother with the slave girl the narrator acknowledges his link to the legacy of slavery. As he questions the woman it becomes apparent that the descent into the music is more than a journey into the African American past; it is a journey to the heart of what America is all about. The tale of miscegenation between the black female slave and the white master, like jazz with its combination of African and European musical elements that forged a new and unique musical form, is a fitting metaphor for the American experience. America is the product of the sometimes voluntary, sometimes involuntary mixing of different peoples. As Ellison declares in "What America Would Be Like Without Blacks" (1970): "Materially, psychologically, and culturally, part of the nation's heritage is Negro American, and whatever it becomes will be shaped in part by the Negro's presence. Which is fortunate, for today it is the black American who puts pressure upon the nation to live up to its ideals" (111). The old woman speaks of her love/hate relationship with her master: "*'I laughs too, but I moans too. He promised to set us free but he never could bring hisself to do it'* " (11). Certainly her experience mirrors America's inability to keep its promise of freedom and equality. Although she loved this master who fathered her sons, she poisoned him because she loves *"Freedom"* more. The narrator questions her about the nature of this freedom and she becomes perplexed and starts to cry. One of her sons attacks the narrator and chases him off: *"'Git outa here and stay, and next time you got questions like that, ask yourself'"* (12). Once again the Invisible Man is told that what he is searching for must come from within. He emerges from the musical depths to the sound of a trumpet and hears Armstrong reiterate his musical question:

> *What did I do*
> *To be so black*
> *And blue?*

And with the conclusion of his Prologue the Invisible Man attempts to answer this question; he begins to narrate the experiences that led him to his notions of invisibility and boomeranging. He has found his ultimate role model in Louis Armstrong and can now can create *his own* "autobiographical chronicle of personal catastrophe expressed lyrically." Through the writing of his story, putting "invisibility down in black and white," the Invisible Man shows that he has found the ability to transcend that is inherent in the blues process.[60] While he emulates the processes of the oral tradition, the Invisible Man also recognizes that as a "talker" he is "without substance, a disembodied voice." He understands the need to give a form to his "black and blue" invisibility: "So why do I write, torturing myself to put it down? Because in spite of myself I've learned some things. Without the possibility of action, all knowledge comes to one labeled 'file and forget,' and I can neither file nor forget" (579). In order to obtain power African Americans must keep their own records in order to subvert "those lies his keepers keep their power by."

In the Epilogue the Invisible Man has his final musical encounter when he considers the line "'Open the window and let the foul air out'" from Armstrong's recording of the Jelly Roll Morton composition "Buddy Bolden's Blues." The reappearance of the jazz man to close the frame around the narrative serves as a confirmation of the lessons the narrator has learned about himself and the way the world moves. Having achieved a transcendence over his "hard times" the narrator realizes that the blues process must go on: "Thus, having tried to give pattern to the chaos which lives within the pattern of your certainties, I must come out, I must emerge" (580-81). However, the pain, the absurdity, the confusion that he knows is awaiting him make the narrator hesitant to leave his hibernation; the narrator does not want to deal with the "foul air." But ultimately the lessons that he has learned during his blues narrative enable him to understand that dealing with the contradictions in life is exactly what makes Armstrong's artistry possible: "Of course Louie was kidding, *he* wouldn't have thrown old

Bad Air out, because it would have broken up the music and the dance, when it was the good music that came from the bell of old Bad Air's horn that counted. Old Bad Air is still around with his music and his dancing and his diversity, and I'll be around with mine" (581). The narrator can now act; he can return to the world because he knows "imagination" is always available as a response to "chaos." Like all the African American music that he encounters throughout *Invisible Man*, Armstrong's jazz variations on the blues provide the narrator (and Ellison) with a paradigm for the representation of a world of "infinite possibility."[61]

Notes for Chapter Three

1. See Eileen Southern, *The Music of Black Americans* for an overview of blues styles and their historical evolution.

2. Johnson's complete recordings, a detailed biography and critical evaluation are available on the Columbia CD *The Complete Recordings* (C2K 46222.)

3. The interview with Young was conducted in Paris in 1959 by Francois Postif. The tape has been circulated among fans and researchers and has never been released officially.

4. For detailed descriptions of the stylistic and historical development of gospel see Southern and Lawrence W. Levine's *Black Culture and Black Consciousness*. Background for this section also came from a three-part series written by the author for *Gambit* newspaper in New Orleans in April and May of 1984.

5. This attitude is exemplified by Sandy Rodgers's Aunt Tempy in Hughes' s *Not Without Laughter*. See Chapter 2 above.

6. As Lawrence Levine asserts: "Musically, they reached back to the traditions of the slave past and out to the rhythms of the secular black musical world around them. They brought into the church not only the sounds of ragtime, blues, and jazz but also the instruments. They accompanied the singing which played a central role in their services with drums, tambourines, triangles, guitars, double basses, saxophones, trumpets, trombones, and whatever else seemed musically appropriate" (180).

7. Quoted in Levine, page 183.

8. Hurston's unpublished manuscript is located in W.P.A. Florida file housed in Washington, D.C. in the Library of Congress.

9. Levine has pointed out that the focus of gospel lyrics is "otherworldly" and features a "total dependence on God," usually substituting Jesus for the Hebrew figures, such as Moses, David and Daniel, who dominated the imagery of the spirituals. These songs, that were composed rather than produced by a folk process, often featured "positive thinking" catch phrases from "American popular culture": "The literacy, the education, the conditions of the outside world had brought with them a cosmology more familiar to modern Western culture" (175-77).

10. Quoted in Levine, page 183.

11. As Michel Fabre states in his introduction to "Blueprint": "Although Wright's attitude toward the Communists greatly varied in later years his attitude throughout his life never disowned one of the

central points of this essay: 'Negro writers must accept the nationalist implications of their lives, but a nationalistic spirit in Negro writing means a nationalism carrying the highest possible pitch of social consciousness. It means a nationalism that is aware of its origins, its limitations, that is aware of the dangers of its position.'"

12. The Wright/Hurston quotations appear in Robert Hemenway's *Zora Neale Hurston: A Literary Biography*. The original sources were as follows: Hurston's review of *Uncle Tom's Children* was published as "Stories of Conflict "in the *Saturday Review* (4/2/38); Wright's comments on *Their Eyes Were Watching God* were published as "Between Laughter and Tears" in *New Masses* (10/5/37).

13. Bernard Bell asserts: "Wright's unqualified rejection of the validity of black folk culture as a way of maintaining or changing arrangements of status, power, and identity in a hostile environment is intellectually, politically, and morally untenable for many" (165).

14. Albert Murray states: "As an actual phenomenon of crucial historical significance the old steam-driven railroad train with its heroic beat, its ceremonial bell, and heraldic as well as narrative whistle goes all the way back not only to the legendary times of John Henry and the steel-driving times that were the heyday of nationwide railroad construction, but also to the ante-bellum period of the mostly metaphorical Underground Railroad that the Fugitive Slaves took from the House of Bondage to the Promised Land Freedom" (*Stomping* 123-24).

15. A variation on this lullaby is featured on the Library of Congress recording *Afro-American Folk Music from Tate and Panola Counties, Mississippi* (AFS L67). Performed by Mary Mabeary, the recorded version has the mother as the parent who will return to soothe the child.

16. While the representation of music may have played a limited role in Wright's foremost fictional efforts the language with which he constructs his prose has been pointed to as a manifestation of black folk elements. As Edward A. Watson has asserted concerning blues language in *Native Son*: "It seems that Wright achieved a subtle yet powerful imaginative success through Bessie Mears, Bigger's girl, whose speech and life-style embodies in no simple way the spirit of the *blues* " (65). He likens Bessie's language to the "tradition of Ma Rainey and Bessie Smith" as her speeches emphasize "the elements of fear, pain and brutality of the earlier blues. . . . Bessie's blues is a poignant reminder of the suffering woman caught up in uncontrollable destructive forces" (66). Both Ellison in "Richard Wright's Blues" (*Shadow and Act*) and Robert B. Steptoe in "Richard Wright & the

Afro-American Literary Tradition" (*Chant of Saints*) discuss Wright's autobiography *Black Boy* as employing blues language and featuring blues incidents.

17. Benjamin Filene has stated, "The image of Leadbelly as popular spokesman attracted Popular Front activists eager to give their left-wing political agenda the flavor of the common people . . . Leadbelly became a regular performer at political meetings and events, and came to be seen, along with Woody Guthrie, as the consummate folk artist" (611). For a detailed account of how the Lomaxes manipulated Leadbelly's career as they constructed a "folk music scene" see Filene's "'Our Singing Country': John and Alan Lomax, Leadbelly, and the Construction of an American Past" in *American Quarterly*, Vol. 43, No. 4 (Dec 1991) (602-24).

18. Filene asserts: "The Lomaxes' emphasis on Leadbelly's "otherness" seems to have been quite intentional . . . John Lomax reflected that "[Leadbelly's] criminal record was securing a hearing for a Negro musician," and that "the terms 'bad nigger' only added to his attraction" (611).

19. Wright comments further on Naturalistic writers in *Black Boy* (274).

20. In *Interviews with Black Writers* by John O'Brien Petry denies any affiliation with Naturalism or any other "school" of writing. She states, "To be absolutely honest about it, it really doesn't interest me" (160).

21. For a thorough and even-handed biographical account and critical evaluation of Holiday see Robert O'Meally's *Lady Day: The Many Faces of Billie Holiday*.

22. According to O'Meally, Holiday had very little to do with the composition of *Lady Sings the Blues*. The "autobiography" was assembled from newspaper clippings, promotional material and old interviews by journalist William Dufty. However, the two quotations cited here are characteristic of Holiday's thoughts on the subjects.

23. The interview was recorded for television the week of Holiday's Nov. 10, 1956 Carnegie Hall concert and the audio portion was released on the Giants of Jazz LP - 1001, *I Wonder Where Our Love Has Gone*.

24. As Gayl Jones asserts in *Liberating Voices*: "the story line achieves flexibility and intricacy from the musical African American oral traditions of jazz and blues" (90). Jones finds that "many black writers see music's potential for modifying the European American fictional forms" and she sees "Solo on the Drums" as an attempt to "bring black musical presence into writing" (92). In the Glossary to

Liberating Voices Jones gives detailed definitions of such terms as "blues," "blues language," and "jazz" in terms of how they influence the structure and composition of African American literature.

25. As Gayl Jones explains: "The author gives an inkling of the problem, tells us there has been a transformation. She introduces the theme, welds the musical procedure to the narrative, and as the story progresses the initial situation is repeated, its contexts amplified, its meaning solved or explored through jazz solos and blues-speech interpolations" (93).

26. The song appears on the Alligator album 4701, *Hound Dog Taylor and the House Rockers (1973).*

27. See above Chapter 2, footnote 20.

28. Gayl Jones suggests that "The drumming has functioned as a kind of catharsis, a purgation ritual. Through his music, Kid Jones has done something, said something. He has 'killed' the marquis effectively in a musical ritual, so he won't have to do it in the world; the central confrontations have been transfigured" (97).

29. The title "Many Thousands Gone" is drawn from the spiritual by the same name (it is alternately called "No More Auction Block"). According to John Bauldie in the liner notes to Bob Dylan's *Bootleg Series: Volumes 1-3* the song "originated in Canada and was sung by Negroes who fled there after Britain abolished slavery in . . . 1833." Dylan recorded the song in 1962 and it was also recorded by Odetta at her 1960 Carnegie Hall concert. Ironically, Baldwin uses a spiritual that is overt in its protest sentiments for the title of an essay attacking protest masking as art.

30. African American musicians appear in the following works of fiction by Baldwin: Gospel music provides the backdrop for John's religious conversion in *Go Tell It on the Mountain* (1952); Rufus, in the first Book of *Another Country* (1962), is a jazz drummer; and Arthur Montana, the main character in *Just Above My Head* (1978), is a gospel singer. "Sonny's Blues" was written in 1948 but was not published until 1957 in *Partisan Review*; it was included in the 1965 collection *Going To Meet the Man.*

31. The technical information on the bebop style was found in Leonard Feather's *Inside Jazz.*

32. In "Blues for Mister Baldwin" Joseph Featherstone finds that the narrator's description of the performance is a "problem of language" because Baldwin fails in "sticking to any one tone." He feels that it is Baldwin's voice being intrusive in the narrative.

33. See Isaiah 51:17-23

34. In "Words and Music: Narrative Ambiguity in Sonny's Blues" by Keith E. Byerman the possibility that Sonny is voluntarily drinking from the cup as a sacrifice for his people is overlooked. Byerman suggests the following possibilities: the narrator is easing Sonny's suffering through his "willingness to be involved in his life; since there is no Biblical reference to the cup "remaining," only being "given" or "taken away", Sonny will either "continue to suffer" or return to "a state of grace" (202).

35. As Baldwin's career progressed he ironically moved closer and closer to Wright in terms of producing literature that clearly took the "protest" approach. As Albert Murray explains in *The Omni-Americans*: "He has relied more and more on the abstract categories of social research and less and less on the poetic insights of the creative artist" (148)

36. The details of Waters's biography were found in Paul Oliver's *The Story of the Blues*; Giles Oakely's *The Devil's Music*; and Jeff Tilton's *Down Home Blues Lyrics*.

37. The line comes from his composition "Mannish Boy."

38. O' Meally calls this aspect of Ellison's craft "his belief in the transcendent value of artistic technique" (38).

39. But as O' Meally warns, "No one formula . . . can explain this capacious novel." O'Meally goes on to cite both "the symbolist tradition of Melville and Hawthorne" and "the vernacular school of Mark Twain and Hemingway" as major influences on *Invisible Man. (Craft* 78).

40. In his essay "The Revolutionary Tradition in Afro-America Literature" Amiri Baraka charges: "Ralph Ellison's *Invisible Man* was the classic work of the fifties in restating and shifting the direction of Afro-American literature. The work puts down both nationalism and Marxism, and opts for *individualism.* This ideological content couched in the purrs of an obviously elegant technique was important in trying to steer Afro-American literature away from protest, away from the revolutionary concerns of the 1930s and early 1940s, and this primarily is the reason this work and its author are so valued by the literary and academic establishments in this country" (320).

41. A literary feud erupted over this issue after Baldwin published the essays on Wright that are discussed earlier in this chapter. Critic Irving Howe championed Wright's position in an essay called "Black Boys and Native Sons, "which also drew Ellison into the fray prompting his essay "The World and the Jug."

42. Robert O'Meally defines Ellison's use of folklore as follows: "Folklore is a dynamic, current process of speaking and singing in certain circumstances. Afro-American folklore-sermons, tales, games,

jokes, boasts, toasts, blues, spirituals-is a rich source for the writer. Here the values, styles, and character types of black American life and culture are preserved and reflected in highly energized, often very eloquent language" (*Craft* 2).

43. C.W. Bigsby asserts in "Improvising America: Ralph Ellison and the Paradox of Form" that jazz functions as a paradigm for Ellison in the following ways: "In terms of writing this tended to be translated into an instructive existentialism, at the level of theme, a picaresque narrative drive, and a prose style that would prove as fluid and flexible, and yet as controlled and subject to the harmonies of character and story, as the jazz musician is free and yet responsive to the necessities of rhythm and mood. In terms of social process it became a description of the means whereby diverse elements are harmonized" (177).

44. In "Ralph Waldo Ellison: Anthropology, Modernism and Jazz" Berndt Ostendorf comments on the function of jazz as a model in challenging the artistic status quo and the relationship of art and protest in Ellison's work.

45. David L. Vanderwerken's "Focusing on the Prologue and the Epilogue" identifies these dualistic images in the Prologue as the key to his approach to teaching the novel.

46. In *The Omni-Americans* Albert Murray suggests that Ellison's commentary on *Black Boy* goes "far beyond the book itself" (161) and that in *Invisible Man* "the possibilities he had talked about in "Richard Wright's Blues" were demonstrated most convincingly" (167)

47. Albert Murray has asserted: "*Invisible Man* was *par excellence* the literary extension of the blues. It was as if Ellison had taken an everyday twelve bar blues tune (by a man from down South sitting in a manhole in New York singing and signifying about how he got there) and scored it for full orchestra" (Murray's italics) (*Omni* 167).

48. George E. Kent's "Ralph Ellison and Afro-American Folk and Cultural Tradition" was one of the first essays to examine the influence of "folk" characters on the Invisible Man.

49. See O'Meally's *The Craft of Ralph Ellison*, Chapter 5 & Pancho Savery's "Not like an arrow, but a boomerang": Ellison's Existential Blues." Both O'Meally and Pancho Savery have analyzed *Invisible Man* in terms of the effects of contact with African American music on the narrator's process of self-definition.

50. Savery says that Trueblood is an "existential hero" who "is in control of what happens because he is in touch with his folk past and therefore knows who he is. He is nobody but himself, while the narrator is nobody but what others have created" (69). O'Meally finds that Trueblood's blues "give eloquent and cathartic expression to his absurd

situation (pointed out by some critics as an oedipal as well as an existential crisis)" (86). Houston Baker's "To Move without Moving: Creativity and Commerce in Ralph Ellison's Trueblood Episode" in *Blues, Ideology* examines the episode in terms of the relation between Ellison's "critical and creative practices and "what might be called the public and private commerce of black art in America" (175).

51. Giles Oakley asserts concerning the real-life Wheatstraw: "Everything comes back to the central idea of the man who has survived every kind of set-back and pain in this world . . . he surfaces up with a careless jaunt to his stride, snapping his fingers at the fates, showing humility to no man" (188). Oakley's description of the self-image Wheatstraw projected makes it clear why Ellison would use him as a model for a folk personage who will attempt to instruct the Invisible Man in the blues sensibility.

52. Savery comments on the Wheatstraw scene that "his first blues encounter in New York is with an exemplar of the city, rather than country, blues" (70). O'Meally asserts that Wheatstraw reminds the narrator that the "southern black folk experience must not be disgarded in the North" and that the narrator "senses not only a complex artistry at work in the blues, but a previously unnoticed degree of personal affirmation" (87-88).

53. Sterling Brown's poem "Ma Rainey" centers around a fictional performance of "Backwater Blues." Rainey assumes the role of communal leader who draws people from miles around because of her charismatic ability to "jes' catch hold of us, somekindaway" (*Collected* 62-63).

54. Savery considers that Mary Rambo's remark about the coffee grounds "conveys the ambiguity or dialectic of the blues . . . more than any other passage in the novel" (71). O'Meally finds that "Bessie's blues sung by Mary Rambo remind the Invisible Man of his responsibility as a black-youth-of-promise to relieve his people's suffering" (89).

55. O'Meally explains that "the many subtle references to sacred folk music serve to enrich the weave of the novel's prose . . . As with the blues, the hero starts out ashamed of the 'primitive' sacred forms and is not freed of his illusions until he recognizes their beauty and wisdom and their value as a bridge to the past" (92).

56. O'Meally asserts that the church song and Tarp's words point out that "Clearly the solution to the problem of who sent the note does lie in the past" and "warns that history repeats" (96).

57. The spiritual at Clifton's funeral is the same song after which Baldwin entitled his essay; see note 29 above. Savery finds in this

performance "that there is and was a tradition for Clifton to fall back on" but the narrator "fails to grasp the implications because he "remains with the Brotherhood" (73). In contrast, O'Meally says that with the song the narrator becomes "fully conscious of the transcendent value of black sacred folk music" (96).

58. See Gates' *The Signifying Monkey* where he discusses how Ellison parodies "Wright's literary structures through repetition and difference" (106).

59. O'Meally asserts that the narrator's doubts are not Ellison's, "the blues . . . do express the complexity of the American scene with special effectiveness" (90).

60. Savery looks upon Armstrong as "the hero of the novel. He is both the first and the last of the narrator's blues visitors" (68). O'Meally finds that in the Prologue "Ellison indicates that by tuning into the most profound meanings of the blues one is put in touch with certain fundamental aspects of Afro-American history and culture." He also suggests Armstrong states the theme of the novel with the line from the Waller song (85-86).

61. Savery feels that Armstrong's return in the Epilogue makes "the novel come full circle (or boomerang)" and that the narrator's comments on Armstrong and the line demonstrate "that the narrator has learned not only to live but to relish the contradiction and ambiguity of life" (74). O'Meally says the line from "Buddy Bolden's Blues" allows the narrator to articulate his decision to "emerge . . . to confront all aspects of his experience" (92).

IV
"The Length of the Music
Was the Only Form"

"I want to say more on my horn than I ever could in ordinary speech."
                    - Eric Dolphy

"People get ready,
There's a train comin'.
Don't need no ticket,
Just get on board."
                    - Curtis Mayfield

"You can be as analytical as you want about what somebody has played, but it's the players who count in the end."
                    - Oscar Peterson

"Tell me sister, how do you feel?
Tell me my brother, brother,
brother, how do you feel?
Do you feel like dancin'?
Get up and let's start dancin'.
Start gettin' the spirit,
The spirit in the dark."
                    - Aretha Franklin

"Seeing is believing and hearing is a bitch."
                    - Lester Young

"Deep in my heart I do believe
We shall overcome someday."
                    - Freedom Song

"There's somebody coming right now and they'll take this music further. They'll expound on it. This music is as old as the hills and it always has been here and always will be. Yeah, I know that's true."
                    - Abbey Lincoln

1.
"THERE MUST BE SOME PEOPLE
WHO LIVED FOR MUSIC":
MARGARET WALKER &
WILLIAM MELVIN KELLEY

During the early years of the 1960s the conviction that African Americans could transcend the limitations of racism through communal effort was perhaps most dramatically expressed in the "freedom songs," such as "Ain't Gonna Let Nobody Turn Me Around," "Oh, Freedom," "We Shall Not Be Moved," and most prominently "We Shall Overcome." The singing of these songs by the participants in boycotts, marches, sit-ins and rallies became emblematic of the civil rights movement's determination to break down the barriers which had denied African Americans their rights as American citizens.

Once again African American culture had produced a musical form that would allow individuals to join together to express both their refusal to submit and the faith that change was on its way. In *Parting the Waters* Taylor Branch describes how three SNCC (Student Nonviolent Coordinating Committee) members, Cordell Reagon, Rutha Harris and Bernice Johnson,[1] came to understand the powerful role the freedom songs could play in drawing people into the civil rights movement. The trio brought their freedom songs to a meeting at the Mount Zion Baptist Church in Albany, Georgia and performed without keyboard accompaniment: "The harmonies and intensities of naked voices became a trademark of the Albany Movement. All sounds, from the soaring gospel descants of the soprano soloists to the thunderous hand-clapping of the congregation, were created by human flesh. The songs harked back to the moods of the slavery spirituals." The civil rights activists found that through unaccompanied performances they could encourage people to express sentiments that normally would have been repressed by Southern racism: "The spirit of the songs could sweep up the crowd, and the young leaders realized that through the songs they could induce humble people to say and feel things that otherwise were beyond them. It amazed them to see people who had inched tentatively into the church take up the verse in full voice, setting themselves against feared authority" (532).

Many of the freedom songs were spirituals or gospel tunes that had emerged directly from the African American folk tradition. The performance of these songs featured the cornerstone characteristics of black music in America: the call and response pattern, polyrhythmic accompaniment, and improvisation. "We Shall Overcome" was the freedom song that most poignantly captured the spirit of the uncompromising determination of the civil rights movement. It became a kind of unofficial anthem and was given widespread recognition when it was referred to in a nationally televised address before Congress by President Lyndon B. Johnson in March of 1965.[2] Although its origins are somewhat obscure, the song's opening and closing phrases, according to Eileen Southern, "point back to the old spiritual[3] *No More Auction Block for Me* —indeed, Martin Luther King, among others, commonly referred to *We Shall Overcome* as a spiritual in his speeches and sermons, obviously because of its strong resemblances to the nineteenth-century slave song" (547). Southern also indicates that the text of the song may have been derived from the "gospel" song "I'll Overcome Some Day" written by Charles Tindley in 1900.[4] While "We Shall Overcome" seems to have evolved into its present form through the 1940s and '50s, its roots reach deep into the African American folk tradition in terms of its origin, content and purpose.

The freedom songs' return to the roots of black folk culture to produce an expressive form critiquing America's racial situation is mirrored in one of the first African American historical novels, Margaret Walker's *Jubilee* (1966). An epic tale that covers the antebellum, Civil War and Reconstruction years, *Jubilee* is a realistic rebuttal to the romanticized stereotypes which *Gone With the Wind* has ingrained in American popular culture's conception of history.[5] Based on the stories of her great-grandmother and great-grandfather that were told to her by her maternal grandmother, Walker chronicles the lives of the mulatto slave woman Vyry Ware Brown and the freeman Randall Ware.

Jubilee is a genuine return to the roots of the African American experience aimed at telling the side of the story that had been heretofore ignored in "official histories." Walker's sources include her grandmother's recollections from family oral history, African American folk materials, slave narratives, documents and formal historical studies.[6] In the essay "How I Wrote *Jubilee* " (1972) Walker divides the extensive research material on Civil War history that she consulted into three categories: the southern white, the northern white, and the Negro viewpoints. She states: "Faced with these three conflicting viewpoints, a novelist in the role of social historian finds it difficult to maintain an 'objective' point of view. Obviously she must choose one or the other—or create her own" (53). Walker creates her own perspective by employing a third person narrator who integrates historical fact, folklore, and a sympathetic kinship with Vyry to deliver a heretofore neglected fictional representation of this momentous American pageant.

Folklore is the most influential element used by Walker in forging her "own" point of view of the events portrayed in *Jubilee*. She explains that it was intended to be "a folk novel based on folk material: folk sayings, folk belief, folkways" ("How" 62). It is through folk materials that Walker is able to invest her black characters with distinctiveness and verisimilitude; it reveals their resourcefulness in the face of a seemingly impossible situation and their conception of themselves as human beings as their oppressors attempt to annihilate all vestiges of dignity and self-worth.

Music is the predominant element from the African American folk tradition in *Jubilee*. The word Jubilee was used by the slaves in the spirituals to exclaim the joy (jubilance?) they would feel upon gaining their emancipation and is found in many of these nineteenth-century "freedom songs."[7] The epigraph to the novel is the lyrics to a "Traditional Negro Spiritual" called "Jubilee":

> We are climbing Jacob's ladder,
> We are climbing Jacob's ladder,
> We are climbing Jacob's ladder,
>   for the year of Jubilee!

> Every round goes higher, higher,
> Every round goes higher, higher,
> Every round goes higher, higher,
>   to the year of Jubilee.

> Do you think I'll make a soldier?
> Do you think I'll make a soldier?
> Do you think I'll make a soldier?
>   in the year of Jubilee?

Thus, *Jubilee* (the novel) is modeled on "Jubilee" (the song) in that it is an expression of the impulse to celebrate the movement toward the acquisition of freedom. Just as the novel takes its title and its overall thematic momentum from traditional music, each of the fifty-eight chapters begins with an epigraph that is taken from the lyrics to a song (occasionally Walker uses a folk saying or rhyme instead of lyrics). It would seem that her source for many of these songs is a collection by Oliver Ditson which was published in the late nineteenth century. She writes of discovering the songbook at a professor's house in Iowa: "This collection contained Civil War songs, Negro folk songs—including spirituals, work songs, popular tunes, and even minstrel songs and favorites I had heard my grandmother say that my great-grandmother had sung" ("How" 60). From time to time the epigraphs provide a title for the chapters and are usually a thematic anticipation of the events, ideas or sentiments that appear in them. Walker's use of musical epigraphs links her novel to the oral folk tradition of African American culture, but it also links her to one of the foundational works of the African American literary tradition, W.E.B. DuBois's *The Souls of Black Folk*. DuBois begins each chapter in his book with a musical transcription from a spiritual. In the final chapter called "Of the Sorrow Songs" he includes a brief explication of how the sentiment expressed in a particular song is thematically related to the chapter it introduces.

Jubilee presents the history of the individual characters as well as an alternative history of the nation as it is embedded in music. An examination of the relationship between various chapters and their musical epigraphs exemplifies this alternative history. The epigraph for chapter 7 is taken from the spiritual "No More Auction Block for Me, " and in the chapter Vyry's beloved Aunt Sally is put on the auction block and sold away. But the lyrics of the song are a refusal to submit so that the chapter also relates the unrest the masters feel because a white woman and her daughter were poisoned by two female slaves. Other acts of subversion by slaves are also mentioned. When Vyry meets the free-born black man Randall Ware for the first time and he plants a seed of hope by promising to buy her freedom. Walker subverts the notion propagated by slave owners that slaves were content with plantation life. The lyrics to "Dixie" open chapter 24, entitled "They made us sing 'Dixie,'" and the chapter delineates the Confederacy's forcing of slaves to work for the war effort. However, the upbeat mood of Southern patriotism featured in "Dixie" is undercut by the revelation that "many of their workers either got away, were mutilated, or shot in the attempt to escape," and the chapter concludes with the text from a reward notice for captured runaways (211-12). Chapter 35, entitled "We'll hang Jeff Davis from a sour apple tree," features an extended epigraph from a slave song that illustrates the slaves' clear understanding of the current political and military situation as well as the keen sense of irony that marks African American folk humor:

> Say, darkeys hab you seen de marster
> Wid de muffstash on his face
> Go long de road sometimes dis mornin
> Like he gwine to leab de place?
> He seen a smoke, way up de ribber
> Whar de Linkum gunboats lay.

> He took hi hat, an lef berry sudden
> An I spec he's run away.
> De marster run? Ha, ha!
> De darkey stay? Ho, ho!
> Hit must be now de kingdom coming
> And de year of jubilo! (268)

The lyrics to "Jump Jim Crow" serve as the epigraph to chapter 48, "Ku Klux Klan don't like no Koons," and the ensuing action includes the brutal beating of Randall Ware and murder of the journeyman who works in his blacksmith shop. The white townspeople are intent on forcing Ware out of Reconstruction politics and off his property, despite the fact that as a freeman he had legally owned it prior to the war. The "Jim Crow" reference in the epigraph is emblematic of the terrorist tactics used by white supremacist groups like the KKK. Walker's use of epigraphs demonstrates the importance of music in her conception of *Jubilee* as a "folk novel."

Music is also represented in *Jubilee* as an integral part of the lives of the African American characters, reflecting Walker's careful study of plantation life as it is portrayed in the slave narratives. They sing in response to the events in their day-to-day lives. They sing as part of their work routine. They sing for entertainment, for themselves and their white masters. Their songs testify to an unshakable faith in an otherworldly reward and also function as vehicles to mask discontent and plans for escape. The epigraphs also provide a key as to how music fits into the plot of the novel. "Swing low, sweet chariot, / Coming for to carry me home . . . " is the epigraph for the first chapter, which is entitled "Death is a mystery that only the squinch owl knows." In black folklore the sound of the screech owl is a harbinger of death; this connects to the epigraph's chariot that carries a person home to eternal rest. The chapter opens with two slaves discussing the superstition after hearing an owl, and the ensuing action focuses on the death watch over Vyry's mother Hetta. When her death is made known to the slave community on this plantation, Brother Ezekiel, who is their preacher and communal leader breaks into "the death chant":

> Soon one morning,
> Death come knocking at my door.
> Soon one morning,
> Death come knocking at my door.
> Soon one morning,
> Death come knocking at my door.
> Oh, my Lord,

Oh, my Lord,
What shall I do? (17)

The interplay of the quotation from the spiritual, the folk superstition and the representation of Brother Ezekiel's musical performance are woven into the fabric of Walker's plot, instilling *Jubilee* with a spirit of authenticity and testifying to the complex culture African American forged despite the dehumanizing effects of subjugation.

As the central character in the novel Vyry is the communal representative of the black women and men who triumphed over the ordeal of life in the nineteenth-century American South.[8] Appropriately, she is a singer with a perceptive understanding of the ability of music from the black folk tradition to function both as a survival mechanism and a subversive weapon. As a teenager she relishes attending the secret "Big Meeting Nights" so she can join in the singing and listen to Brother Ezekiel preach: "There was wonderful and high-spirited singing, such as Vyry remembered long afterward, and she tried to remember and sing the songs they sang . . . ." She is also drawn to Brother Ezekiel's sermons on the Old Testament, particularly "Moses and the story of his leading the children of Israel out of Egypt" (44-45). Although at first "Vyry did not understand that these meetings served a double purpose," (46-47) she is being initiated into the community and begins to apply the folk expressions to the situation of herself and her people.

One of the most important links in Walker's reconstruction of her personal and racial heritage is the passing along of the African American music-making process. After her mother's death Vyry is raised by Aunt Sally, and she learns an important lesson about singing from the older woman. When Vyry hears Aunt Sally singing while working in the kitchen she knows it is "a true sign of trouble." Although Aunt Sally loves to sing, she only does so in the Big House when she is "deeply troubled," and everyone, including "Big Missy," knows they must leave her alone. Vyry comes to an understanding of how music helps Aunt Sally deal with life: "Vyry always loved to hear her sing, but the songs often puzzled her before she grew to associate them with Aunt Sally's mood and mind, her anger and resentment that she could voice in no other way" (71). After Vyry has her first child she sinks into despair because Ware is unsuccessful in attempting to purchase her freedom. Her one source of solace comes through emulating Aunt Sally's musical example:

Only evil could happen, and more evil, and it was this evil
that peopled all her fear. Nevertheless she began to

unburden herself as Aunt Sally had by lifting her voice in
song. She was surprised to hear the dark rich voice of
Aunt Sally come out of her throat. She was surprised to
discover how much she enjoyed singing and what a relief
she felt when she sang. The days always went faster
singing. (150-51)

After the war as Vyry runs the decimated plantation she passes the
musical tradition along to her children: "In the twilight when the
smoldering ashes were cooled by the dusk and the starry night and the
glistening dew, they sat out on Marse John's veranda and sang, the
children and Vyry and Innis Brown with Miss Lillian rocking, apart
from all around her. The summer then was an idyll, a season of peace,
when all the agitation of the violent world around them seemed
suspended, and they felt secure" (297). Singing together not only
provides Vyry and her family with entertainment and relief from their
physical work but helps them to develop a sense of community. The
music acts as a buffer in a world turned upside down and imbues them
with hope because it links them to the endurance of Aunt Sally and past
generations.

African American generations continue to pass along the musical
heritage that is depicted in *Jubilee*. Walker herself was the recipient of
this heritage through her grandmother's telling her of the songs she had
learned from her mother—fictionalized as Vyry. And this musical
legacy played a large role in the shaping of the novel. Like Vyry, who
follows her creative impulses and draws strength from the African
American folk tradition during a time of great crisis for her people,
Walker produced a novel for the tumultuous years of the 1960s that
looked to the past to produce a work of fiction that could function as a
model for communal perseverance.

Another 1960s African American novel that explores a return to
the roots of folk culture in response to racism is William Melvin
Kelley's *A Drop of Patience* (1965).[9] The novel chronicles the career of
the Ludlow Washington, a blind jazz musician, from his early
experiences near the Gulf Coast through his ascent to the top of New
York's modern jazz scene during the years after World War II. After a
humiliating mental breakdown resulting from his realization of his
position as a black man in America, Ludlow rejects the belated
recognition of the entertainment industry and resolves to find a small
black church where the congregation will genuinely understand his
music. The pivotal role Ludlow plays in the evolution of the "New
Music" is loosely modeled on the alto saxophonist Charlie Parker and
the development of "bebop." It is never stated what horn Ludlow plays,

and seemingly Kelley omits the name of the specific instrument to attempts to make one-to-one correspondences between the novel's characters and Parker and his contemporaries. Kelley employs a double-voiced narration[10] by allowing Ludlow to tell his own story through brief "INTERVIEW. . . " segments that precede each of the six parts of the novel. These segments are juxtaposed with third-person narrated chapters that amplify the events and ideas presented in the interview quotation. This technique lends authenticity to the narrative because the lion's share of primary sources that make up jazz history comes from such transcribed interviews of jazz artists describing their experiences and explaining their musical approaches.[11] Kelley's use of the interview segments also strengthens the narrative's link to the oral tradition of black folk culture—the source of the jazz that Ludlow creates.

The quotations that comprise these segments may have originated in an interview that Ludlow gives in the final part of the third person narrative. After seven years of scuffling to survive because he has been ostracized for his breakdown, a black college student named Harriet Lewis interviews Ludlow for her school newspaper. The love and care that she eventually gives him reconnects Ludlow with his roots in the black community and he once again takes control of his life. The interview is important to Ludlow because it boosts his ego: "Surprised and a little flattered that someone, even a college girl, should still want to interview him, he submitted to her questioning" (212). When Harriet searches the blind man out to read him her article he reacts to the story he has told with surprise: "It was strange to listen to his words being spoken by someone else. When she finished, she asked him if he approved. 'I really sound like that?'" (214).Coming near the end of the narrated portion of his life, the interview allows Ludlow to look back over his experiences and orient the direction he will take in the future.

The protagonist's blindness in *A Drop of Patience* sets up dual influences on his life that intersect on the stage of a downtown New York night club in the act of self-debasement that marks his mental collapse. Living in a world of sound and feeling, Ludlow pours his energy into musical creativity as he develops a masterful technique and an innovative style that has a far reaching influence on the conception of jazz improvisation. The inability to see makes the absurdity of American racism even more pronounced for this man who literally is unable to distinguish black from white.

Ludlow's relationship with the music goes through a series of transitions beginning with his earliest instructions on piano in the home for blind black boys where his father leaves him at age five. Given a horn to learn when he is nine years old, Ludlow recognizes that the

music can at least give him the chance to earn a living. As he says in
the interview segment that opens Part Two: "But I did practice good,
because I could tell music was better than a tin cup on somebody's
corner" (25). At sixteen Ludlow is made the ward of the black band
leader Bud Rodney, who had heard the young musician win the "State
Championship" the previous year. Obligated to perform for Rodney
until his eighteenth birthday, Ludlow aspires to lead his own group
some day but is content with his ability to earn a living. Working
regularly for Rodney in a black night club, Ludlow's attitude toward
music-making changes when the premiere jazz singer of the day, Inez
Cunningham, attends a set. His friend, the trombonist Otis Hardie,
describes her enthusiastic response to Ludlow's solos which surprises
the young horn man: "It had never really occurred to him before that
anyone could be moved by his playing" (37). He begins to recognize
the possibilities that can arise from being a musician: "There must be
some people who lived for music, to play it and hear it played. Perhaps
Inez Cunningham was a person like that. There was no other reason for
her to come to a bar filled with drunks and prostitutes" (38). The singer
lavishes praise on the young horn player and offers him a job touring
with her band, but he refuses because Rodney has a legal hold on him.

With the exception of Ludlow and Hardie, Rodney's band is made
up of older musicians who run through a standard repertoire of popular
jazz and blues tunes. Although Rodney often tries to censure the young
musician, he cannot prevent Ludlow from experimenting with a new
approach to improvisation. Ludlow's innovations follow the pattern
typical of folk-derived African American artistic expression in that he
reaches back into the tradition and bases his new concepts on the
playing of an older pianist named Norman Spencer. As Ludlow
explains in the interview segment from Part Three:

> So I was with Bud Rodney, but after a while I didn't like
> what he was making me play. I mean, I started to really
> listen to some things Norman Spencer was doing on
> piano—like breaking up time a little. He was going boom-
> boom-boom-boom with his left, but the right was going
> boom-da-boom-boom, da-da-boom-da, and like that. Of
> course, he wasn't one of us young boys. It was just his
> way because he was really an old-time player. (67)

Ludlow is ahead of his time in the conception of jazz improvisation that
he develops from listening to Spencer. This is evident during a
performance of an old ballad with Rodney's band. Ludlow is puzzled by
a "happy and warm" feeling he has after taking his solo and realizes this

results from his being able to express memories of his family and life before the blind home. After the solo Rodney reacts with anger, "'What the hell that supposed to be . . . You call that music?'" (73). Ludlow does not understand the pianist's comments and asks Hardie about them at the close of the set: "'The ballad?' Hardie sucked his tongue. 'I don't know. I heard it, man, but I couldn't tell you what you was doing. You wasn't even in time sometimes, you know, like Norman Spencer? Hell man, I can't tell you.' Hardie was perplexed" (73). After Ludlow has left Rodney and made a name for himself touring and recording with Inez Cunningham, the two young musicians are reunited as members of a big band. Hardie compliments Ludlow on the particular effectiveness of his eight-bar solo on a Cunningham record. But Ludlow has grown beyond the singer's format and replies: "'I left because of them God damn little eight-bar solos. They wasn't enough. To play something good, or hear it, you got to have eight choruses.'" Ludlow's need for more space to stretch out as a soloist indicates that he is still expanding his musical horizons, while the trombonist reveals that he has finally come to grasp what Ludlow had been doing on the ballad that night with Rodney's band: "Hardie was timid. 'Them eight bars was pretty anyways. . . . Remember that time back with Rodney when we played that old ballad and you did them things to it and Rodney bawled you out? Them eight bars was just like that'" (130). Hardie tells his friend of the tremendous influence his conception is having on the jazz world; this shocks Ludlow because he had felt that the only thing that separated him from other players was technical facility: "He had known too that he was tired of what music sounded like—heavy and loud— and so at sessions he had suggested to the other men how they might play a certain song. But he had never thought of this as a new style; he was simply trying to get a sound to the music that he liked" (131). Even with the hindsight he has in the interview Ludlow is self-effacing when confronted with the reputation of having invented modern jazz. In the interview segment featured in Part Four he says that the music arose from a collaborative effort at Harlem jam sessions. He once again credits Norman Spencer with helping him define his approach:

> If I did invent it, like they say, I invented it back in New Marsails in Bud Rodney's band, or maybe even before that, in the blind home. Because all my life I been playing what I liked. Take Norman Spencer. He coulda been the one who invented it himself. He was doing new things way back in the twenties. I only listened and played what I liked in him and that was that. I didn't decide one day— blam!—I'd play something new, because I been playing

> pretty much the same since I was thirteen, except now
> maybe I can play a little faster. But that ain't genius.
> That's just practicing. (127)

Although Ludlow consistently downplays his role as an innovator
his attitude toward the role music plays in his life transforms
dramatically from his perception that it "was better than a tin cup on
somebody's corner." Like Charlie Parker, Dizzy Gillespie, Thelonious
Monk, Bud Powell and the other musicians who are credited with the
development of bebop, Ludlow finds that his engagement with the
music is not about making money but rather is about the pursuit of a
creative impulse. Ludlow becomes a musical associate of Norman
Spencer after moving to New York; he looks upon the older musician
as a teacher, not someone he copies but someone who "made him
think." One night Ludlow goes to jam with Spencer at the club in
Harlem, which is the only place where the pianist will perform. Ludlow
is perplexed over what compels him to play music and asks Spencer
why he plays. He refuses to accept the taciturn old man's answer that it
is the only thing he knows how to do, and Spencer replies: "'Some folks
around think we artists, like classical musicians. Maybe we are.'" The
pianist goes on to explain:

> 'Ludlow, there only two reasons why people do things—
> because they want to and because they got to. The only
> time you can do something good is when you want to.
> Now maybe sometimes you can want to do something so
> bad that after a while it's like you got to. But now instead
> of being made to do it by someone else, you making
> yourself do it, and then maybe you an artist. Okay, now
> take you. You could be playing like everybody else and
> then instead of being in O'Gee's band, he'd be in yours.
> For some reason you don't play like no one else. But ain't
> nobody forcing you to be different. So maybe you better
> forget about money because if you really cared about it,
> you'd be playing the way that makes the most money.'
> (137).

Yet, the younger man still has trouble grasping the difference
between being an artist and a paid entertainer, and Spencer reaches
back into the folk responses of the black oral tradition and slips Ludlow
into the dirty dozens: "'Hell, boy, I don't know. Ask your mama!'"
(138). Nevertheless, Ludlow eventually does come to see himself as an
artist and resents the lack of respect he finds in audiences. This is

evidenced as he is leading his own group at a New York club during the celebration of the Allied victory over the Japanese. Ludlow is livid that the partying customers do not even "pretend to listen" (153).

The evening of his discussion with Spencer about the motivation for playing music is also significant because Ludlow is exposed to two different attitudes concerning how blacks should deal with whites. Ludlow's upbringing did little to prepare him for interacting with white people. He was raised in an all black blind home and his tenure with Rodney was in the heart of the black community. His seven years on the road had been with black bands in a segregated country. The night of his talk with Spencer in Harlem Ludlow is shocked when he is told a group of white patrons have entered the club. The scenario of the races finding a meeting ground in the black music club is one that has been represented in African American fiction with, at best, ambiguity. Kelley renders the situation from Spencer's point of view: "'They pushed us all together up here, but they still won't leave us alone. They got the idea they missing something, so they dress up and come here to see. I don't show them nothing'" (138). The white man ("old pasty-faced Charlie") who approaches Spencer and Ludlow is obviously well versed in the music and careers of the two jazz men, but the old pianist holds true to his advice to "don't show them nothing" as he replies through an obsequious minstrel mask, "'Oh, no, boss. Poor old colored jazz music player like me shouldn't never get thanked by no white man, boss. You the boss, boss.'" As the conversation continues Ludlow feels sorry for the white man who is drunk but also sincere in his admiration for their music. The white man invites the jazz men to a party at his house, revealing his unconsciously patronizing attitude: "'You don't have to play if you don't want to . . . but you can if you want to'" (139).[12] When Ludlow tells Spencer the man "didn't seem too bad," the pianist lets out the feelings that he has masked:

> White folks ain't never bad, Ludlow. They just weak. At least the ones we got here is weak. Here they round you up and push you in a slum, all the time telling you how much they love you. You take the Germans. Right now, they rounding up Jews and killing them. But they ain't spouting no shit about loving them. The white folks we got here ain't nearly that strong. You mark my words, don't never depend on no white man for nothing. He ain't strong enough to keep his promises.' (140)

Ludlow says that he will remember the advice and the old man replies, "'Make sure you do.'" These words take on a haunting quality later in the novel when broken faith between a white and Ludlow leads to his breakdown.

On the way downtown to the party Ludlow participates in a conversation with a young tenor saxophonist named Reno Tems that presents him with a completely different perspective on the relationship between blacks and whites. Ludlow tries out his question about the reason for playing music on the younger man:

> 'Because it's the black man's music!' All at once the boy was not at all timid. Ludlow smiled. 'And we got to keep on working at it so everybody in the world'll know the black man created it.'
>
> Ludlow snorted. 'I met some white boys who doing good things.'
>
> 'They just copying us, that's all. We do all the creating. Like you.'
>
> Ludlow winced. 'Listen, you do the playing and forget all this other stuff. When you up there trying to put something together, you ain't got time to think about all that mess!' (142-43)

Ludlow does not seem to accept Reno's expression of black pride and shows that he truly does live in a world of sound; he does not want to be concerned with "all that mess" and judges other musicians by what they play and not by the color of their skin. However, his behavior at the party indicates that he has learned from both Spencer's and Reno's approaches. He dislikes a white Southern woman who he feels is "trying singlehanded to make up for all the South's crimes." He takes his cue from Spencer's trickster strategy and leads her along, fabricating a tale of how the Klan blinded him and killed Reno's father and raped his mother. Ludlow plays on her patronizing guilt, hoping to set his friend up to get "that white ass," by telling her that Reno is "one bitter nigger" who needs "sympathy and help." But Ludlow also meets the host's black maid, and in his interaction with her he exhibits a sense of the black pride of which Reno had spoken. The role of the African American musician as a communal leader is evidenced in the maid's recognizing Ludlow and her familiarity with his music. Ludlow asks how white people live and she replies that "'They either try too hard or not hard enough.'" When she says that her boss tries too hard Ludlow wants to know if he should play when the host asks him. She tells him, "'A little bit for him and a lot for me.'" Later, as they play he thinks of the woman: "Ludlow did not forget that somewhere near the kitchen the maid was standing, probably on tired feet, listening" (148). Ludlow feels a special bond with this black woman, a bond that allows her to have a special understanding of the music he creates. Surrounded by dissipated whites the jazz man keeps this woman in mind because he senses what Reno meant when he declared, "'It's the black man's music!'"

Ludlow is finally free to question his true position as a black man in America after recognition of his musical innovations allows him to focus on the personal side of his life. The creative aspect of Ludlow's life seems to have fallen into place by the end of World War II. He is in demand because of the influence he has had on the development of the music and finds steady work leading his own group: "The New Music, as it was called, had now caught on, and people all over the country wanted to hear it played by those who had done the most to create it" (180). With the achievement of artistic success and financial security Ludlow looks for personal fulfillment. True to his inclination not to judge people by skin color he falls in love with a white woman named Ragan. He misses the warning signs that she is, like Spencer warned him about whites, not strong enough to keep her promises. When she discovers that she is pregnant she refuses to marry Ludlow and abandons him. The betrayal forces Ludlow to question his status as a black man in white-dominated America. While on a break one night at a club Ludlow asks Reno, "'What you think white folks want from us?'" The younger musician replies: "'Most of them want to think we're not dangerous. And that means they don't want us to be human. Because if I learned anything at all in college, it's that everybody's just naturally dangerous'" (198-99). Ludlow asks Reno to lead him to the street and he makes his way to a nearby magic store and purchases a tin of "stage make-up, like they use in minstrel shows. Blackface." He returns to the club, covers his face with the make-up and mounts the bandstand:

> He began to sweat; his head was throbbing steadily now and he had trouble remembering what he planned to do. 'Ain't out here to play music tonight, folks. No sir!' He tried to make himself sound as ignorant as he could. He was imitating the minstrels. 'Going to tell you folks some funny stories and sing some songs.' He waited for laughter; there was less now. 'You understand now? Good. You see, I ain't dangerous. Honest!' Such pleas were against the rules, he knew. He was supposed to perform. On that basis alone, they would decide if he was dangerous. (202)

Ludlow's realization that white America, embodied in Ragan, refuses to accept his humanity triggers a ritual act of self-debasement in which he transforms himself from a creative master into a minstrel buffoon. His minstrel performance in the jazz club, a space where he had thought of himself as an honored celebrant, echoes Brother Tod Clifton's "falling out of history" and putting on a sidewalk Sambo show when he detects the Brotherhood's betrayal of blacks in *Invisible Man*. In an ironic testament to his humanity, Ludlow is completely disarmed by his love for a white woman; he has lost contact with his culture and is unable to adopt either the open defiance of Reno's black pride or the mask of Spencer's trickster strategy. He abandons "the black man's music" because he is "dangerous" when engaged in the act of jazz creation, an act that is inherently subversive of racist preconceptions. And Ludlow's blackface is not Spencer's mask because he fails to separate the mask from the man who is behind it. He does not wear the mask to "get over" on "the man," rather, he actually tries to become a puppet that does not challenge but only entertains the white audience.

Ludlow's reconnection to African American culture comes seven years after his breakdown. Although he earns a hand-to-mouth existence through various gigs, "little dances, rock bands, a couple records," the creative impulse still burns within the horn man. As he states in the interview segment from Part Six: "Hell, I'd been thinking about a lot of things in the hospitals, and I'd been practicing. I was still out front. Only nobody knew it yet. Anyway, I couldn't get much work. No one'd hire any group I'd got together. They was all afraid I'd put on another minstrel show" (207). The spark that ignites Ludlow's spiritual revival comes when Hardie secures his old friend a spot in a jam session at a big jazz concert downtown. Hardie still recognizes Ludlow's importance as an innovator as he recalls helping him from the stage the night of his breakdown: "'Remember I said you couldn't die because I wouldn't know what to play?'" (210). It is at this concert that Harriet interviews the legendary jazz man. The relationship they develop allows Ludlow to get back in touch with his roots—one of the first things she does is bring him to a concert of West African music—and redefine his identity as a black artist. They are both working at a black resort in the mountains when Harriet returns from a trip to New York with a copy of a jazz magazine. She is excited because it contains an article about Ludlow entitled "Why Do We Waste Our Geniuses?"[13] Inspired by Ludlow's improvisations on the recording of the concert jam session, the critic asserts that the jazz man's playing is better than ever. He reviews Ludlow's career and makes a futile attempt to trace him in Harlem:

> *' That was where the trail ended. Disappointed, I returned*
> *home and listened to all of Ludlow Washington's records,*
> *starting with Inez Cunningham, ending with the concert.*
> *The emotion I experienced while listening to these*
> *uniformly brilliant performances was one of admiration,*
> *respect, gratitude and shame—the last because I realized*
> *that I, and all of us who love jazz, had been guilty of a*
> *grave crime. We had wasted, neglected, the only*
> *undisputed genius jazz has produced in the last two*
> *decades; we have allowed him to spend the last seven*
> *years in cheap hotels, playing in bad rock-and-roll bands.*
> *But our neglect, however bad that may be, is not the worst*
> *crime. We have cheated ourselves of the best music we*
> *will probably hear in our lifetime. Now you understand*
> *the title of this essay: 'Why do we waste our geniuses ?"*
> (Kelley's italics) (229)

Despite Harriet's enthusiasm, Ludlow is far from thrilled with the magazine article. Considering that the time frame for these events is during the mid-1950s, the critic is most probably a white man. Perhaps Ludlow thinks that the critic, like the host of the downtown party, is trying too hard. Or the jazz man may have learned to follow Spencer's advice and not trust whites. He may have adopted Reno's perspective and rejects a white man's evaluation of the "black man's music." Nevertheless he does not share Harriet's opinion that the article is an open invitation for him to return to the New York jazz scene in triumph: "He thought of New York as it had been for him seven years before. He remembered himself standing on the stage, under dry heat, playing his best into the face of tinkling glasses, ringing telephones, belling cash registers, screaming waiters, jingling money, booming laughter, and cackling women. Even when he was popular, there had not been much appreciation" (230). He finds it more appealing to play for the dancers at the black summer resort because "a person had to be listening to dance." Ludlow also thinks back to Spencer's descriptions of "'the old Harlem rent parties'" where folks "'was enjoying what you was doing,'" and wonders if "'perhaps Harlem was not New York at all.'" Ludlow explains to Harriet: "'But if I go back and take their money, I got to live like they tell me. You got to be careful who you take money from in this world'" (231). Years before Ludlow had decided that he was not playing for money; he aspired to be an artist to whom people listened. But he has refined his "vision" of his role as a musician. Ludlow wants to play for his own people, a sympathetic audience—like the maid at the downtown party—who can understand what he is expressing in the sounds creates: "There were other, better places to go. He might find that store-front church, or perhaps a church on a dirt road in the South, no more than a shack, with a congregation of twelve or so, without an organ to help their high, shaky voices carry the tunes of their hymns. A place like that would need a good musician" (237). The jazz man has rejected the crass commercialism of the American entertainment industry. He has rejected the white world that can accept him as a paid performer but not as a human being. Ludlow recognizes his role as a ritual leader for his people. He longs to be engaged with the audience, to participate in the call and response of the black music-making process. His rites of passage have led him home to the heart of the African American community.[14]

2.
"THE SOUND BAKED INSIDE THEIR HEADS": AMIRI BARAKA & HENRY DUMAS

The recording of the "Freedom Now Suite" by drummer Max Roach in the summer of 1960 dramatically revealed the ability of music derived from the black folk idiom to produce new and innovative forms which express the tenor of the times for African Americans. Roach's career as a jazz artist personifies the evolutionary nature of the black music heritage in America.[15] In 1942 at the age of seventeen he was playing drums in Charlie Parker's band at Clarke Monroe's Uptown House in Harlem. The young drummer was also attending the legendary after hours jam sessions at Minton's where an inner circle of modern jazz artists was expanding the jazz vocabulary with the innovations that came to be called bebop. He modeled his approach to the drums on Kenny Clarke's ground breaking use of the top cymbal, rather than the bass drum, to keep a steady beat. Roach mastered and expanded this technique and came to be regarded as the definitive bop drumming stylist. During the 1950s Roach led his own group with trumpeter Clifford Brown and pioneered "hard bop," a soulful, driving, blues-inflected bebop derivative that developed as the East Coast answer to the smooth, airy, relaxed "cool" jazz that flourished on the West Coast. By 1960 Roach had become an accomplished composer and arranger, and with the release of "Freedom Now Suite" he made it clear that his music was a forum for an experimental approach to improvisation as well as an expression of African American insistence for revolutionary change in American race relations.

"Freedom Now Suite" anticipated many aspects of African American political, social and historical consciousness that came to the forefront during the 1960s. Songs such as "Driva' Man" and "Freedom Day" examined the roots of the African American experience. The former depicts the brutality of slavery, while the latter celebrates Emancipation. "Driva' Man" is particularly notable because the veteran tenor saxophonist Coleman Hawkins's horn is the male voice that complements vocalist Abbey Lincoln's slave woman persona. Lincoln's dramatization of the lyrics are matched by Hawkins' version of the story contained in his gruff, wailing saxophone improvisation. The presence of this original "voice" of the jazz saxophone interacting with musicians from two succeeding generations illustrates the viability of the jazz tradition. The centerpiece of "Freedom Now Suite" is a composition that Roach originally conceived as a ballet, "Tryptich: Prayer/Protest/Peace." A duet between Roach's drumming and Lincoln's non-verbal vocals, the African American tradition of meaning embedded in sound is perfectly illustrated as the two musicians make an impressionistic journey from mournful plea to railing outrage to tranquil fulfillment. "Tryptich" represents Roach's vision of the African American movement toward genuine freedom. The second half of "Freedom Now Suite" consists of two compositions that signal the resurgence of interest black Americans had in reconnecting with their African heritage. "All Africa" links various manifestations of the African diaspora through the interplay of drums including Roach's African American jazz stylings, Michael (Babatunde) Olatunji's traditional Nigerian drumming and the Afro-Cuban percussion of Ray Mantilla and Tomas du Vall. The piece opens with Lincoln singing Oscar Brown, Jr.'s lyrics which acknowledge the role of music as a cultural conduit in African-derived culture:

> The beat has a rich and magnificent history,
> Full of adventure, excitement and mystery.
> Some of it bitter and some of it sweet,
> But all of it part of the beat, the beat, the beat . . .
> They say it began with a chant and a hum
> And a black hand laid on a native drum.

This is followed by an extended percussion jam over which Lincoln calls a litany of African tribal names and Olatunji responds with a saying related to the issue of freedom from the tribe. The final performance on the album is "Tears for Johannesburg," an instrumental statement linking the struggle of African Americans to acquire equal rights to the battle against apartheid in South Africa. Roach's pan-African perspective broadens the attack on racism to an international level. His music communicates an insistence that piecemeal conciliation is unsatisfactory; conditions that are intolerable to black people worldwide must be amended. "Freedom Now Suite" is a landmark in African American music; it combines artistic virtuosity with political imperative, tradition with innovation, and a sense of history with a vision for the future.

The African American writers who came together to form the Black Arts Movement in the mid-1960s attempted to create works that were informed by many of the same principles that surfaced in the "Freedom Now Suite." The Black Arts Movement's artistic productions were characterized by a political commitment to African American independence and empowerment, an awareness and celebration of the black cultural heritage—including a connection to African roots and an affirmation of the unity of African people throughout the Diaspora. As Amiri Baraka (LeRoi Jones),[16] the most important catalyst for the Black Arts Movement, suggests in the essay "The Revolutionary Tradition in Afro-American Literature" (1984): "Its political line, at its most positive, was that literature must be a weapon of revolutionary struggle, that it must serve the black revolution. And its writers . . . its publications, its community black arts theaters, its manifestos [sic] and activism, were meant as real manifestations of black culture-black art as a weapon of liberation" (321).

Black Arts Movement writers consistently looked to African American music as an aesthetic paradigm for the production of art that would function as a revolutionary weapon.[17] In the essay "Towards a Black Aesthetic" (1968) Hoyt W. Fuller uses black musicians to describe the work of a group of Chicago writers who are moving "toward a definition of a black aesthetic": "The writers are deliberately striving to invest their work with the distinctive styles and rhythms and colors of the ghetto, with those peculiar qualities which, for example characterize the music of a John Coltrane or a Charlie Parker or a Ray Charles" (9). In his "Introduction to Black Aesthetics in Music" (1970) Jimmy Stewart amplifies this sense of Black music-making as a paradigm:

> African philosophy and metaphysics have always been animated by a total vision of life; so we, as legatees of that vision of the world, have manifested that index of our culture in the only approximation we could: in our music. This is observable in a formal sense in the music we have produced in the West, but more significantly in that music's inner dynamic. In the inner workings of our music

has been the ideal paradigm of the understanding of the creative process as a movement *with* existence. (Stewart's italics) (79-80)

Stewart emphasizes that the creative impulse in African-derived culture is process oriented; the creative black musician constantly strives to achieve new heights of emotive expressiveness in terms of spontaneity and inventiveness in improvisation or rhythmic interplay. Artistic production in this tradition is integral to day-to-day life. The appropriateness of the music-making process as a demonstration of an essential "blackness" is elaborated in Ron Wellburn's "The Black Aesthetic Imperative" (1970). Wellburn looks at the black musician as the leader in "the expression of true black sensibility" and, like Baraka, sees black art as a revolutionary weapon. He asserts that the musician can "do more damage to the oppressor's image of himself than heavily armed urban guerrillas" and calls upon all African Americans to "re-establish ourselves as musicians . . . at least become a drummer or learn to play on a simple reed flute" (128-29).[18] The implication of establishing black musicians as artistic paradigms for writers is pointedly articulated by Larry Neal in "And Shine Swam On" (1968), his Afterword for *Black Fire* :

> The key to where black people have to go is in music. Our music has always been the most dominant manifestation of what we are and feel, literature was just an afterthought, the step taken by the Negro bourgeoisie who desired acceptance on the white man's terms. And that is precisely why the literature has failed. It was the case of one elite addressing another elite.
> But our music is something else. The best of it has always operated at the core of our lives, forcing itself upon us as in a ritual. It has always, somehow, represented the collective psyche. Black literature must attempt to achieve that same sense of collective ritual, but directed at the destruction of useless, dead ideas. Further, it can be a ritual that affirms our highest possibilities, but is yet honest with us. (654-55)

Neal wants to invest an egalitarian sensibility in African American literature; he wants writers to impact the people in the same way that musicians are able to touch their audiences with "soul." He continues: "The poet must become a performer, the way James Brown is a performer—loud, gaudy and racy . . . He must learn to embellish the context in which the work is executed; and, where possible, link the work to all usable aspects of the music . . . Poets must learn to sing, dance and chant their works, tearing into the substance of their individual and collective experiences" (655). Neal's focus on poetry and his demand for a literature that is oriented toward live performance and direct interaction with an audience explains why so much of the imaginative output of Black Arts Movement writers was in the form of poetry or drama rather than fiction.[19] Musical techniques and elements could be adapted and incorporated into poetry and drama with much greater facility and immediacy than fiction. However, two stunning exceptions to this are the short stories "The Screamers" (1963) by Baraka and "Will the Circle Be Unbroken?" (1966)[20] by Henry Dumas.

Like his Black Arts Movement colleagues, Baraka regarded music as the preeminent form of African American artistic expression. As he declares in "The Myth of a Negro Literature" (1962): "There has never been an equivalent to Duke Ellington or Louis Armstrong in Negro Writing, and even the best of contemporary literature written by Negroes cannot yet be compared to the fantastic beauty of the music of Charlie Parker" (191). One of Baraka's main reasons for asserting that music has been such an accurate reflector of the African American psyche corresponds with Neal's suggestion that literature was a "bourgeoisie" form of expression. In *Blues People* (1963) Baraka states:

> Only Negro music, because, perhaps, it drew its strength and beauty out of the depth of the black man's soul, and because to a large extent its traditions could be carried on by the 'lowest classes' of Negroes, has been able to survive the constant and willful dilutions of the black middle class and the persistent calls to oblivion made by the mainstream of society. Of, course, that mainstream wrought very definite and very constant changes upon the *form* of the American Negro's music, but the emotional significance and vitality at its core remain, to this day, unaltered. (Baraka's italics) (131) [21]

While Baraka finds that black musicians have constantly constructed new forms to express an essential sense of African American identity, "the emotional significance and vitality at its core," black writers "developed an emotional allegiance to the middle-class (middle-brow) culture of America" and thus produced literature that "was always an example of 'culture' in the narrow sense of 'cultivation' or 'sophistication' in an individual within their own group" (131-32).

The influence of Baraka's rejection of black middle-class and mainstream American values on his writing is evidenced in his attraction to the avant-garde and free form experimentation of the Beat Generation writers.[22] He identified with their rejection and subversion of traditional forms and accepted values but ultimately came to reject their valuelessness. For Baraka, dropping out of the mainstream and adopting a bohemian lifestyle was inadequate; the black writer must be engaged in direct action to foster change for the whole race. Although an exaltation of jazz musicians had been central to the work of many Beat writers, Baraka eventually looked to the black musical artist as a role model for his rejection of the bohemian individualism of the Beats.[23] The saxophonist John Coltrane became the ultimate artistic model for Baraka. As he states in the essay "New Black Music" (1965): "Trane is a mature swan whose wing span was a whole world. But he also shows us how to murder the popular song. To do away with weak Western forms. He is a beautiful philosopher" (174). Like Coltrane with his saxophone solos, Baraka attacks conventional forms with his writing.[24]

Baraka attacks the traditional form of the short story in "The Screamers," which develops like an extended Coltrane improvisation in a surrealistic swirl of seemingly disjointed imagery, plot information and commentary.[25] The story is set in the mid-1950s at The Graham, a Newark jazz club, where a young, black middle-class narrator describes the surrounding scene and performance by the saxophonist/band leader Lynn Hope. The saxophonist finds an infectious rhythmic groove and constructs a solo that draws the band and audience into a conga line that marches into the Newark streets only to be attacked by the police and firemen who misunderstand the ritual nature of the performance. The ability of the black musician to create forms that express the essential spirit of African Americans influences the narration of the story. As the saxophonist's performance develops, the disjointed nature of the narrator's description gives way to a more lucid relation of the events and his interpretation of the experience. Lynn Hope's music enables the narrator to make sense, to find direction and meaning, to impose *form* on the life that the black community leads in America.

Baraka's rejection of middle-class black life and its identification with mainstream America is reflected in the narrator of "The Screamers" who is looking to escape his middle-class background and identify with the working class.[26] The narrator clearly feels left out of the club's inner circle: "A yellow girl will not dance with me, nor will Teddy's people" (71). He wishes he could capture that essence of blackness that the working class patrons and the musicians exude:

A greasy hipness, down-ness, nobody in our camp
believed (having social-worker mothers and postman
fathers; or living squeezed in lightskinned projects with
adulterers and proud skinny ladies with soft voices). The
theory, the spectrum, this sound baked inside their heads,
and still rub sweaty against those lesser lights. Those
niggers. Laundromat workers, beauticians, pregnant short-
haired jail bait separated all from 'us,' but in this vat we
sweated gladly for each other. And rubbed. And Lynn
could be a common hero, from whatever side we saw him.
(71-72)

The club and the music provide the narrator with an opportunity to
enter into working class life. Lynn, the "common hero," is the leader
who brings the stratified black community together through his
articulation of "this sound baked inside their heads."[27] The narrator
elaborates on his disaffection from the black middle class and
mainstream America when he declares, "You see, I left America on the
first fast boat" (74). His faith that he can get in touch with an authentic
black approach to life through the music motivates the narrator to come
to The Graham to hear Lynn Hope:

Willing for any experience, any image, any further
separation from where my good grades were sure to lead.
Frightened of post offices, lawyer's offices, doctor's cars,
the deaths of clean politicians. Or of the imaginary fat
man, advertising cemeteries to his "good colored friends."
Lynn's screams erased them all, and I thought myself
intrepid white commando from the West. Plunged into
noise and flesh, and their form become an ethic. (74-75)

Self-conscious about his middle-class upbringing, the narrator locates
his "ethic," the way he will lead his life, in the "screams" of the
saxophonist's "form." The music not only overcomes barriers between
classes but also brings individuals together in a sensual ritual: "Any
meat you clung to was yours those few minutes without interruption.
The length of the music was the only form" (75). The performance in
the club is a orgiastic group experience in which audience members
look to reach the height of sensual pleasure, "All extremes were popular
with that crowd" (75). Lynn senses their dissatisfaction, "We had not
completely come" (77), and when he finds his groove the crowd joins
with him in a communal orgasm: "And he screamed it so the veins in is

face stood out like neon. 'Uhh, yeh, Uhh, yeh, Uhh yeh,' we all screamed to push him further" (78).

The soundtrack for this group frenzy is a blues-based saxophone style known as the "honk."[28] With the bebop players demanding to be looked upon as artists and refusing to provide backdrop for dancers, the honk laid the foundation for the raw, steady grooves of rhythm and blues. The narrator describes this sound which "became a basis for thought" in working class black clubs all over America:

> The repeated rhythmic figure, a screamed riff, pushed in its insistence past music. It was hatred and frustration, secrecy and despair. It spurted out of the diphthong culture, and reinforced the black cults of emotion. There was no compromise, no dreary sophistication, only the elegance of something that is too ugly to be described, and is diluted only at the agent's peril. All the saxophonists of that world were honkers, Illinois, Gator, Big Jay, Jug, the great sounds of our day. Ethnic historians, actors, priests of the unconscious. (76)

The narrator connects his litany of saxophonists—Illinois Jacquet, Willis "Gatortail" Jackson, Big Jay McNeely[29] and Gene "Jug" Ammons—to oral tradition and the roots of African American expressive culture. He also acknowledges their role as ritual leaders who pass along the story of the race's experiences in America through sound and rhythm. The sound was raw and gut- wrenching and the rhythm was primal and pounding. Beauty and sophistication have no place in this form in which "the innovators searched for uglier modes" (76). Throughout his analyses of African American music, Baraka associates this effusion of unrefined emotion with the expression of an essential black sensibility.[30] The honkers were also known for acrobatic histrionics: waving their horns violently, falling to their knees, rolling on their backs, walking the bar. Variations on these extra-musical acts, almost anti-musical acts from the white Western perspective, are described by the narrator. He recounts his witnessing of "the completely nihilistic act" by McNeeley: "The first Dada coon of the age, jumped and stomped and yowled and finally sensed the only other space that form allowed" (76). The saxophonist, like the European Dada artists, attacks conventional forms.[31] The description of the recalled scene continues, comparing Big Jay to the painter Marcel Duchamp's desecration of "legitimate art": "On his back screaming was the Mona Lisa with the mustache, as crude and simple" (77).[32]

Lynn Hope knows that he must top Big Jay's performance in order to maintain his position as ritual leader at The Graham, and the audience recognizes when he has found the form that gives definition to their lives as black Americans: "Then Lynn got his riff, that rhythmic figure we knew he would repeat, the honked note that would be his personal evaluation of the world" (78). As the audience screams in unison with Lynn's riff he leads his band off the stage and into the crowd. Although he retains the role of leader, the saxophonist completely breaks down the separation between artist and audience. The form of the honked riff also eliminates the stratification in the club that had troubled the narrator as he waited for the music to begin. They are a community united through music and dance: "There was confusion and stumbling, but there were no real fights. The thing they wanted was right there and easily accessible. No one could stop you from getting in that line." When the celebration of their blackness can no longer be contained in the club, "Lynn thought further, and made to destroy the ghetto." The movement of the conga line into the streets of Newark is a ritual destruction, a joyful triumph, a refusal to submit in song and dance: "We screamed and screamed at the clear image of ourselves as we should always be. Ecstatic, completed, involved in a secret communal expression. It would be the form of the sweetest revolution, to hucklebuck into the fallen capital, and let the oppressors lindy hop out" (79).[33] Their revolution is sweet because it is absorptive, a revolution that hopes to convert rather than destroy its oppressors. But when the representatives of the dominant culture, the police and fire departments, arrive, they cannot understand the form, "What was it, a labor riot? Anarchists? A nigger strike?" (79). Just as white America fails to understand that African American music is more than mere entertainment, the authorities misunderstand Lynn's spontaneous display of cultural pride and unity. The conga line is attacked with billy clubs and firehoses, and "America's responsible immigrants," who are doing the dirty work of the true power brokers, create a riot: "The knives came out, the razors, all the Biggers who would not be bent, counterattacked or came up behind the civil servants smashing them with coke bottles and aerials." The narrator continues to march with Lynn, the band and "a few other fools" until they get "halfway up the stairs" of the club: "Then we broke our different ways, to save whatever it was each of us thought we loved" (80). Baraka's evocation of Bigger Thomas is appropriate in describing the African Americans involved in this riot because they are cornered and pushed into acts of senseless violence by white oppression. Baraka also seems to echo Wright's insistence that the nationalism of folk-derived expression be transcended by a commitment to a political agenda. The members of the conga line may differ from Bigger in that they have embraced their cultural heritage in a ritual celebration, but they have not found a suitable political outlet for the energy Lynn Hope has channeled. Their ritual is ineffective and their transcendence is transitory when confronted with the brutality of American racism. The saxophonist, the band and the narrator cling to the form as they attempt to return to the safe haven of the jazz club but are forced to break "our different ways." The unity that the music has engendered is again fragmented, and the individual impulse to save themselves, "whatever it was each of us thought we loved," supersedes communal interests. Although, as the saxophonist's name implies, there is "Hope" that the "secret communal expression" will bring them back together, they must have an agenda for direct action if they are to impose their form on the realities of American existence with any permanence.

Henry Dumas's short story "Will the Circle Be Unbroken?" takes the Black Arts Movement concept of African American music as a revolutionary weapon a step further than "The Screamers." In the essay "The Changing Same (R&B and New Black Music)" (1966) Baraka refers his readers to the Dumas story for insight into the "total function of 'free music'" (the avant-garde explorations of such musicians as Coltrane, Albert Ayler, Ornette Coleman and Sun Ra): "Understand the implications of music as an autonomous *judge* of civilizations" (Baraka's italics) (186). Certainly, the music in the story does function as judge, and it also functions as executioner. White people who enter the Sound Barrier Club immediately die when they listen to the music created by the saxophonist Probe Adams. Although it is set in Harlem of the 1960s there is a myth-like quality to this story and the characters exude an archetypal significance. Baraka's essay "Henry Dumas: Afro-Surreal Expressionist" (1988) comments on this aspect of Dumas's fiction: "The stories are fables; a mythological presence pervades. They are morality tales, magical, resonating dream emotions and images; shifting ambiguous terror, mystery, implied revelation. But they are also stories of real life, now or whenever, constructed in weirdness and poetry in which the contemporaneity of essential themes is clear" (164). The fable-like quality of Dumas's writing is seen in the description of the instrument Probe plays in addition to soprano saxophone, the afro-horn, "the newest axe to cut the deadwood of the world" (109):

> There are only three afro-horns in the world. They were forged from a rare metal found only in Africa and South America. No one knows who forged the horns, but the general opinion among musicologists is that it was the Egyptians. One European museum guards an afro-horn.

The other is supposed to be somewhere on the West Coast
of Mexico, among a tribe of Indians. Probe grew into his
from a black peddler who claimed to have traveled a
thousand miles just to give it to his son. From that day on,
Probe's sax handled like a child, a child waiting for itself
to grow out of itself. (113-14)

There is certainly a sense of mystery, myth and magic in the
description, but issues that concern the contemporary black artist are
integrated into this fabulous tale. The modern musician is linked to an
ancient artistic heritage. The Europeans, who look at art in terms of
artifacts, keep the afro-horn a prisoner in a museum, while the black
American and the Mexican Indian, representatives of two cultures that
look upon art as a process that is integrated into daily life, make use of
the instrument and expect the traditional to foster something new.

Like so many other Black Arts writers Dumas finds a sense of
community and a sense of racial identity in African American music.[34]
As he declares in his poem "Listen To the Sound of My Horn" :

Listen to the sound of my horn, my people,
          this rhythm of years long past.
Listen to the sound of my horn, I say,
          Great music and I . . . have come at last!
(*Knees* 79)

This ability to reach a spiritual communion through music is also
exhibited in his short story, "The Voice" (1965).[35] Three members of a
Harlem soul group, The Emotions, question the nature of existence and
their relationship as black men to God after the sudden death of their
lead singer. A visit to the home of their deceased friend immerses the
three young men in the black community as they are surrounded by
family members, visitors from down South and the scent of a home-
cooked meal. They join with the dead singer's guitar-playing brother in
a spontaneous performance—their first since the death: "We sang from
our souls, and before long everybody was standing round listening.
Spencer's mother was trying not to cry. And then all of a sudden Blake
caught a note, and we all heard it and we came to his aid. We got to
feeling good, and the people backed us up with some hand-clapping.
Spence should have been there then, because we were all singing and
making one voice" (175). The performance allows them to go on with
their lives; they can draw spiritual strength from the communal culture
and lead a meaningful black existence in a white-dominated world.

While "Will the Circle Be Unbroken?" takes its title from a old-time religious hymn, the music's sense of black spirituality comes from a cosmic mysticism rather than a down-home Christian fervor. Probe is a mysterious figure who has returned from "exile" and rumors are widespread about his "new sound." The music Probe and his band create is "a spiraling circle," and the individual lines the seven musicians play weave together "into a blanket." The community that will result from the "coming circle" is depicted as an unborn child: "The black audience, unaware at first of its collectiveness, had begun to move in a soundless rhythm as if it were the tiny twitchings of an embryo" (109).

"Will the Circle Be Unbroken?" and "The Voice" share the perspective that a black community can be created through music-making. Yet, the two stories feature diametrically opposed views on the aesthetic criteria used to judge the African American artistic production—an issue of central concern to Black Arts Movement writers. In "The Voice" The Emotions meet a rabbi who tells them he enjoys their singing. The narrator is surprised but ultimately finds a validation for his music in the white man's comment: "How could he enjoy our singing? We were singing soul. He was white. How could he even pretend to understand? We didnt [sic] say anything. Maybe we were better than we thought, if a white man liked our sound" (166). He knows he is making music that is characteristically black, but he allows the music to be judged by a critical standard from outside the culture. Like many of the Motown acts and other soul artists of the 1960s, the narrator of "The Voice" is a self-taught, grass-roots musician who is producing popular music—music that is basically aimed at mass consumption. The issue of art versus entertainment would not be as crucial to a soul performer as it would to a free jazz innovator.

The music is regarded as an emblem of their blackness by Probe and the other musicians in "Will the Circle Be Unbroken?." It is the medium through which they will construct a new African American community, and they demand the right to develop it independent of outside influences. White patrons are banned from The Sound Barrier Club because the "new sound" is lethal to white listeners; a sign that the doorman holds declares: "'We cannot allow non-Brothers because of the danger involved with extensions'" (112). The central conflict in the story arises when three whites insist on being allowed to enter. The leader of the trio is Jan, a tenor saxophonist who "had blown with Probe six years ago on the West Coast." He discounts "this new philosophy the musicians were talking about" and fundamentally misunderstands the function of music in black culture: "He had known many Negro musicians and theirs was no different from any other artist's struggles to be himself, including his own" (110). Jan fails to recognize the communal nature of black artistic expression. Both of Jan's companions ("two of the hippest ofays in town") have written about jazz, and he feels they will gain entrance "if anybody could break the circle of the Sound Club." Ron, a Yale graduate, has written many articles that have helped black musicians, particularly Probe. He has also tried to be a blues singer: "The best compliment he ever got was from Mississippi John or Muddy Waters, one of the two, during a civil rights rally in Alabama. He had spontaneously leaped up during the rally and played from his soul. Muddy was in the audience, and later told Ron: 'Boy, you keep that up, you gwine get me back on the plantation'" (110). Although he has "knocked around the music world" and knows he can capture "the depth of the black man's psyche," Ron has also failed to comprehend the fundamental nature of black music. His insincere and patronizing attitude is illustrated by his inability to distinguish between Mississippi John Hurt and Muddy Waters. Through his foolish arrogance he actually takes a comparison between himself and the blues master seriously and completely misses the sarcastic irony of Muddy's "compliment." Tasha is a "Vassar girl" who has had a love affair with the fictional trombonist Oliver Fullerton. Part of the biography she has started has been published in *Down Beat* , and she is now "noted as a critic and authority on the Fullerton movement." Fullerton's career declined from a drug problem after his affair with Tasha. She believes if they had married his career would have been a success: "She still loved him. It was her own love, protected deep inside her, encased, her little black secret and her passport to the inner world that Oliver had died trying to enter. It would be only a matter of time. She would translate love into an honest appraisal of black music" (111). Like Ron, Tasha possesses a tremendous ego and her focus is on herself and not on understanding black music. The three whites are warned about the effect of Probe's music, and Jan thinks, "It was incredible that all the spades believed this thing about the lethal vibrations from the new sound" (112). Although he considers himself a "brother" and a "blood" because he has played with Probe, his thinking in terms of "spades" reveals his incapacity to understand the significance of the music. The flaw in the three whites' approach to black music is similar to a point Baraka makes in the essay "Jazz and the White Critic" (1963). Like the white critics Baraka is attacking, Jan and his friends fail to see that "Negro music is essentially the expression of an attitude, or a collection of attitudes, about the world, and only secondarily an attitude about the way music is made" (13). Ironically, the three whites gain admission to the club through the intercession of an Irish policeman, who "had never seen anything worthwhile from niggers in Harlem" (113). It seems the well-meaning but misguided and patronizing enthusiasts are more threatening "invaders" than the blatant racist who strolls away, and they suffer the consequences of hearing Probe's new sound.[36]

As the creation of the new sound develops Dumas intensifies the birth imagery.[37] The three whites go into "the dark cavern which led to the music." Their reverse journey up the birth canal will lead to their death. Aware of their presence, Probe "tightened the circle. Movement began from within it, shaking without breaking balance. He had to prepare the womb for the afro-horn." Probe functions as a kind of midwife preparing for the imminent birth signaled by the contractions and internal movement. But before he can handle the "vibrations" of the afro-horn he must call for "motives." The three whites, who "clung to the wall" remind him of the treatment his people have received in a white world: "There sat the city of Samson. The white pillars imposing . . . but how easy it is to tear the building down with motives." Probe who is "healed of his blindness, born anew of spirit" puts down his saxophone and lifts "*his axe*" (113). The music of the afro-horn combines with the other instruments, particularly Magwa's drum, to repair the fissure the entrance of the whites has made in the circle and to greet the emerging child:

> *Inside the center of the gyrations is an atom stripped of time, black. The gathering of the hunters, deeper. Coming, laced in the energy of the sun. He is blowing. Magwa's hands. Reverence of skin. Under the single voices is the child of a woman, black They are building back the wall, crumbling under the disturbance.* (Dumas's italics) (114)

The three whites slump over immediately when they are hit with the "shock waves" of "Probe's first statement on the afro-horn." With the circle returned to wholeness the birth finally occurs: "The musicians stood. The horn and Probe drew up the shadows from the audience. A child climbed upon the chords of sound, growing out of the circle of the womb, searching with fingers and then with motive . . . ." (114-15). As the performance ends the audience notices the three dead people, confirming the rumors about the power of Probe's new sound: "'It's true then. It's true . . .'" (115). The black musician's role as communal leader has gone beyond ritual; Probe's jazz, a black form, has been effective in repulsing the white "invaders" who overstep the self-defined black boundaries. The musical performance at the Sound Barrier Club is an archetypal triumph. By drawing upon an instrument that can be traced back to ancient Egypt the contemporary black artist has created a new black life—a life that is resistant to the intrusion of outsiders.

Yet, "Will the Circle Be Unbroken?" is more than just a parable outlining the creation of an all black community. The story is also representative of the Black Arts Movement's insistence that there be black criteria for the evaluation of black art, a black aesthetic. Larry Neal comments on this aspect of Dumas' story in the essay "Henry Dumas: Literary Landmark" (1987):

> What you see is a raveling, and unraveling, a collecting. So now we had music as a force of judgment. We also had a place, ritually, symbolically, a place where whites can't go—a psychic zone that should not be intruded upon. That explained it to a certain extent.
>
> We didn't want the white critics in there, I think the object was for black people to find out who they were without someone overlooking their shoulder. Black people had a feeling of always being on stage for white folks. It was time, some of us thought, to be in certain contexts socially, unashamedly on our own, and to define ourselves on our own terms without someone else intervening in the definition. (315)

The theme of self-definition seems to be of paramount importance to Dumas. It is the whites who come to "break the circle" and attempt to impose their definitions on the artistic productions of African Americans—not the racist Irish cop who "didn't think the sounds were worth listening to"—who are judged and executed by the music of Probe's afro-horn. Dumas explores the construction of a black aesthetic through an classic scenario in African American literature. Throughout the tradition black writers who have represented the music have been concerned with whites misinterpreting the sounds produced by black musicians. For the black writer, whether it is Douglass trying to insure that the spirituals are not perceived as a sign of contentment or Dunbar viewing whites who come to the Banner Club to hear the ragtime "puffessor" as dissolute and patronizing, McKay portraying the vice squad masked as music enthusiasts or Kelley pointing out that white jazz fans barely even listen when Ludlow plays, the intrusion of whites into the ritual arena where black music is created is emblematic of white America's denial of the essential humanity of African Americans.[38] The exclusionary nature of The Sound Barrier Club—the musicians actually build a wall in sound—is a culmination of this representation. Probe wields "the newest axe to cut the deadwood of the world" and constructs an autonomous black community. Thus, in "Will the Circle Be Unbroken?" the African American musician is both the communal leader and the artistic paradigm. Revolutionary and creative, visionary and traditional, independent and nurturing, he is the ultimate representative of the Black Arts Movement's approach to the hostile environment that blacks must face in America.

Notes for Chapter Four

1. Johnson (who later became Bernice Johnson Reagon) is leader of the folk group Sweet Honey In The Rock (a folk group that employs the a cappella form) and is the Smithsonian Institute's Curator of the Division of Community Life, Department of Social and Art History.

2. See Fuld, page 510.

3. See above Chapter 3, note 29.

4. See Chapter 3, page 159. The term "gospel" did not come into use for black religious music until later in the century. See Southern, *The Music Of Black America* for more on Tindley (450-51).

5. See "A Critical Background" in Lorraine Hansberry's *The Drinking Gourd* (1961) in which she discusses similar intentions for her never produced teleplay. Like *Jubilee*, Hansberry's work is a revisionist history of slavery and its title is taken from a spiritual.

6. According to Bernard Bell in *The Afro-American Novel and Its Tradition*, the novel is a "neo-slave narrative based primarily on folk materials and Vyry's quest for freedom" in which "Walker's task . . . was to create fiction from the oral tradition of her family and the recorded history of the nation" (286).

7. See Chapter One above on "jubilee" in the songs that appear in the texts of William Wells Brown.

8. In "Music as Theme: The Blues Mode in the Works of Margaret Walker" Eleanor Traylor asserts: "Music is the leitmotif of Margaret Walker's *Jubilee*. The celebrant of the novel is a singer. Her songs articulate progressive stages in her life; they amplify its meaning. Through her songs, the personal history of Vyry, Elvira Ware Brown, central dramatic figure, actual maternal great grandmother of the author, merges with the history of a community, of a time, of a place, of a space-a mythical zone-within the history of world story" (513).

9. The title comes from *Othello* 4.2.

10. See Gayl Jones's "Multiple-Voiced Blues: Sherley A. Williams's 'Someone Sweet Angel Chile' in *Liberating Voices* (38-43).

11. Whitney Balliett's "People Who Shoot Doves Out of Season" asserts that the novel's voices are "wholly authoritative" but finds that "Kelley's characters, though, tend to spring from his ideas, rather than the other way around. If he were to press deeper into the ordinary hearts he writes of, instead of forcing them to grow on intellectual trellises, he would help us know our own hearts" (178).

12. The scenario is a classic one; in August Wilson's *Ma Rainey's Black Bottom*, the blues singer says of her manager: "He's been my

manager for six years, always talking about sticking together, and the only time he had me in his house was to sing for some friends" (79).

13. Bernard Bell suggests that the novel is "a fable of American neglect of the creative gift of black jazz musicians" (296).

14. In *Give Birth to Brightness* Shirley Anne Williams asserts: "Ludlow returns to the group experience which produced him, realizing at the novel's end that the pursuit of fame as a jazz artist in night clubs and concert halls is unimportant compared to the need of Black people for Black musicians who will speak to them and for them in the forums of their own communities. It is also his need, for in order to be at peace with himself he has to be with his own people" (145).

15. The information on Roach's career is from Leonard Feather's *Inside Jazz* and *The Encyclopedia of Jazz* and Nat Hentoff's liner notes to *Freedom Now Suite*.

16 Born Everett LeRoy Jones in 1934, the writer changed his first name to LeRoi in 1952. In 1967 he changed his name to Imamu Ameer Baraka, which he eventually altered to Amiri Baraka (Harris, *Reader* xxxi-ii). He will be referred to as Baraka throughout this chapter.

17. For a critique of the Black Arts Movement writer's attempts to define a black aesthetic see David Lionel Smith's "The Black Arts Movement and Its Critics" in *American Literary History*, (93-110).

18. In "Are Black Musicians Serious?" Haki Madhubuti (Don L. Lee) finds that black musicians produce "the most advanced and developed forms of creative expression that Afrikan people have retained in this country," but he also takes them to task for being too individualistic and not organizing themselves to avoid exploitation— which would be an much needed paradigm for many black Americans.

19. David L. Smith suggests that this aspect of the Black Arts Movement "opened up exciting new possibilities of artistic experimentation, and it sought to redefine the relationship between writer and audience. In effect, this meant both liabilities and opportunities for writers, audiences, and critics" (101).

20. The story was first published in *Negro Digest* 16 (November 1966) : 76-80 and was collected in *Ark of Bones* (1974).

21. This quotation is basically a revision of an section from "The Myth of a Negro Literature" (191).

22. For more on Baraka's association with the Beats see Gayle Jones (112-4) and particularly William J. Harris's *Jazz Aesthetic*, Chapters 2 & 3.

23. Harris has suggested: "From the white avant-garde Baraka learned how to write and think about poetry, but from jazz he learned how to reject, invert, and transform what the white avant-garde had taught him" (17).

24. Harris uses the term "jazz aesthetic" to describe Baraka's application of Coltrane's destruction of Western forms and their subsequent reconstruction as black forms in his approach to writing: "Baraka also wants to take weak Western forms, rip them asunder, and create something new out of the rubble. He transposes Coltrane's musical ideas to poetry, using them to turn white poetic forms backwards and upside down. This murderous impulse is behind all the forms of Baraka's aesthetic and art" (15). Kimberly W. Benston's "Late Coltrane: A Re-Membering of Orpheus" expands on this concept of Coltrane as a destroyer of Western forms. Benston also discusses how black music informs the language and structure of contemporary black poetry.

25. Gayl Jones asserts that "The Screamers" "is like a free-form jazz solo. Many readers find it difficult because of its adroit blurring and blending of visual and temporal details, its shifts in time, setting, and emotional sequences; its fragments of biography, history, and sociopolitical commentary. Reading the story, then, is like solving a puzzle of space, time, character, chronology, event, and description" (115-16).

26. Many of the details of the narrator's life correspond to Baraka's own biography, particularly the reference to a postal worker father and a social worker mother. As Harris asserts concerning autobiography in Baraka's poetry: "Because Baraka is so committed to the autobiographical mode to use the standard New Critical device of referring to the 'I' of a Baraka poem as a persona is to miss its spirit if not its meaning" (41).

27. In *Blues People* Baraka traces this class stratification back to slavery and accuses black writers with its perpetuation: "The idea of the 'separation,' the strata, had developed within the group. The thin division of the field hand from the house servant had widened, and the legacy of the house servant was given voice constantly in the work of early Negro writers" (131). Ralph Ellison takes exception to Baraka's approach to black American culture through the blues. In his review of *Blues People* Ellison quips: "The tremendous burden of sociology which Jones would place upon this body of music is enough to give even the blues the blues" (*Shadow* 249).

28 For Baraka's musicological analysis of the "honk" see *Blues People* (172).

29 In both "The Screamers" and *Blues People* Baraka spells the saxophonist's name "McNeeley"; however, it is spelt "McNeely" in *The Jazz Encyclopedia.*

30. This type of description is pervasive throughout *Blues People*; for example, he uses it in reference to Charlie Parker (30) and Coltrane and Sonny Rollins (227). It is featured in the later poem "AM/TRAK" (*Reader* 267-72) where "honk" and "scream" are used to describe Coltrane's essential cry of his blackness. Benston comments on this in *Baraka: The Renegade and the Mask*: "He esteems in black music the qualities indicative of Africanesque emotiveness: the shout, holler or 'scream'; atonality; improvisation; communal modes" (83).

31. Gayl Jones discusses "dada" in relation to Baraka (111).

32. Harris finds that the honker's act goes beyond the painter's artistic statement: "As in Duchamp's famous mock defacing of the Mona Lisa, in Baraka's story McNeely defaces high art in order to create something new and vital. In Baraka's view, both he and Duchamp are involved in creative destruction. But Duchamp's graffiti are finally not as complete as Baraka's: the French artist's work stays within the house of art, while Baraka's goes out into the street" (33).

33. Harris explains: "For Baraka, dancing is synonymous with political activism; thus, dancing . . . means affirming ethnic authenticity and engaging in radical political acts" (106).

34. In "Elemental Wisdom in *Goodbye, Sweetwater* : Suggestions for Further Study" Eugenia Collier states: "It is apparent (from his poems as well as his stories) that Dumas loved black music and found in it the strength, the ancestral ties that black people have always found. Music, like the river, ties us to the generations who labored and sang out their sorrow and looked to each other and to their religion for sustenance" (197).

35. According to the editor the story was probably completed in 1965. It was first published in the posthumous collection *Rope Of Wind* (1979).

36. The white liberal as villain is pointed out by Donald P. Costello in "Black Man as Victim" in relation to Baraka's *Dutchman*: "Whitey can tell the black man nothing because whitey can understand nothing. As early as 1961, Jones had written: 'Liberals think that they are peculiarly qualified to tell American Negroes and the other oppressed peoples of the world how to wage their struggles.' In *Dutchman*, the Jones reply to whitey is 'It's none of your business'" (209).

37. In *Baraka: The Renegade and the Mask* Benston suggests that, "The horn . . . penetrates the womb-like circle of the black collective and helps to conceive the black child, the fresh promise of liberated Afro-consciousness" (72).

38. In *Not Without Laughter* Hughes finds the mingling of blacks and whites "freely on equal terms" in the Bottoms where blues and jazz and spirituals are part of daily life to be ironic since Tempy aspires to be white and refuses to listen to these sounds. He does not seem to find the presence of whites to be an intrusion. However, the white man in Chicago who tells Sandy that black musicians are clowns is obviously an example of concern over misinterpretation of the music. The one significant example of an exception to this view of whites as intruders seems to be "Sonny's Blues." The climatic jazz session takes place downtown and seemingly there are whites who are part of the community the musicians forge through their performance of the blues; Baldwin may feel that whites can understand the music and have a sympathetic kinship with blacks.

Coda:
"What Good Is a Liturgy
Without a Text?"

"The music is the magic of a secret world,
It's a world that is always within."
- Abbey Lincoln

The journey from the nineteenth-century Maryland plantation where Frederick Douglass discovers the impulse to resist enslavement in the sound of the spirituals ("Every tone was a testimony . . . ") to the 1960s Harlem jazz club where Probe Adams creates shock waves of "truer vibrations" on his afro-horn that kill white "invaders" is emblematic of the pervasive influence African American music has had on black writers. The fictional representation of music has been an accurate barometer of the artistic, social and political concerns of writers throughout the development of the African American literary tradition. Even though Baraka's honking saxophonist Lynn Hope leading a conga line of screaming black men and women through the streets of Newark is a long way from William Wells Brown's house servant Sam leading a secret call/response celebration of the master's death behind the "Big House" in Natchez, the music still functions in these fictional representations as a mode of survival, resistance and transcendence despite American racism. While the music has consistently been a symbol of the communal/individual relationship in black American culture, black writers have also used it as index of their evolving definition of an African American sensibility. Ante-bellum writers looked upon the spirituals as totems of hope for a better day. Yet, the music's subversion was indirect; the defiance was masked in religious imagery and performances were often held in secret. Black Arts Movement writers considered music a revolutionary weapon; the defiance was open and direct.

In the century between Brown and Baraka, the representation of music in black fiction went through a dramatic metamorphosis. The examination of the tradition of representing music within *the* tradition of African American literature illustrates that black writers were continuously informed by black music and musicians in terms of subject matter, thematic concerns and artistic paradigms. African American writers developed a number of tropes for representing music and musicians in fiction which can trace their roots back to the pre-fictional slave narratives that laid the foundation for the black literary tradition in America. Music and musicians play a variety of archetypal roles in the depiction of African American life. On a very concrete level the music provides a way out of a limited situation; it provides a viable option to break down the strictures of racism. Individuals who follow this route to overcome these limitations then become role models for the race and inspire further effort in the communal struggle toward freedom. The creation of African American musical forms—for both artist and audience—is accompanied by a way of looking at the world, a method of survival, a mode of personal transcendence, whether it is a channel for emotional release or a means of material uplift, a trickster strategy or a defiant challenge. The black musician who demonstrates these approaches to life takes on the role of communal spokesperson or ritual leader. Ultimately, the music is a manifestation of an African American sensibility that links artist and audience to a communal heritage. The music provides a cultural conduit that reaches back to oral traditions and keeps alive the spirit and the memory of transcendent survival and triumph and provides the impetus to forge ahead creatively. The music's connection to this sensibility and the techniques of the oral tradition also furnishes linguistic, structural and compositional models for African American writers.

In much of the writing of the Black Arts Movement it would seem that the representation of music had reached a kind of apex; the music had almost become synonymous with some essence of "blackness." However, the Black Arts Movement did not have the last word on the definition of an African American sensibility, and the representation of black music continued to evolve after the movement declined. Even Baraka, the movement's most stalwart proponent, eventually renounced its ethnocentricity in favor of a "Third World Marxist" perspective and revised his conception of black consciousness. As he declares in "The Revolutionary Tradition in Afro-American Literature": "It became embroiled in cultural nationalism, bourgeois nationalism, substituting mistrust and hatred of white people for scientific analysis of the real enemies of black people, until by the middle seventies a dead end had been reached that could only be surmounted by a complete change of world view, ideology" (321).

The adoption of Marxist ideology by no means diminished Baraka's devotion to the representation of African American music and other elements from the oral tradition in his production of innovative performance-oriented forms. The creative acts of black musicians which are represented in the poetry and drama Baraka has produced over the last three decades are paradigms for political engagement. In "AM/TRAK" (1979), his biographical paean to Coltrane, Baraka asserts:

From the endless sessions
money lord hovers oer us
capitalism beats our ass
dope & juice wont change it
Trane, blow, oh scream yeh, anyway. (270)

Baraka's "In the Tradition" (1983), an extended poem dedicated to the jazz saxophonist Arthur Blythe (Baraka has recorded it with a jazz ensemble), is the ultimate melding of the black musical and literary tradition aimed at Marxist revolutionary action. The arrangement of his written language approximates the rhythm and phrasing of a saxophone improvisation, as exemplified by the following excerpt:

in the tradition

1/4 notes
eighth notes
16th notes
32nds, 64ths, 128ths, silver blue
presidents
of Langston & Langston Manifestos
Tell us again about the negro artist
& the racial mountain so we will not
be negro artists, Mckay Banjoes and
Homes in Harlem, Blue Black Boys &
Little Richard Wrights, Tradition of
For My People Margaret Walker & David Walker & Jr Walker
& Walker Smith Sweet Ray Leonard Rockin in Rhythm w/
Musical Dukes,
What is this tradition Basied on, we Blue Black Ward strugglin
against a Big White Fog, Africa people, our fingerprints are
everywhere
on you america, our fingerprints are everywhere, Cesaire told
you . . . . (305)

In a consummate example of the black oral tradition's ability to renew itself Baraka blows (screams? honks?) a litany that brings together black writers (particularly those who have represented music in their work) with black musicians and the titles of songs and books in a railing improvisational attack on racism and economic exploitation. Baraka's "Third World Marxist" work is a testament to African American music's ability to lead black writers to new and exciting modes of creative expression.

The post-Black Arts Movement era has seen a blossoming of innovative and powerful African American fiction. The representation of music continues to play a key role in the development of this fiction as evidenced by such novels as Al Young's *Snakes* (1970), Ishmael Reed's *Mumbo Jumbo* (1972), Gayl Jones's *Corregidora* (1975), Toni Morrison's *Song of Solomon* (1977) and *Jazz* (1992), Alice Walker's *The Color Purple* (1982), Ntozake Shange's *Betsey Brown* (1985), Nathaniel Mackey's *Bedouin Hornbook* (1986) and *Djbot Baghostus's Run* (1993) and Xam Cartiér's *Be-Bop, Re-Bop* (1987) and *Muse-Echo Blues* (1991). African American music along with the tropes black writers developed and refined in representing the music and musicians inform these novels in a variety ways. But the most telling index of their success is the individual writer's ability to create a distinctive black "voice." The attainment of this voice in fiction is the equivalent of the remarkable sense of "swing" that is expressed in the Basie band's performance of a Kansas City blues or the orgasmic surge of "soul" James Brown and Aretha Franklin conjure as they work a rhythmic groove or the "scream" Coltrane's tenor saxophone evokes. "Listen" to Gayl Jones in *Corregidora*:

> *They call it the devil blues. It ride your back. It devil you.*
> I bit my lip singing. I troubled my mind, took my rocker down by the river again. It was as if I wanted them to see what he'd done, hear it. All those blues feelings. That time I asked him to try to understand my feeling ways. That's what I called it. My feeling ways. My voice felt like it was screaming. What do they say about pleasure mixed with pain? (Jones's italics) (52)

The ability of contemporary African American writers to capture this feeling in fiction with the vibrancy and spontaneity that has characterized the music is a result of the fact that they have a tradition of representing music to draw on—the lineage from Douglass to Dumas that was examined in this study. Music is not only in the content of African American fiction; it is in the language itself. Albert Murray's assertion in *Stomping the Blues* that the soul, the swing, the groove in African American music is the result of artistic technique and awareness of a tradition rather than some spontaneous outpouring of emotion can be applied to the articulation of a distinctly African American voice in fiction by contemporary black writers:

> It is not a matter of having the blues and giving direct
> personal release to raw emotion brought on by suffering.

It is a matter of mastering the elements of craft required by the idiom. It is a matter of idiomatic orientation and the refinement of auditory sensibility in terms of idiomatic nuance. It is a far greater matter of convention, and hence tradition, than of impulse. (126)

Improvisation on a tradition and the construction of a black voice with the written word are central to Henry Louis Gates, Jr.'s theory of tropological revision in the African American literature, *The Signifying Monkey* (1988). Gates asserts that the African American literary tradition has been constructed through black writers "Signifyin(g)" on or repeating and revising tropes which appear in the works of other black writers: "When one Signifies upon another text, by tropological revision or repetition and difference, the double-voiced utterance allows us to chart discrete formal relationships in Afro-American literary history. Signifyin(g), then, is a metaphor for textual revision" (88). This Signifyin(g) relationship is apparent in the representation of music in African American fiction. The blues singer in Gayl Jones's *Corregidora* is constantly retelling the tragic legacy of slavery that has been passed down through the female generations of her family. When she speaks of "please mixed with pain" in her "blues feelings," it seems to be a conscious Signify(ing) on Ellison's classic definition of the blues as "an impulse to keep the painful details and episodes of a brutal experience alive . . . by squeezing from it a near-tragic, near-comic lyricism." Gates calls attention to a Signifyin(g) relationship in the representation of black music in fiction in his chapter on Alice Walker's *The Color Purple* through the connection he makes between the country blues man Tea Cake in *Their Eyes Were Watching God* and the Classic Blues singer Shug Avery in Walker's novel. Appropriately, Gates looks to African American music as a model for his concept of tropological revision:

Improvisation, of course, so fundamental to the very idea of jazz, is 'nothing more' than repetition and revision. In this sort of revision, again where meaning is fixed, it is the realignment of the signifier that is the signal trait of expressive genius. The more mundane the fixed text ('April in Paris' by Charlie Parker, 'My Favorite Things' by John Coltrane), the more dramatic is the Signifyin(g) revision. It is this principle of repetition and difference, this practice of intertextuality, which has been so crucial to the black vernacular forms of Signifyin(g), jazz—and even its antecedents, the blues, the spirituals, and

ragtime—and which is the source of my trope for black
intertextuality in the Afro-American formal literary
tradition. (63-64)

One of the primary objectives of Gates's theory of Signifyin(g) is
to study "the relationship between black vernacular and formal
traditions" (xii). The representation of music in African American
fiction enables black writers to construct a bridge between the oral and
literary heritage. The importance of this oral/literary bridge to African
American culture is one of the main themes in Morrison's novel *Song of
Solomon*. The representation of music is a key to the novel's meaning
and structure; Milkman Dead discovers his family history and a sense
of pride for his racial heritage in a folk song that surfaces throughout
the novel.

The oral tradition in the form of the folk song provides Milkman
with the knowledge he needs to transcend the limitations of his
mundane, disconnected existence. But Milkman also comes to
understand that the permanence of the written word enables a literary
culture to control an oral culture:

> He read the road signs with interest now, wondering what
> lay beneath the names. The Algonquins had named the
> territory he lived in Great Water, *michi gami*. How many
> dead lives and fading memories were buried in and
> beneath the names of the places in this country. Under the
> recorded names were other names, just as 'Macon Dead,'
> recorded for all time in some dusty file, hid from view the
> real names of people, places, and things. Names that had
> meaning. No wonder Pilate put hers in her ear. When you
> know your name, you should hang on to it, for unless it is
> noted down and remembered, it will die when you do.
> (329)

Morrison acknowledges the importance of the oral tradition in keeping
African Americans in touch with their heritage. Yet, she also
emphasizes how crucial it is for black culture to forge the techniques
and wisdom of that oral tradition into a literary tradition. Representing
music plays a key role in Morrison's accomplishment of that feat in
Song of Solomon.

The establishment of a black literary tradition that is linked to the
oral tradition is the agenda for Ishmael Reed's *Mumbo Jumbo*. In a
strikingly innovative example of a contemporary black writer
improvising on the established tropes of representing music in African

American fiction, Reed spans the entire history of African-derived artistic sensibility in a kind of whirlwind post-modern jazz solo: William Wells Brown, Paul Laurence Dunbar, James Weldon Johnson, Claude McKay, the Harlem Renaissance, Richard Wright, Ralph Ellison and the Black Arts Movement, Scott Joplin, W. C. Handy, Bessie Smith, Fats Waller, Cab Calloway, Louis Armstrong, Mahalia Jackson, Charlie Parker, John Coltrane and Otis Redding all make an appearance in *Mumbo Jumbo*. Reed takes the representation of music to a new level in that the musical hero in the novel is actually the distinctive feeling of African American music. The feeling, the spirit, the groove is (dis)embodied in *Mumbo Jumbo* as "Jes Grew," the anti-plague that enlivens its host and manifests itself through music-making, singing and dancing. Signifyin(g) on James Weldon Johnson's use of the term "jes grew" to describe the emergence of ragtime from black folk culture, Reed adopts it as the (dis)embodiment of the creative energy of the African American oral tradition:

> 'It belonged to nobody,' Johnson said. 'Its word were unprintable but its tune irresistible.' Jes Grew, the Something or Other that led Charlie Parker to scale the Everests of the Chord. Riff fly skid dip soar and gave his Alto Godspeed. Jes Grew that touched John Coltrane's Tenor; that tinged the voice of Otis Redding. . . .' (211)

The motivation for the spread of Jes Grew across America is the search for its ancient text, which representatives of the dominant white culture have kidnapped in order to dissipate its infectious energy: "*So Jes Grew is seeking its words. Its text. For what good is a liturgy without a text '*" (Reed's italics) (6). Of course, Jes Grew's search for its text is Reed's metaphor for the attempt to translate the feeling and techniques of black oral expression into a written form and establish a genuine African American literary tradition—which Reed does in the novel. *Mumbo Jumbo* is a testament to the ongoing quest of the black writer to create fiction that conforms to Duke Ellington's classic guideline: "It don't mean a thing if it ain't got that swing!"

Selected Bibliography

Andrews, William L. Introduction. *Three Classic African American Novels.* New York: Mentor, 1990. 7-21.

------. "The Novelization of Voice in Early African American Narrative." *PMLA.* 105.1 (1990): 23-34.

------. *To Tell a Free Story: The First Century of Afro-American Autobiography, 1760-1865.* Urbana: U of Illinois P, 1986.

Baker, Jr., Houston A. *Black Literature in America.* New York: McGraw-Hill, 1971.

------. *Blues, Ideology, and Afro-American Literature.* Chicago: U of Chicago P, 1984.

Baldwin, James. "The Discovery of Whar It Means to be an American." *Nobody.* 3-12.

------. "Everybody's Protest Novel." *Notes.* 13-23.

------. *Go Tell It on the Mountain.* 1953. New York: Dell, 1969.

------. "Many Thousands Gone." *Notes.* 24-45.

------. *Nobody Knows My Name.* New York: Dell, 1961.

------. *Notes of a Native Son.* Boston: Beacon, 1955.

------. "Sonny's Blues." 1948. *Going to Meet the Man.* New York: Dial P, 1965. 101-41.

Baraka, Amiri (LeRoi Jones). "AM/TRAK" *Baraka Reader.* 267-72.

------. *Black Music.* New York: William Morrow, 1967.

------. *Blues People.* New York: William Morrow, 1963.

------. "The Changing Same (R&B and New Black Music)." *Black Music.* 180-211.

------. "Coltrane Live At Birdland." *Black Music.* 63-68.

------. *Dutchman.* New York: William Morrow, 1964.

------. "Henry Dumas: Afro-Surreal Expressionist." *Black American Literature Forum.* 22.2 (1988) : 164-66.

------. "In The Tradition" *Baraka Reader.* 302-10.

------. "Jazz and the White Critic." *Black Music.* 11-20.

------. "A Jazz Great: John Coltrane." *Black Music.* 56-62.

------. *The LeRoi Jones/Amiri Baraka Reader.* Ed. William J. Harris. New York: Thunder's Mouth P, 1991.

------. "The Myth of Negro of a Negro Literature." 1962. *Black Expression.* Ed. Addison Gayle, Jr. New York: Weybright and Talley, 1969. 190-97.

------. "New Black Music: A Concert in Benefit of The Black Arts Repertory Theatre/School Live." 1965 *Black Music.* 172-76.

------ . "The Revolutionary Tradition in Afro-American Literature."
    Baraka Reader. 311-22.
------ . "The Screamers." 1963. *Tales.* New York: Grove P, 1967. 71-
    80.
------ , and Amina Baraka. *The Music: Reflections on Jazz and Blues.*
    New York: William Morrow, 1987.
Balliet, Whitney. "People Who Shoot Doves Out of Season." *The New
    Yorker.* 14 May 1965 : 174-78.
Bauldie, John. Liner Notes. *Bootleg Series Volumes 1-3.* Bob Dylan.
    Columbia Records, 1991.
Bell, Bernard W. *The Afro-American Novel and Its Tradition.*
    Amherst: U of Mass P, 1987.
Benston, Kimberly W. *Baraka: The Renegade and the Mask.* New
    Haven: Yale UP, 1976.
------ . "Late Coltrane: A Re-membering of Orpheus." *Chant of Saints.*
    Ed. Michael S. Harper and Robert B. Stepto. Urbana: U of
    Illinois P, 1979. 413-24.
------ . "Performing Blackness: Re/Placing Afro-American Poetry."
    Afro-American Literary Studies in the 1990s. Ed. Houston A.
    Baker, Jr. & Patricia Redmond. Chicago: U of Chicago P,
    1989. 164-93.
Bibb, Henry. *Narrative of the Life and Adventures of Henry Bibb, an
    American Slave.* 1845. *Puttin' On Ole Massa.* Ed. Gilbert
    Osofsky. New York: Harper & Row, 1969.
Bigsby, C. W. E. "Improvising America: Ralph Ellison and the
    Paradox of Form." *Speaking for You: The Vision of Ralph
    Ellison.* Ed. Kimberly W. Benston. Washington, D.C.:
    Howard UP, 1987. 173-83.
Bradford, Sarah. *Harriet Tubman: The Moses of Her People.* (1886)
    Gloucester, Mass.: Peter Smith, 1981.
Branch, Taylor. *Parting The Waters: America in the King Years, 1954-
    63.* New York: Simon and Schuster, 1988.
Brooks, Gwendolyn. Afterword. *Contending Forces.* By Pauline E.
    Hopkins. Carbondale: Southern Illinois UP, 1978.
Brown, Sterling. "The Blues as Folk Poetry." *The Book of Negro
    Folklore.* Ed. Langston Hughes & Arna Bontemps. New York:
    Dodd, Mead & Comp, 1958. 371-86.
------ . *The Collected Poems of Sterling A. Brown.* Ed. Michael S.
    Harper. New York: Harper and Row, 1980.
------ . "Spirituals." *The Book of Negro Folklore.* Ed. Langston
    Hughes & Arna Bontemps. New York: Dodd, Mead & Comp,
    1958. 279-89.

Brown, William Wells. *The Anti-Slavery Harp: A Collection of Songs for Anti-Slavery Meetins*. Boston: Bela Marsh, 1848.

------. *Clotel; or, The President's Daughter*. 1853. *Three Classic African-American Novels*. Ed. Henry Louis Gates, Jr. New York: Vintage Classics, 1990. 5-223.

------. *The Escape or A Leap for Freedom*. 1858. New York: Prologue P, 1969.

------. *Narrative of William Wells Brown, a Fugitive Slave*. 1847. *Puttin' On Ole Massa*. Ed. Gilbert Osofsky. New York: Harper & Row, 1969.

------. *My Southern Home: or, The South and Its People*. Boston: A.G. Brown, 1880.

Bruce, Jr., Dickson. *Black American Writing from the Nadir: The Evolution of a Literary Tradition 1877 - 1915*. Baton Rouge: Louisiana State UP, 1989.

Byerman, Keith E. "Words and Music: Narrative Ambiguity in Sonny's Blues.'" *Critical Essays on James Baldwin*. Ed. Fred K. Standley & Nancy V. Burt. Boston: G.K. Hall, 1988. 198-204.

Callahan, John F. "The Historical Frequencies of Ralph Waldo Ellison." *Chant of Saints*. Ed. Michael S. Harper and Robert B. Stepto. Urbana: U of Illinois P, 1979. 33-52.

Carby, Hazel. Introduction. *The Magazine Novels of Pauline Hopkins*. New York: Oxford UP, 1988, xxix-l.

------. *Reconstructing Womanhood: The Emergence of the Afro-American Woman Novelist*. New York: Oxford UP, 1987.

------. "It Jus Be's Dat Way Sometime: The Sexual Politics of Women's Blues." *Feminisms*. Ed. Robyn R. Warhol & Diane Price Herndle. New Brunswick: Rutgers UP, 1991. 746-58.

Cartiér, Xam. *Be-Bop, Re-Bop*. New York: Ballantine, 1987.

------. *Muse-Echo Blues*. New York: Ballantine, 1991.

Collier, Eugenia. "Elemental Wisdom in *Goodbye, Sweetwater* : Suggestions for Further Study." *Black American Literature Forum*. 22.2 (1988) : 192-99.

Costello, Donald P. "Black Man as Victim." *Five Black Writers*. Ed. Donald B. Gibson. New York: New York U P, 1970. 206-14.

de Jongh, James L. "Notes on Henry Dumas's Harlem." *Black American Literature Forum*. 22.2 (1988) : 218-20.

Delany, Martin R. *Blake; or the Huts of America*. (1861-2) Boston: Beacon, 1970.

Douglass, Frederick. *My Bondage and My Freedom*. 1855. New York: Dover P, 1969.

------ . *Narrative of the Life of Frederick Douglass, an American Slave.* 1845. *The Classic Slave Narratives.* Ed. Henry Louis Gates, Jr. New York: Mentor, 1987. 241-331.

DuBois, W. E. B. *The Souls of Black Folk.* 1903. New York: Penguin Books, 1989.

Dumas, Henry. *Ark of Bones and Other Stories.* New York: Random House, 1974.

------ . *Goodbye, Sweetwater: New & Selected Stories.* Ed. Eugene B. Redmond. New York: Thunder's Mouth P, 1988.

------ . *Knees of a Natural Man: The Selected Poetry of Henry Dumas.* Ed. Eugene B. Redmond. New York: Thunder's Mouth P, 1989.

------ . *Rope of Wind and Other Stories.* New York: Random House, 1979.

------ . "The Voice." *Rope of Wind.* 159-75.

------ . "Will the Circle Be Unbroken?" 1966. *Ark of Bones.* 107-15.

Dunbar, Paul Laurence. *The Complete Poems of Paul Laurence Dunbar.* New York: Dodd, Mead, 1970.

------ . *The Sport of the Gods.* New York: Dodd, Mead, 1902.

Eady, Cornelius. *The Gathering of My Name.* Pittsburgh: Carnegie Mellon UP, 1991.

Ellison, Ralph. "A Coupla Scalped Indians." 1956. *Black Literature in America.* Ed. Houston A. Baker, Jr. New York: McGraw-Hill, 1971. 321-31.

------ . "The Art of Fiction." *Shadow.* 167-86.

------ . "As the Spirit Moves Mahalia." *Shadow.* 213-20.

------ . "Beating That Boy." *Shadow.* 95-101.

------ . "Blues People." *Shadow.* 247-60.

------ . "Change the Joke and Slip the Yoke." *Shadow.* 45-59.

------ . "The Charlie Christian Story." *Shadow.* 233-40.

------ . *Going to the Territory.* New York: Random House, 1986.

------ . *Invisible Man.* 1952. New York: Vintage, 1989.

------ . "Living With Music." *Shadow.* 187-198.

------ . "Mister Toussan." 1941. *Black American Literature: Fiction.* Ed. Darwin T. Turner. Columbus, Ohio: Charles E. Merrill, 1969. 95-102.

------ . "On Bird, Bird-Watching, and Jazz." *Shadow.* 221-232.

------ . "Remembering Jimmy." *Shadow.* 24-46.

------ . "Richard Wright's Blues." *Shadow.* 77-94.

------ . *Shadow and Act.* 1964. New York: Vintage, 1972.

------ . "What America Would Like Without Blacks." *Territory.* 104-12.

------ . "The World and the Jug." *Shadow.* 107-43.

------ . "The World and the Jug." *Shadow*. 107-43.
Farrison, William Edward. *William Wells Brown: Author and Reformer*. Chicago: U of Chicago P, 1969.
Feather, Leonard. *The Encyclopedia of Jazz*. New York: Horizon P, 1960.
------ . *Inside Jazz*. 1949. New York: Da Capo, 1978.
Featherstone, Joseph. "Blues for Mister Baldwin." *Critical Essays on James Baldwin*. Ed. Fred K. Standley & Nancy V. Burt. Boston: G.K. Hall, 1988. 152-55.
Filene, Benjamin. "'Our Singing Country': John and Alan Lomax, Leadbelly, and the Construction of an American Past." *American Quarterly*. 43.4 (1991) : 602-24.
Fisher, Miles Mark. *Negro Slave Songs in the United States*. 1953. New York: Carol Publishing Group, 1990.
Floyd, Samuel J., Ed. *Black Music in the Harlem Renaissance: A Collection of Essays*. New York: Greenwood P, 1990.
Forest, Leon. "Luminosity from the Lower Frequencies." *Speaking for You: The Vision of Ralph Ellison*. Ed. Kimberly W. Benston. Washington, D.C.: Howard UP, 1987. 173-83.
Freedman, Samuel G. "What Black Writers Owe to Music." *New York Times*. 14 October 1984, 2.1&7.
Fuld, James J. *The Book of World-Famous Music: Classical, Popular, Folk*. New York: Crown P: 1966.
Fuller, Hoyt W. "Towards A Black Aesthetic." Gayle 3-11.
Gayle, Jr., Addison. Ed. *The Black Aesthetic*. 1971. Garden City, N.Y.: Anchor, 1972.
Gates, Jr. Henry Louis. Introduction. *The Classic Slave Narratives*. New York: Mentor, 1987. ix-xviii.
------ . *The Signifying Monkey*. New York: Oxford UP, 1988.
Giles, James R. *Claude McKay*. Boston: Twayne P, 1976.
Giovanni, Nikki. *Re:Creation*. Detroit: Broadside P, 1970.
------ . *Gemini.*. New York: Penguin Books, 1971.
Handy, William Christopher. "The Heart of the Blues." 1940. Southern. *Readings*. 212-26.
Hansberry, Lorraine. *The Drinking Gourd*. 1960. *The Collected Last Plays*. Ed. Robert Nemiroff. New York: New American Library, 1983.
Harper, Michael S. *Dear John, Dear Coltrane*. Pittsburgh: U of Pittsburgh P, 1970.
------ . *Images of Kin*. Urbana: U of Illinois P, 1977.
------ . *Nightmare Begins Responsibility*. Urbana: U of Illinois P, 1975.
------ . *Song: I Want a Witness*. Pittsburgh: U of Pittsburgh P, 1972.
Harris, William J. "'I Write The Blues:' An Interview With Al

------ . *The Poetry and Poetics of Amiri Baraka: The Jazz Aesthetic.*
Columbia: U of Missouri, 1985.

Heermance, J. Noel. *William Wells Brown and* Clotelle: *A Portrait of
the Artist in the First Negro Novel.* Archon Books, 1969.

Hemenway, Robert. *Zora Neale Hurston: A Literary Biography.*
Urbana: U of Illinois P, 1977.

Henderson, Stephen. Introduction: "The Forms of Things Unknown."
*Understanding the New Black Poetry: Black Speech and Black
Music as Poetic References.* New York: William Morrow, 1973.

Hentoff, Nat. Liner Notes. *We Insist! Max Roach's Freedom Now
Suite.* Columbia, 1980.

Holiday, Billie. Interview. *I Wonder Where Our Love Has Gone.* By
Mike Wallace. New York. Nov. 1956. Giants of Jazz LP-
1001.

------ , with William Dufty. *Lady Sings the Blues.* New York: Lancer,
1956.

hooks, bell. "Writing the Subject: Reading *The Color Purple.*"
Reading Black, Reading Feminist. Ed. Henry Louis Gates, Jr.
New York: Meridian, 1990. 454-470.

Hopkins, Pauline E. *Contending Forces: A Romance Illustrative Life
North and South.* 1900. Carbondale: Southern Illinois UP,
1978.

------ . *Of One Blood Or, the Hidden Self.* 1902-3. *The Magazine
Novels of Pauline Hopkins.* New York: Oxford UP, 1988.

Howe, Irving. "Black Boys and Native Sons." *Five Black Writers.* Ed.
Donald B. Gibson. New York: New York U P, 1970. 254-70.

Hughes, Langston. *Ask Your Mama:12 Moods for Jazz.* New York:
Knopf, 1961.

------ . *The Langston Hughes Reader.* New York: George Brazilles,
1958.

------ . "The Negro Writer and the Racial Mountain." 1926. *Black
Expression.* Ed. Addison Gayle, Jr. New York: Weybright
and Talley, 1969, 258-63.

------ . *Not Without Laughter.* 1930. New York: Alfred Knopf, 1969.

------ . *Selected Poems of Langston Hughes.* 1959. New York: Knopf,
1973.

------ , and Milton Meltzer. *Black Magic: A Pictorial History of Black
Entertainers in America.* New York: Bonanza Books, 1967.

------ , and Zora Neale Hurston. Mule Bone: A Comedy of Negro Life.
1931. New York: Harper Perennial, 1991. 45-153.

Hurston, Zora Neale. "The Bone of Contention." *Mule Bone.* New
York: Harper Perennial, 1991. 27-39.

------ . "How It Feels to Be Colored Me." 1928. *I Love Myself When I'm Laughing*. Ed. Alice Walker. New York: Feminist P, 1979, 152-5.

------ . Introduction. "Ever Been Down." Audiotape. Rec. June 1939. Jacksonville, Florida. Archive of Folk Music, Library of Congress, Washington, D.C. AFS 3138 B1.

------ . "The Sanctified Church" W. P. A. manuscript, 1939. Florida file, Library of Congress, Washington, D.C.

------ . "Sweat." 1926. *I Love Myself When I'm Laughing*. Ed. Alice Walker. New York: Feminist P, 1979, 152-55.

------ . *Their Eyes Were Watching God*. 1937. New York: Perennial Library, 1990.

Jackson, Blyden. *A History of Afro-American Literature - Volume 1: The Long Beginning, 1746-1895*. Baton Rouge: Louisiana State UP, 1989.

Jacobs, Harriet. *Incidents in the Life of a Slave Girl*. 1861. *The Classic Slave Narratives*. Ed. Henry Louis Gates, Jr. New York: Mentor, 1987. 335-515.

Jemie, Onwuchekwa. "Jazz, Jive, and Jam." 1976. *Langston Hughes: Modern Critical Views*. Ed. Harold Bloom. New York: Chelsea House, 1989. 71-91.

Johnson, James Weldon. *The Autobiography of an Ex-Coloured Man*. 1912. New York: Vintage Books, 1989.

------ . *Black Manhattan*. 1930. New York: DaCapo, 1991.

------ . *God's Trombone: Seven Negro Sermons in Verse*. New York: Viking, 1927.

------- . Preface. *The Book of American Negro Spirituals*. New York: Viking, 1925. 11-50.

------ . Preface To The First Edition. 1921. *The Book of American Negro Poetry*. New York: Harcourt, Brace & World, 1958. 9-48.

Johnson, Patricia A., and Walter C. Farrell, Jr. "How Langston Hughes Used The Blues." *MELUS* 6.1 (1979): 55-63.

Jones, Gayl. *Corregidora*. Boston: Beacon, 1975.

------ . *Eva's Man*. New York: Random House, 1976.

------ . *Liberating Voices: Oral Tradition in African American Literature*. Cambridge: Harvard UP, 1991.

------ . *The White Rat*. Boston: Beacon, 1977.

Keil, Charles. *Urban Blues*. Chicago: U of Chicago P, 1966.

Kelley, William Melvin. *A Different Drummer*. New York: Doubleday, 1962.

------ . *A Drop of Patience*. New York: Doubleday, 1965.

------ . *Dem.* New York: Doubleday, 1967.

------ . *Dunfords travels everywheres.* New York: Doubleday, 1970.

Kent, George E. "Hughes and the Afro-American Folk and Cultural Tradition." 1972. *Langston Hughes: Modern Critical Views.* Ed. Harold Bloom. New York: Chelsea House, 1989. 17-36.

------ . "Ralph Ellison and Afro-American Folk and Cultural Tradition." 1970. *Ralph Ellison: A Collection of Critical Essays.* Ed. John Hersey. Englewood N. J.: Prentice Hall, 1974. 160-70.

Lenz, Gunter H. "Symbolic Space, Communal Rituals, and the Surreality of the Urban Ghetto: Harlem in Black Literature from the 1920s to the 1960s." *Callaloo* 35 (1988) : 309-45.

Levine, Lawrence W. *Black Culture and Black Consciousness.* New York: Oxford UP, 1977.

Lewis, David Levering. *When Harlem Was In Vogue.* New York: Oxford UP, 1981

Lieb, Sandra. *Mother of the Blues: A Study of Ma Rainey.* U of Mass P, 1981.

Locke, Alain. *The Negro and His Music.* 1936. New York: Arno P & New York Times, 1969.

------ . *The New Negro: An Interpretation.* 1925. New York: Arno P & New York Times, 1968.

Lomax, Alan. Letter to Oliver Strunk. 3 August 1935. Archive of Folk Music. Library of Congress, Washington, D.C.

------ . "Zora Neale Hurston: A Life of Negro Folklore." *Sing Out.* 10 (October- November 1961) : 12-13.

Mackey, Nathaniel. *Bedouin Hornbook.* Lexington: U of Kentucky P, 1986.

------ . "The Changing Same: Black Music in the Poetry of Amiri Baraka." *Imamu Amiri Baraka: A Collection of Critical Essays.* Ed. Kimberly W. Benston. Engelwood Cliffs, N.J.: Prentice Hall, 1978. 119-34.

------ . *Djbot Baghostus's Run.* Los Angeles: Sun & Moon P, 1993.

------ . *Eroding Witness.* Urbana: U of Illinois P, 1985.

Madhubuti Haki (Don L. Lee). "Are Black Musicians Serious?" *From Plan to Planet Life Studies: The Need for Afrikan Minds and Institutions.* Detroit, Broadside P, 1973

------ . *Don't Cry Scream.* Detroit: Broadside P, 1969.

Martin, Reginald. *Ishmael Reed and the New Black Aesthetic Critics.* New York: St. Martin's P, 1988.

McKay, Claude. *Banjo.* 1929 New York: Harcourt, 1957.

------ . *Home to Harlem.* New York: Harper, 1928.

Miller, Floyd J. Introduction *Blake; or, the Huts of America* (1861-62)
By Martin R. Delany Boston: Beacon, 1970, xi-xxix.
Morrison, Toni. *Jazz.* New York: Alfred Knopf, 1992.
------ . *Song of Solomon.* 1977. New York: Signet, 1978.
Murray, Albert. "Comping for Basie." *The Invention of Ethnicity.* Ed.
Werner Sollors. New York: Oxford UP, 1989, 209-25.
------ . "Duke Ellington Vamps 'Til Ready." *Chant of Saints.* Ed.
Michael S. Harper and Robert B. Stepto. Urbana: U of Illinois P,
1979. 440-44.
------ . *The Hero and The Blues.* Columbia: U of Missouri P, 1973.
------ . *The Omni-Americans: New Perspectives on Black Experience
and American Culture.* New York: Outerbridge & Dienstfrey,
1970.
------ . *Stomping the Blues.* New York: McGraw-Hill, 1976.
Neal, Larry. An Afterword: "And Shine Swam On." *Black Fire.* Ed.
LeRoi Jones & Larry Neal. New York: William Morrow, 1968.
638-56.
------ . "Ellison's Zoot Suit." *Ralph Ellison: A Collection of Critical
Essays.* Ed. John Hersey. Englewood N.J.: Prentice Hall, 1974.
58-79.
------ . "Henry Dumas: Literary Landmark." *Black American
Literature Forum.* 22.2 (1988) : 313-15.
------ . *Hoodoo Hollerin' Bebop Ghosts.* Washington, D.C.: Howard
UP, 1974.
------ . *Visions of a Liberated Future: Black Arts Movement Writings.*
New York: Thunder's Mouth P, 1989.
Northup, Solomon. *Twelve Years A Slave.* 1853. *Puttin' On Ole
Massa.* Ed. Gilbert Osofsky. New York: Harper & Row, 1969.
Oakley, Giles. *The Devil's Music: A History of the Blues.* New York:
Harcourt, Brace, Jovanovich, 1976.
O'Brien, John, Ed. *Interviews With Black Writers.* New York:
Liveright, 1973.
Oliver, Paul. *The Story of the Blues.* 1969. Rodman, Pa.: Chilton
Books, 1975.
O'Meally, Robert. *The Craft of Ralph Ellison.* Cambridge: Harvard
UP, 1980.
------ . *Lady Day: The Many Faces of Billie Holiday.* New York:
Arcade P, 1991.
------ . "Riffs and Rituals: Folklore in the Work of Ralph Ellison."
Afro-American Literature: The Reconstruction of Instruction. Ed.
Dexter Fisher & Robert Steptoe, New York: Modern Language
Association of America, 1979. 154-69.

Ostendorf, Berndt. "Ralph Waldo Ellison: Anthropology, Modernism
    and Jazz." *New Essays on* Invisible Man. Ed. Robert O'Meally.
    Cambridge: Cambridge UP, 1988. 95-121.
Petry, Ann. "Solo on the Drums." 1947. *Miss Muriel and Other
    Stories*. Boston: Beacon, 1971. 235-42.
------ . *The Street*. 1946. Boston: Beacon, 1985.
Rampersad, Arnold. "Henry Dumas's World of Fiction." *Black
    American Literature Forum*. 22.2 (1988) : 329-32.
Reed, Ishmael. *Flight to Canada*. New York: Random House, 1976.
------ . *Mumbo Jumbo*. 1972. New York: Atheneum, 1988.
------ . *New and Collected Poems*. New York: Atheneum, 1989.
------ . *Writin' Is Fightin': Thirty-seven Years of Boxing on Paper*.
    New York: Atheneum, 1988.
Reilly, John M. "'Sonny's Blues': James Baldwin's Image of Black
    Community." 1970. *James Baldwin: A Collection of Critical
    Essays*. Ed. Kenneth Kinnamon. Englewood Cliffs, N. J.: Prentice
    Hall, 1974. 139-46.
Roy, Darlene. "Henry Dumas—Master Storyteller." *Black American
    Literature Forum*. 22.2 (1988) : 343-45.
Sanchez, Sonia. *Home Coming*. Detroit: Broadside P, 1969.
------ . *Homegirls and Handgrenades*. New York: Thunder's Mouth P,
    1984.
------ . *Under A Soprano Sky*. Trenton, N.J.: Africa World P, 1987.
------ . *We A BaddDDD People*. Detroit: Broadside P, 1970
Savery, Pancho. "'Not like an arrow, but a boomerang': Ellison's
    Existential Blues." *Approaches to Teaching Ellison's* Invisible
    Man. Ed. Susan Resneck Pan & Pancho Savery. New York:
    Modern Language Association of America, 1989. 119-23.
Shange, Ntozake. *A Daughter's Geography*. New York: St. Martin's P,
    1983.
------ . *Betsey Brown*. New York: St. Martin's P, 1985.
------ . *for colored girls who have contemplated suicide when the
    rainbow is enuf*. New York: St. Martin's P, 1976.
------ . *The Love Space Demands: A Continuing Saga*. New York: St.
    Martin's P, 1991.
------ . *nappy edges*. New York: St. Martin's P, 1978.
------ . *Ridin' the Moon in Texas: Word Paintings*. New York: St.
    Martin's P, 1987.
------ . *Sassafrass, Cypress and Indigo*. New York: St. Martin's P,
    1982.
------ . *See No Evil: Prefaces, Essays and Accounts 1976-1983*. San
    Francisco: Momo's P, 1984.
------ . *three pieces*. New York: St. Martin's Press, 1981.

Smith, David Lionel. "The Black Arts Movement and Its Critics." *American Literary History* 3.1 (1991): 93-110.

Sollors, Werner. *Beyond Ethnicity: Consent and Descent in American Culture.* New York: Oxford UP, 1986.

Southern, Eileen. *The Music of Black Americans: A History.* New York: Norton, 1971.

------ , Ed. *Readings in Black American Music.* 2nd ed. New York: Norton, 1983.

Stearns, Marshall W. *The Story of Jazz.* New York: Oxford UP, 1956.

Steptoe, Robert B. *From Behind the Veil: A Study of Afro-American Narrative.* Urbana: U of Illinois P, 1979.

------ . "I Thought I Knew These People: Richard Wright & The Afro-American Literary Tradition." *Chant of Saints.* Ed. Michael S. Harper and Robert B. Steptoe. Urbana: U of Illinois P, 1979. 123-35.

Stewart, Jimmy. "Introduction to Black Aesthetics in Music." Gayle 77-91.

Takaki, Ronald T. *Violence in the Black Imagination.* New York: Capricorn Books, 1972.

Tanner, Tony. "The Music of Invisibility." *Ralph Ellison: A Collection of Critical Essays.* Ed. John Hersey. Englewood N. J.: Prentice Hall, 1974. 80-94

Taylor, Gordon O. "Learning to Listen to Lower Frequencies." *Approaches to Teaching Ellison's Invisible Man.* Ed. Susan Resneck Pan & Pancho Savery. New York: Modern Language Association of America, 1989. 119-23.

Thomas, J. C. *Chasin' the Trane: The Music and Mystique of John Coltrane.* 1975. New York: Da Capo, 1985.

Tilton, Jeff Todd. *Downhome Blues Lyrics: An Anthology from the Post-World War II Era.* Urbana: U of Illinois P, 1990.

Tracy, Steven C. *Langston Hughes & The Blues.* Urbana: U of Illinois P, 1988.

Traylor, Eleanor. "Music as Theme: The Blues Mode in the Works of Margaret Walker." *Black Women Writers (1950-1980).* Ed. Mari Evans. New York: Doubleday, 1984. 511-25.

Vanderwerken, David L. "Focusing on the Prologue and the Epilogue." *Approaches to Teaching Ellison's Invisible Man.* Ed. Susan Resneck Pan & Pancho Savery. New York: Modern Language Association of America, 1989. 119-23.

Walcutt, Charles Child. "Theodore Dreiser and the Divided Stream." *The Stature of Theodore Dreiser.* Ed. Alfred Kazin and Charles Shapiro. Bloomington; U of Indiana P, 1955. 246-69.

Walker, Alice. *The Color Purple*. 1982. New York: Pocket Books, 1985.
------ . *In Love and Trouble*. New York: Harcourt, Brace, Jovanovich, 1973.
------ . *In Search of Our Mother's Gardens*. New York: Harcourt, Brace, Jovanovich, 1983.
Walker, Margaret. *For My People*. 1942. New York: Arno, 1968.
------ . *How I Wrote Jubilee*. New York: The Feminist P, 1990.
------ . *Jubilee*. Boston: Houghton Mifflin, 1966.
------ . *This Is My Century: New and Collected Poems*. Athens, Georgia: U of Georgia P, 1988.
Washington, Booker T. *Up From Slavery*. 1901. New York: Penguin, 1986.
Watson, Edward A. "Bessie's Blues." *New Letters*. 38 (1971) : 64-70.
Wellburn, Ron. "The Black Aesthetic Imperative." Gayle 126-42.
Whalum, Wendell Phillips. "James Weldon Johnson's Theories and Performance Practices of Afro-American Folksong." *Phylon*. 32.4 (Winter 1971): 383-95.
Wilentz, Gay. "'If You Surrender to the Air': Folk Legends of Flight and Resistance in African American Literature." *MELUS* 16.1 (Spring 1989-90) : 21-32.
Williams, Sherley A. "The Blues Roots of Contemporary Afro-American Poetry." *Chant of Saints*. Ed. Michael S. Harper and Robert B. Stepto. Urbana: U of Illinois P, 1979. 123-35.
------ . *Give Birth to Brightness: A Thematic Study in Neo-Black Literature*. New York: Dial P, 1972.
------ . *The Peacock Poems*. Middleton, Conn.: Wesleyan UP, 1975.
------ . "Someone Sweet Angel Child." *Chant of Saints*. Ed. Michael S. Harper and Robert B. Stepto. Urbana: U of Illinois P, 1979.
Wilson, August. *Ma Rainey's Black Bottom*. New York: New American Library, 1985.
Wright, Richard. "Blueprint for Negro Writing." 1937. *Richard Wright Reader*. Ed. Ellen Wright & Michel Fabre. New York: Harper & Row, 1978. 36-49.
------ . Foreword. 1959. *The Meaning of the Blues*. 1960 By Paul Oliver. New York: Collier, 1966. 7-12.
------ . "How Bigger Was Born." *Native Son*. 1940. New York: Harper & Row, 1966. xii-xxiv.
------ . "The Literature of Negro in the United States." from *White Man, Listen!* 1957. *Black Expression*. Ed. Addison Gayle, Jr. New York: Weybright and Talley, 1969. 198-229.
------ . *Native Son*. 1940. New York: Harper & Row, 1966.

------ . *12 Million Black Voices: A Folk History of the Negro in the U.S.* 1941.

------ . *Richard Wright Reader.* Ed. Ellen Wright & Michel Fabre. New York: Harper & Row, 1978.

------ . *Uncle Tom's Children.* 1939. New York: Harper & Row, 1965.

Yellin, Jean Fagan. *The Intricate Knot: Black Figures in American Literature, 1776-1863.* New York: New York UP, 1972.

Young, Al. *Bodies and Souls.* Berkeley: Creative Arts Book Co, 1981.

------ . *The Blues Don't Change.* Baton Rouge: Louisiana State UP, 1982.

------ . *Kinds of Blue.* Berkeley: Creative Arts Book Co, 1984.

------ . *Snakes.* New York: Holt, Rinehart, Winston, 1970.

------ . *The Song Turning Back Into Itself.* New York: Holt, Rinehart, Winston, 1971.

------ . *Things Ain't What They Used To Be.* Berkeley: Creative Arts Book Co, 1987.

------ , and Janet Coleman. *Mingus/Mingus: Two Memoirs.* New York: Limelight Editions, 1991.

Young, Lester. Unreleased interview. Francois Postif. Paris 1959.

Selected Discography

The following discography features information on specific recordings mentioned in this study and respresentative recordings of many of the artists and/or musical styles cited. Except where noted, the recordings are compact discs.

African American Community Gospel. Smithsonian/Folkways, 1994.
African American Gospel:The Pioneering Composers.
     Smithsonian/Folkways, 1994.
African American Spirituals: The Concert Tradition.
     Smithsonian/Folkways, 1994.
Afro-American Folk Music from Tate and Panola Counties Misissippi.
     Rec. 1942-71. LP. Library of Congress AFS L67, 1978.
Afro-American Spirituals, Work Songs, and Ballads. Audiocassette.
     Library of Congress Music Division-Recording Laboratory. L-3,
     n.d.
Armstrong, Louis. "(What Did I Do to Be So) Black and Blue." Rec.
     22 July 1929. *Volume V: Louis in New York*. Columbia, 1990.
Basie, Count. *Blues By Basie*. Rec. 1939-50. LP. Columbia, 1980.
Berry, Chuck. *The Great Twenty Eight*. MCA, 1984.
Better Boot That Thing: Great Women Blues Singers of the 1920's. Rec.
     1927-30. Bluebird, 1992.
Blues Piano—Chicago Plus. Rec. 1951-54. LP. Atlantic, 1972.
Broonzy, Big Bill. *Good Time Tonight*. Rec. 1930-40. Columbia, 1990.
Brown, James. *Star Time*. Polydor, 1991.
Calloway, Cab. *Masterpieces 12*. Rec. 1932-42. Jazz Archives, n.d.
Carr, Leroy. "Shady Lane Blues." Rec. 20 Februray 1934, *Blues
     Before Sunrise*. Portrait, 1989.
Charles, Ray. *The Birth of Soul.*. Atlantic, 1991.
Coltrane, John. *A Love Supreme*. Rec. 9 Dec. 1964. Impulse, 1986.
------ . *My Favorite Things*. Rec. October 1960. Atlantic, 1961.
Dixon, Willie. *The Big Three Trio*. Columbia, 1991.
Dolphy, Eric. *Copenhagen Concert*. Rec. 8 Sept. 1961. LP. Prestige,
     1973.
Domino, Fats. *"They Call Me the Fat Man . . ."* EMI, 1991.
Ellington, Duke. *The Beginning: Volume One*. Rec. 1926-28. LP.
     MCA, n.d.
------ . *Hot In Harlem: Volume Two*. Rec. 1928-29. MCA, n.d.
------ . *Rockin' In Rhythm' Volume Three*. Rec. 1929-31. MCA, n.d.
Fuller, Blind Boy. *East Coast Piedmont Style*. Rec. 1935-39.
     Columbia, 1991.

Franklin, Aretha. *Spirit in the Dark*. LP. Atlantic, 1970.
------. *Queen of Soul*. Atlantic, 1992.
Georgia Sea Island Songs. Rec. 1935 & 1961. LP. New World, 1977.
Gillespie, Dizzy. *Manteca*. Rec. 1947-49. LP. Camden, 1979.
Gordon, Dexter. *Sophisticated Giant*. Rec. 1977. LP. Columbia, 1977.
Hines, Earl "Fatha". *The Grand Terrace Band*. Rec. 1939-42. LP. Camden, 1979.
Holiday, Billie. *The Complete Decca Recordings*. Rec. 1945-50. GRP, 1991.
------. *The First Verve Sessions*. Rec. 1952-54. LP. Verve,1976.
-------. *The Golden Years*. Rec. 1933-41. LP. Columbia, 1962.
Howlin' Wolf. *Change My Way*. Rec. 1958-1963. LP. Chess, 1977.
Hurt, Mississippi John. *The Best of Mississippi John Hurt*. Rec. 15 April 1965. Vanguard, 1987.
Jackson, Mahalia. *Essence of Mahalia Jackson*. Columbia, 1994.
------. *Live at Newport 1958*. Columbia, 1994.
Jacobs, Little Walter. *Confessin' the Blues*. Rec. 1953-1963. LP. Chess, 1977.
James, Elmore. "Mean Mistreatin' Mama." Rec. 1961. *King of the Slide Guitar*. Capricorn, 1992.
Jacquet, Illinois. *How High the Moon*. Rec. 20 Aug. 1968 & 16 Sept. 1969. LP. Prestige, 1975.
Johnson, Budd. *Let's Swing*. Rec. 2 Dec. 1960. LP. Swingville, n.d.
------, and Phil Woods. *The Old Dude & the Fundance Kid*. Rec. 4 Feb. 1984. LP. Uptown, 1985.
Johnson, Robert. *The Complete Recordings*. Rec. 1936-7. Columbia, 1990.
Leadbelly. *King of the 12-String Guitar*. Rec. 1935. Columbia, 1991.
Lincoln, Abbey (Aminata Moseka). *Devil's Got Your Tongue*. Verve, 1992.
------. *You Gotta Pay The Band*. Verve, 1991.
Little Richard (Penniman). *The Georgia Peach*. Rec. 1955-57. Speciality, 1991.
McTell, Blind Willie. *Atlanta Twelve String*. Rec. 1949. LP. Atlantic, 1972.
Mean Mothers: Independent Women's Blues, Volume 1. Rec. 1931-49. Rosetta, n.d.
Memphis Minnie. *Hoodoo Lady (1933-1937)*. Columbia, 1991.
Memphis Slim. *Born with the Blues*. Jewel, n.d.
Monk, Thelonious. *Live at the Five Spot: Discovery!* Rec. 1957. Blue Note, 1993.
------. *Misterioso*. Rec. August 1958. LP. Riverside, n.d.

Morton, Jelly Roll. *1923-24*. Milestone, 1992.
Mulebone: Music Composed and Performed by Taj Mahal. Lyrics by Langston Hughes. Gramavision, 1991.
Negro Religious Field Recordings 1934-1942 from Louisiana, Mississsippi and Tennessee. Document, n.d.
Negro Religious Songs and Services. Audiocassette. Library of Congress Music Division—Recording Laboratory. L-10, n.d.
Nicholas, Big Nick. *Big and Warm.* LP. India Navigation, 1983.
------. *Big Nick.* LP. India Navigation, 1985.
Parker, Charlie. *The Very Best of Bird.* Rec. 1946-47. Warner Bros., 1977.
Patton, Charlie. *King of the Delta Blues.* Yazoo, 1991.
Powell, Bud. *The Complete Blue Note and Roost Recordings.* Rec. 1947-58. Blue Note, 1994.
Preachin' the Gospel: Holy Blues. Columbia, 1991.
Precious Lord: Recordings of the Great Gospel Songs of Thomas A. Dorsey. Columbia, 1994.
Rainey, Ma. *Ma Rainey.* Rec. 1924-28. Milestone, 1992.
Redding, Otis. *The Ultimate Otis Redding.* Warner Bros., 1986.
Roach, Max. *We Insist! Max Roach's Freedom Now Suite.* Rec. 31 August & 6 September 1960. LP. Columbia, 1980.
Smith, Bessie. "Back Water Blues." Rec. 17 Feb. 1927. *Nobody's Blues But Mine.* LP. Columbia, 1972.
Sounds of the South: A Musical Journey from the Georgia Sea Islands to the Mississippi Delta. Rec. by Alan Lomax. Atlantic, 1994.
Staple Singers. *Freedom Highway.* Columbia, 1991.
Sweet Honey In The Rock. *In This Land.* EarthBeat!, 1992.
Taylor, Hound Dog. "Wild About You Baby." *Hound Dog Taylor and the HouseRockers.* LP. Alligator, 1973.
Waller, Fats. *The Fats Waller Piano Solos: Turn on the Heat.* RCA, 1991.
Waters, Muddy. "I Love the Life I Live, I Live the Life I Love." Rec. 1 December 1956. *Trouble No More..* MCA , 1989.
------. "Mannish Boy." *The Last Waltz.* The Band. Rec. November 1976. Warner Bros. 1978.
Webster, Ben, with Coleman Hawkins. *Tenor Giants.* Rec. 1957-59. LP. Verve, 1977.
Wheatstraw, Peetie. "Good Woman Blues." LP. *Piano Blues.* RBF, n.d.
Williams, Mary Lou. *Mary Lou Williams 1944.* Classics, 1995.
Williamson, Sonny Boy. *King Biscuit Time.* Rec. 1951. LP. Arhoolie, n.d.
Young, Lester. *Lester Swings.* Rec. 1945-51. LP. Verve, 1977.

Index